WHEN IT'S
DARKNESS
ON
THE DELTA

WHEN IT'S DARKNESS ON THE DELTA

HOW AMERICA'S RICHEST SOIL BECAME ITS POOREST LAND

W. RALPH EUBANKS

BEACON PRESS, BOSTON

BEACON PRESS
24 Farnsworth Street
Boston, Massachusetts
www.beacon.org

Beacon Press books
are published under the auspices of
the Unitarian Universalist Association of Congregations.

29 28 27 26   8 7 6 5 4 3 2 1

This book is printed on acid-free paper that meets the uncoated paper
ANSI/NISO specifications for permanence as revised in 1992.

Text design and composition by Kim Arney

A portion of chapter 1, "The Dimming Mystique of Mileston," was published
in the *Oxford American*, nos. 109–110 (Spring–Summer 2020). Portions of
chapters 14 and 15 were published in *Outside* (Summer 2023) under the
title "Mississippi Delta: Returning Home to Its Haunted Past."

All photographs © W. Ralph Eubanks, except the Mileston Store,
by Marion Post Wolcott, 1939, FSA/OWI Collection, Prints and Photographs
Division, Library of Congress; and the Stansel Plantation, by Rory Doyle.

*Library of Congress Cataloguing-in-Publication
Data is available for this title.*
Hardcover ISBN: 978-0-8070-4532-9
E-book ISBN: 978-0-8070-4533-6
Audiobook: 978-0-8070-2236-8

The authorized representative in the EU for product safety and
compliance is Easy Access System Europe 16879218, Mustamäe tee 50,
10621 Tallinn, Estonia: http://beacon.org/eu-contact.

For my father, Warren Eubanks,
who taught me to love the Mississippi Delta
and whose presence I still feel while traveling its roads

Thus the very existence of the blues tradition is irrefutable evidence that those who evolved it respond to the vicissitudes of the human condition not with hysterics and desperation, but through the wisdom of poetry informed by pragmatic insight.

—ALBERT MURRAY, *The Blue Devils of Nada*

CONTENTS

PALIMPSEST

*Here are no hills, no rocks, no thin earth barely
hiding the stones beneath, but pure soil endlessly deep,
dark and sweet, dripping fatness.*

—DAVID L. COHN, *Where I Was Born and Raised*

Despite its expansiveness, beauty, and the lush loamy richness of the soil, suffering and injustice permeate visions of the Mississippi Delta landscape as much as the wail of the blues, a musical form inspired by the pain and inequities this land has inflicted on its people. But near the dimming of the day a warm light envelops this Southern plain. At dusk, the skies above Mississippi Delta fields glow with red and orange as if the sky were a fireplace. Maybe it is the expansiveness of the land that creates this light. Whatever it is, for a brief part of the day beauty soothes the ghostlike silence that seems to howl across this wide and often empty place.

The Delta is two hundred miles long and flat as far as the eye can see. At sunset it seems as if the sky consumes the land and gives texture to the fields below it. The glow of the Delta at dusk has always cast a spell over me, a soothing incantation that beckons me each time I return. Yet over time, I have come to realize that the Delta is a palimpsest, a place where what the land means and how it and its people are seen has been erased and written over time and time again. Looking back, I realize that during my boyhood I witnessed this land's waning days as a cotton kingdom. By the time I left Mississippi in the late 1970s, the common belief was catfish farming would succeed cotton farming, but those days have now faded as well. By the 1990s, casinos began to dot former cotton fields on the landscape of impoverished Tunica County. Now those casinos employ less than a third of the people they did when gambling in the Delta was at its peak.

Today they are selling the Delta as a place tourists can visit to gamble in a casino and see the land that gave birth to the blues. Yet the question remains as to whether selling the Delta blues to tourists imposes a new mythology on this land, one that overshadows harsher realities that have yet to be confronted. Blues tourism focuses more on the personas of those who created the music and often glances over how the music was created out of pain and as a means to protest the circumstances that created that pain. What often gets overlooked or pushed to the margins when attracting tourist dollars is the relationship between the blues and the labor of the Black bodies who cleared the Delta, built the levees to protect the land, and cultivated and picked the crops. Generational pain and trauma cannot be packaged into something attractive to vacationers. Does turning the blues into a commodity create a new economic foundation for the Delta or is it simply another form of cultural erasure? Should the pain of the past captured in the blues be commodified in the present?

The Delta's history and the questions it raises stand as part of a multilayered record, which means the past and the present often collide in this place of overlaid stories. That also means the past is erased as much as its traces linger on in the landscape of the present. But for someone who has spent time in the Mississippi Delta his entire life, the presence of the past can feel quite sudden and forceful. When I happen to encounter memory and history crashing together, I tend to pay attention.

That is exactly what happened one afternoon when I encountered two dusty white shotgun houses at the corner of my field of vision as I was driving. Immediately, I pulled to the side of the road and stopped. They stood haloed by the glow of the late afternoon sun, reminding me of a collection of photographs taken by Marion Post Wolcott as she drove down these very same roads as a Farm Security Administration (FSA) photographer during the Great Depression. Faintly whitewashed, the buildings appeared unoccupied, but from my recollection of Wolcott's sepia-toned photographs, I could imagine a whole family gathered outside on the visibly absent front porch, with the dark loamy Delta soil beneath their feet as they dangled above the ground.

Entire families who worked under the feudal system of sharecropping once lived in houses like these, because one-room shanties were deemed sufficient for them by the lords of the land who held them in bondage despite the end of slavery. Sharecropping was slavery's successor system, and the circumstances of these tenant farmers bore a profound similarity to the peculiar institution: white planters owned the land in the vast cotton fields and Black laborers were given what was deemed their share when the crops were harvested. The sharecroppers owned nothing, and at the end of farming season they were sometimes left with nothing. In the 1930s, the average sharecropper earned between $250 and $500 each year, the equivalent of a net income of less than $10,000 today. Fast forward to today and the economic legacy of sharecropping is reflected in educational outcomes, employment, and poverty, all of which fall below the levels measured in parts of Mississippi that were never part of the Delta's plantation economy.

It has been more than half a century since automated cotton-picking machines ended sharecropping and its exploitation. Houses like the one I saw off in the distance were abandoned as people left for Chicago and other points north and west. Consequently, few visible footprints of that old system appear on the horizon. When they do, they cast a haunting shadow as a vivid reminder of a not-so-distant unenlightened past. As someone who sometimes thinks in photographs, seeing a former tenant farmer's residence provides evidence of what once was. Encountering in living color the black-and-white world of the past also makes me want to know the story behind the photographs these structures suggest.

Since that afternoon, I've learned that soon after taking her photographs of the Delta, Marion Post Wolcott's notoriously flinty boss, Roy Stryker, wrote to her while she was in the nearby town of Greenville. Before complaining that she had not provided a telegraph address—FSA photographers were required to report on the condition of the film they had shot so that photographs could be processed quickly—Stryker commented about her Mississippi Delta photographs, "They are going to be an extremely valuable collection." Stryker added, "I would say you have made some very accurate observations."[1] Indeed she had.

While Dorothea Lange's famous photograph of a plantation overseer—featuring a proud-looking corpulent man holding his foot on a car bumper with four expressionless Black men behind him—captured a sense of permanence regarding the sharecropping system, some of Wolcott's Delta photographs also captured a sign of a change that was chipping away at the plantation system, a shift that also led people to abandon those same shotgun houses she photographed. "We were very much delighted with your discovery of the prosperous Negro community," Roy Stryker wrote to Wolcott in the same letter in 1939. That community was Mileston, a Farm Security Administration resettlement project on the southeastern edge of the Delta and just twenty miles to the east of the shotgun houses I spotted.

In the late 1930s, the FSA Resettlement Administration made 110 former sharecropping families landowners in this part of Mississippi's Holmes County. Rather than being subjected to the paternalism of working for a plantation owner and overseer, families at Mileston owned their land. Over a hundred houses were also built for these families, as well as a school and a community center. What Wolcott captured with her camera was a community in transition from tenant farming to landowning.

In addition to her photograph of the plantation overseer, Lange also took photographs of a radical and visionary experiment in American agriculture that was happening in the heart of the Delta. The Delta Cooperative Farm, like Mileston, was run by former sharecroppers and included nineteen Black families and twelve white families. These families shared in the profits and produce of the farm. So, in addition to the overseer and sharecroppers Lange memorialized in her photographs, both she and Marion Post Wolcott encountered change on the Delta landscape. The place Wolcott photographed was so different from the rest of the Delta that it was considered a prosperous community.

What the camera did not capture was the independent spirit that flourished among the people in Mileston, as well as at the Delta Cooperative Farm and its successor, the Providence Cooperative Farm. It was that independent and radical spirit that attracted my father to Mileston in 1949 and my mother in 1951 when they married. Unlike a sharecropping system in which the tenants owned nothing, landowning bred a radical sense of possibility. When they arrived, my parents were proud to be a part of a community that pushed against the norms that were set for Black rural life at the time. Mileston existed in a space that felt free from the Delta of plantations and plantation owners. But that did not last. By the mid-1950s, the entire Delta became a dangerous place for Black people who yearned for independence and pushed against the cultural and social norms of the time. In 1956, my family left the Delta. Even though I did not grow up in this rich, flat expanse of land, my father brought me here regularly. Had he not feared for his young family's life, he would never have left. Sadly, it was the tensions that sprang out of the changes rendered by Mileston and Providence Farm that led them to leave.

Depression-era photographs often spring to mind when I see something evocative of the Delta's past on the landscape. They are a tool to help me see the truth in a place that is often shrouded in myth. If a photograph captures a past reality and freezes it in time, mythology can shield the actuality of the past from the light of day and obscure what is real. It often overwhelms reality, as it does in a song from 1932 that has become the unofficial anthem of the Delta:

When it's darkness on the Delta
That's the time my heart is light
When it's darkness on the Delta
Let me linger in the shelter of the night.

The lyrics continue with descriptions of "lounging on the levee" and "cotton all around me," evoking a romantic idea of the Delta as a place of leisure, with "darkies singing sweet and low" thrown in, perpetuating the lie that the people picking that cotton all around them were happy. Of course, the three Tin Pan Alley songwriters who wrote "(When It's) Darkness on the Delta" never set foot on a levee or ever saw a field of cotton. But "Darkness on the Delta" is an anthem that was always popular with the white planter class and was played at cotillions and other dances. In the very same year that "Darkness on the Delta" was released, Cab Calloway and the Boswell Sisters separately recorded two Fats Waller songs about life in the Delta, "Old Yazoo" and "Down on the Delta."[2] Both songs are free of romantic ideas about the Delta landscape and its people, so they have disappeared from memory.

The songs that originated in those vast fields of cotton are grittier than those written about the Delta from the West Side of Manhattan. On cotton plantations in Mississippi, African Americans like Son House were singing, "The blues ain't nothing but a low-down shakin' chill." There was a lot more worry about the weight of life in the Delta than there were ever people lounging on the levee. As anyone who has listened to a blues song knows, there are more songs about trouble brewing and people finding some way to leave that trouble behind. More bad luck and trouble rose out of those vast fields of cotton than anyone will ever know.

When Robert F. Kennedy visited the Delta in 1967, he got a sense of the poverty and anguish that led the people to transform their troubles into music. Visiting a Delta sharecropper's home, Kennedy saw none of the romance of the Delta. What he encountered led him to whisper to his aide Peter Edelman, "I've been to third-world countries, and I've never seen anything like this." John Stennis, the segregation senator of Mississippi, was so embarrassed by the impoverished circumstances Kennedy encountered among his constituents that Stennis suggested $10 million in emergency aid. At the same time, he denied that Kennedy found any evidence of hunger or malnutrition, calling the findings "a gross libel and slander against Mississippi." Many of the problems Robert Kennedy witnessed have persisted—today nearly 21 percent of the Delta's population lacks adequate access to food—but it is unimaginable that a member of the US Senate today would appropriate or even suggest appropriating money to help cure any of the ills of the Delta.

It is even questionable whether those in political power in Mississippi even care about the plight of the Delta. The best indicator of that is spending for K–12 education, which across Mississippi is underfunded by $176 million, according to the state's own public school funding formula.[3] In the Delta town of Greenville, education was underfunded by $1.4 million for 2023–24 and by $38 million cumulatively since 2008. This is a town in which poverty is among the worst in the nation: 32.2 percent of Greenville's residents live below the poverty line. The median income is $35,148. As the town has lost population and its school system has become more segregated, the city has been on a steady decline despite its label as "Queen of the Delta." But Greenville is only a queen from the past who has now been dethroned.

By seeking to ignore or diminish the significance of the Delta's history, the past becomes obscured by mythology and influences how the powerful see the place. I once had a Mississippi politician announce to me with a hint of pride in his voice that without the Delta, the economic ranking of the state of Mississippi would be significantly higher, perhaps close to twenty-fifth in the nation. Time and time again, I heard others make the same proclamation. When I did some fact-checking and learned that the Delta is less than 20 percent of the state's population, I began to wonder whether this statement was only a way of saying that Mississippi needs to rid itself of the Black and the poor. Whether the Delta is counted or not, Mississippi is still a poor state. Probe even deeper, and the same politician will blame the people of the Delta for their plight, despite glaring evidence in the public record over the past half-century of Mississippi's systematic efforts to keep economic and political power out of the hands of Black Delta residents. The willful blindness to the poverty and pain of the people of the Delta is part of the story of the Delta.

While many turn a blind eye to the Delta, others have looked at the place seeking to discern some form of truth. Mississippi Freedom Summer leader Bob Moses was one of them. "In probably five years . . . the automation of the plantation will be completed," Moses noted in a speech at Stanford University in 1964, noticing exactly what Mississippi's white political class chose to ignore at the time.

> The labor market on the plantation will be very well stabilized and at a very low point. And the people who come off those plantations will be unemployed and unemployable in our society. They will be permanently unemployed because, first, they don't have the skills. And there isn't anywhere, in our whole country, a system for teaching them how to read and write. Because that was nobody's problem who had power, who had resources, who had money, who could tackle that problem.[4]

If you look at the Delta today, you see how prescient Bob Moses's observations were. Not only are the poorest counties in the Mississippi Delta also the ones with the highest concentration of the slave population in 1860, they are also the ones in which sharecropping and farm labor were the predominant means of employment more than a century later at the end of the 1960s. The ghosts of slavery, sharecropping, and Jim Crow haunt the Delta.

When my family arrived in the Delta, no one counted on the transformational role automation and mechanization would come to play in farming—that they would eliminate the need for people to work in the fields and leave unskilled farmworkers jobless. Small farmers had not yet been pushed out by agribusiness. Complicating today's Mississippi Delta is access to education, which continues to be a civil rights issue in this part of the state. In the Delta's poorest counties, in which nearly half the student population lives at poverty level, there is not only insufficient school funding but in many schools, there are not enough teachers. The beginning of the school year is no longer delayed for cotton-picking season, as it was during my childhood, but the gaps in funding and staffing mean the educational outcomes are not much better than they were fifty years ago. During the COVID-19 pandemic, when school moved online rather than in person, many students could not attend school since the Delta ranks last in the state in high-speed household internet access. Much of the Delta lacks access to fast wired broadband at home. Students were given shiny new tablets to continue their learning during the pandemic, which is of little use when many of them had no internet service.

Even before the pandemic, a Mississippi judge ruled that the legislature is not obliged to fully fund schools in the state, a ruling that hit poor districts across the Delta with a wallop. So, education has not become the great equalizer for opportunity many hoped it would become after the end of segregation. And when students graduate, one of the largest employers in the area today is a network of local prisons, both public and private, whose population—both inmates and guards—is largely African American and drawn from the Delta's native sons and daughters.

My father thought Black farmers owning their own land and profiting from it was what would lift the Delta out of poverty. With only a few exceptions, that has not happened. Sharecropper shacks from my father's time, like those I stumbled across, pop up occasionally on the landscape, but many of them have only been abandoned, destroyed, or replaced by rusting trailer homes. As I drive through the Delta, I wonder what, if anything, could change the fortunes of this place. And I am overcome with pangs of survivor's guilt that my family escaped. What draws me back is both the connection I feel to this land and a sense that my family committed a breach by leaving it behind.

The long flat expanses of dark loamy soil of the Delta were created when, not long before the Civil War, the land was partially cleared of jungle-thick stands of trees, mostly hardwood and pine, through the toil of enslaved people. Later, more land was cleared by the descendants of those slaves. The land was cleared to exploit its rich soil and turn this land into a cotton kingdom. Now that the wealthy people who cleared the Delta have extracted riches from this created space, it is being abandoned and the poor can take what little is left.

This land is filled with stories, which for some reason people feel compelled to tell me on dusty roads and sagging front porches with the wind blowing beneath my feet. These stories unfurl like the terse lines of a blues song sketching an epic tale. But they are wrapped up in the long-term impact of neglect and the human cruelty undergirding the social and economic stagnation that seems to have been willed on this place. Each time I think nothing brighter than the deep pitch of night exists in the Delta, I find some source of light that guides me to my next destination, shows me my next story. Yes, trauma is imprinted on the landscape of this expansive alluvial plain, across time and generations. You can see it and feel it in the abandoned towns, buildings, shotgun shacks, and the vast fields that surround them. Confronting and easing that trauma in some way is what brought my family to the Delta. In the end, the continuous presence of racial violence forced my family to leave. It is my need to confront this long bright line of pain that draws me back and urges me to tell the story of this place.

But this story is not just my story to tell. It is the story of the people of the Delta who never left, who continue to embrace and practice that radical spirit of progress that attracted my family here. These are the people who have been working to transform the Delta because long ago they realized that no one is coming to save them.

The land called the Mississippi Delta was shaped by the great river that runs alongside its western edge. To begin to reckon with the forces that shaped the Delta, we must confront the poverty and strife over time that shaped the land and its people as much as the river itself. The journey through the Delta in these pages is personal and historical, and the voices that narrate this story come from the past and the present. Only by looking at both the forces of history and the way we live now can we begin to understand not only the Mississippi Delta, but also the forces of inequality that have shaped America itself.

That means the story of the people of the Delta is not just a Mississippi story. Nor is it just a Southern story. At its very core, the Delta's story is an American story. The idea of American exceptionalism has rendered the Delta and other places like it invisible since the story of the Delta is exceptional in only disturbing ways. By reckoning with the story of the Delta, we as Americans can also begin to confront the other disadvantaged places like it that dot the American landscape, from sea to shining sea.

WHEN IT'S
DARKNESS
ON
THE DELTA

CHAPTER 1

THE DIMMING MYSTIQUE OF MILESTON

I'm goin' away, to a world unknown
I'm goin' away, to a world unknown
I'm worried now, but I won't be worried long

—CHARLEY PATTON, "Down the Dirt Road Blues"

If a place as rich and tortured as the Mississippi Delta did not exist, some raconteur south of the Mason–Dixon line would have to make it up. The American South is a place filled with stories and storytellers, and a fertile imagination nurtured in this deeply haunted region would surely invent a tale of a swampy, seemingly untamable wilderness of dark, rich soil that men and women conquered just to make it their own. For some the Delta is a place that magically rose out of a tangled wilderness, much like the mansion Sutpen's Hundred did in the William Faulkner novel *Absalom, Absalom!* The tragic character Quentin Compson observes that the mansion's owner, Thomas Sutpen, would "watch his mansion rise, carried plank by plank and brick by brick out of the swamp where the clay and timber waited." It's almost as if the slaves who labored to clear the land of the Delta were mere passive observers of the place's creation. One day it was cleared, and overnight the cotton crop became king.

The mansion known as Sutpen's Hundred that sprang from Faulkner's imagination may have been built on the soil of his fictional Yoknapatawpha County, but its inspiration came from the Mississippi Delta and the people who chose to tame that land. Faulkner knew that within the story of the Mississippi Delta lies the story of the American South, one that largely lives in legend, with a wrinkle of truth thrown in. In the Delta's haunted ground, you can also find the roots of the South's relationship with a system of patriarchy, racism, and social stratification. Without the influence of slavery, white supremacy, and social class, the Delta as we know it would have never existed. Indeed, the Delta was built on those very forces.

But the Delta's story is not just about the sins of the South; it is also a story of America and this country's thirst and ambition for transformation and reinvention. It was first settled by planters who—after taming the land—would remake the Delta in their own vision and image. When Mississippi became a state in 1817, the Delta was firmly in the hands of the Choctaw Nation. Of course, the Choctaw were removed from the land and white settlers subsequently arrived between 1825 and 1827. Moving into what was once called the "Yazoo Bottoms" to farm its rich soil offered the chance to make a fortune, but given the labor entailed in clearing the land, it required a lot of money and a lot of slaves. This was not a place for a thrifty farmer with a strong work ethic and a dream.

Though the Delta is a Southern space, it's also an ancient one. Formally known as the Yazoo-Mississippi Delta—named for the rivers that made and shaped it—the region was formed long before national political and racial divisions were projected onto our borders and our consciousness. If you go back fifteen thousand years, when glaciers were melting and what's now the Mississippi River flooded often, the lower Mississippi valleys were buried under a thick coating of alluvium. Dark, fertile soil was deposited here, creating some of the richest agricultural land in the world.

The eastern side of the Delta is defined by a line of bluffs, some rising two hundred feet—hence my childhood memory of a dramatic drop upon entering the Delta—and the western boundary is the Mississippi River itself. The result is a huge, flat plain that extends roughly from Memphis, Tennessee, to Vicksburg, Mississippi. The Delta is the most photographed part of the state, making some people think it's bigger than it really is. But it's still quite large: it totals 7,110 square miles, about one-seventh of Mississippi's area.

The fields of the modern-day Delta serve as a direct contrast to the primordial environment. When I drive up from the south into the Delta, I head north out of Yazoo City and then along the Delta's eastern edge, with bluffs visible off in the distance. As I drive, I think about how these agricultural expanses are essentially a created environment. This land was not flat and largely treeless until it was cleared by slaves and the descendants of slaves, who farmed under a system of sharecropping that mirrored the inequities of bondage.

With the region's labor and wealth tied up in the peculiar institution of slavery, Delta planters had a stake in maintaining an economy based on cheap labor. The migration of one-fourth to one-third of the Black work-force to Southern urban areas in the years immediately after emancipation confirmed the fears of cotton planters about the shift from slave to wage labor. In 1869, one proposed alternative to what planters saw as an overde-pendence on Black labor was to bring in Chinese immigrant labor. Cotton plantation owners saw two possible outcomes from pursuing this course of action: the Chinese immigrants would permanently replace the loss of the Black population, or they would create competition between the two groups that would compel former slaves to resume their submissive status on plantations. But when the Chinese arrived, they found the wages were low and lost interest in the work because they would not tolerate the ex-ploitation by the planters. Though they came in small numbers, eventually most of the Chinese were operating small grocery stores that catered to a largely Black clientele.

The case was the same with Italian workers, mostly from Sicily, who also immigrated to the Delta in the 1900s. Delta planter William Alexander Percy deemed that Italians did not "fit in" with the Delta's tenant farming system because they were too independent and aggressive, meaning they could not be controlled and intimidated like Black laborers could be. Other ethnic groups, like the Lebanese, also found their way to the Delta. Jew-ish merchants and planters were also part of the cultural landscape. While we often think of the Delta through the lens of a racial binary, it is a place with a complex ethnic, racial, and cultural milieu. Yet it is the Black-white divide that has dominated the way we look at the Delta, given the connec-tion between Black labor and the institution of slavery. While other ethnic groups were also subject to forms of racial intimidation and discrimination, Black people were granted a status directly tied to their previous condition of servitude, which placed them below the status of recent immigrants.

After emancipation and the end of the Civil War, residents needed to find a way to exert white control over Black labor, given that immigrant labor failed to fill the void left by Black out-migration. Using the political weight of Delta politicians—as the state's most prosperous region, the Delta wielded a great deal of political power in those days—in 1866 Mississippi enacted the Black Codes, which kept Blacks from leasing land and becom-ing independent farmers. After the Republican Party gained a majority in Congress in 1866, it passed the Reconstruction Act, placed the South un-der military rule, and repealed the Black Codes. At the time of the codes' repeal in 1867, Delta planters were still in search of some way to procure labor for their farms as cheaply as possible. And the newly freed slaves wanted to have some autonomy. But these newly freed men and women had no means to rent land, buy farm supplies and seeds, or get credit to start a farm. At the same time, the white farmers were looking for a way to shift some of the risk of their cotton crop onto those who worked the land. So it was within the marketplace that a compromise was reached, and a system called sharecropping was born.

Sharecropping allowed a tenant the use of the land for farming in exchange for a share in the profits of the crop. The system grew because of the expanding labor requirements of the Delta's then-booming plantation economy. Although sharecroppers were both Black and white, those in the Delta were largely Black. In addition to Delta freedmen, by the 1890s planters even recruited Black refugees fleeing the failing farm economy of Mississippi's Hill Country.

Virtually every Black farmer hoped the system of sharecropping would be a first step toward landownership. Delta Blacks, much to the concern of whites, registered to vote in large numbers and elected Republican office holders they thought would eventually deliver on the promise made after slavery of "40 acres and a mule." But by 1880, with the demise of Reconstruction and the disenfranchisement of Blacks that came with that demise, there was no governmental intervention on behalf of Black farmers that led to their owning a piece of land.

From the people who lived the pain of hard work and marginalization, the art form of the blues came into being. It's a music whose origins and history are as primeval as the land that gave it birth. Howard Odum, a sociologist, collected songs in the Delta between 1905 and 1908, but he didn't call them "the blues." What Odum failed to realize at the time is that the blues is music that tells the story of the lives its practitioners lived and was sung to ease the pain of their daily survival. Later, folklorist Alan Lomax noticed that the singing of what we would today call "field hollers"—a form of call and response—was another musical art form shaped by the labor of Black people in the Delta. These field hollers are now considered a direct precursor to the blues. The Delta's greatest export, the blues is a light that comes from the darkest part of this region's soul.

The prospect of moving from sharecropping to being a landowner is not material for the blues, something sung after crying out the proclamation

"Woke up this morning . . ." That's why when talk began of an experiment that would lead to Black farmers owning their own land, it was hard for people in the Delta to believe it. This un-blues-like twist of fate would not take place until the wake of the Great Depression and the New Deal, and it occurred through a resettlement program developed by President Franklin D. Roosevelt's Farm Security Administration that came to several Delta communities, including a community in Holmes County called Mileston.

The names of tiny hamlets collide with each other as I drive along Highway 49 through the Mississippi Delta. A town named Eden hints that a section of this flat expansive terrain once felt more like a paradise than it may seem at the current moment, looking more abandoned than idyllic. The sign pointing toward the town of Egypt conjures up the voice of Burl Ives as Big Daddy in *Cat on a Hot Tin Roof*, growling in his famous baritone that you are driving through some of the richest land this side of the valley Nile.

It's easy to overlook these communities that dot the Delta landscape or to write them off as merely the slowly decaying detritus of King Cotton. They feel a bit like footnotes that can be scanned and skimmed, their details of interest only to an elect few and of marginal significance to the masses. But if you begin to wipe the dust off the names of places in the Mississippi Delta, different stories begin to emerge. And like most Mississippi stories, they hold their surprises tightly.

One of those places is the tiny community of Mileston, named for the plantation that once encompassed the land where the town now sits. It rests on the western edge of Holmes County, south of the muddy and slow-moving Big Black River and just north of Bee Lake. It was this place that Marion Post Wolcott documented in more than one hundred Farm Security Administration photographs in the 1930s. Eventually, the land of the Mileston Plantation that she captured with her camera was purchased by the federal government and sold in pieces to some of the same sharecroppers she froze in time with her camera as they chopped cotton.

Mileston is a place I, too, would probably ignore without looking back had my family not once lived on this land. Two of my sisters were born here. Before I was born, my parents lived right next door to what was once the Mileston store and post office, on the same spot immortalized in Wolcott's photographs. It was nothing special, just a standard two-bedroom house built by the government for the resettlement project that made sharecroppers on this land independent farmers. Both of these buildings are gone now, but I can imagine them on the seemingly deserted stretch of Delta land in the same way that I can sense the youthful spirit of my parents whenever I am here. To be honest, I visit Mileston more than I do my parents' graves; it is here in the Delta that I can again imagine them as vibrant people.

My father arrived in Mileston young and idealistic in 1949, with a newly minted agronomy degree from Tuskegee Institute. He worked at the tail end of the transition of this land from sharecropping to landowning. At night he taught GED classes and farming techniques to World War II veterans like himself, and by day vocational agriculture at the local school. When my parents married, my mother joined my father in Mileston in 1951—they met while at Tuskegee—and she became a teacher in this community as well as the girls' basketball coach for the high school.

I'd always wondered what brought my parents to the Delta from their own now-deserted south Alabama towns of Edna and Prestwick. When I asked, my normally loquacious father would just say one word: opportunity. Ten years ago, I began investigating, learning of the connection between the opportunity my father was seeking and the remnants of a dream initiated by Franklin D. Roosevelt's New Deal.

To understand this connection between my father's opportunity and the New Deal, I had to go back to the Great Mississippi Flood of 1927. Secretary of Commerce Herbert Hoover was placed in charge of all flood relief efforts by then president Calvin Coolidge. During the flood, 330,000 Black Delta residents were moved to 154 relief camps. Over 13,000 "refugees" near Greenville, Mississippi, were evacuated to an unbroken levee—and stranded there for days without food or clean water—while boats arrived to evacuate white women and children. As conditions deteriorated for Black residents in the aftermath of the flood, word slowly filtered north, and the scandal threatened to derail Hoover's presidential ambitions.

Hoover in turn appointed Tuskegee Institute president Robert Moton to oversee a "colored advisory commission" to investigate the treatment of Black Delta residents during the flood. A protégé of Booker T. Washington, Moton was a believer in accommodation, not confrontation. Hoover promised Moton that he intended to divide the land of bankrupt planters into small Black-owned farms if he won the presidency. In turn, Moton did Hoover's bidding and encouraged Black refugees to stay in their relief camps. In his appeal, Moton insisted that "whatever might be said to the contrary, the white man of the South loves the Negro. Many who have gone north have not found conditions as they had expected. . . . There is less reason now for Negroes to leave the South than ever before."[1]

With the help of Moton, Hoover avoided scandal and won the presidency. But he did not keep his promise to Moton. When Franklin Delano Roosevelt challenged Hoover's reelection, Moton and his Tuskegee machine backed Roosevelt. It was Roosevelt's New Deal that kept its promise to Moton. In the late 1930s, the Farm Security Administration, an agency of FDR's New Deal, established a series of model farming and industrial communities, thirteen of which were reserved for Blacks. Given the connection between the Mississippi Delta and Tuskegee Institute forged by Moton, it would follow that a young Tuskegee graduate would be encouraged to move there to work with Black farmers. Mileston was a place very much aligned with Tuskegee's particular idea of racial uplift.

The land that was once the Mileston Plantation became the only Black resettlement community in Mississippi. With the purchase of ten thousand acres of rich Delta farmland and a capital investment of $886,436, the federal government hoped to transform the lives of 110 families of former Black sharecroppers who would live there as landowners. The Great Depression made the land affordable.

The Depression hit the Delta cotton industry hard, with cotton prices dropping from a high of 12 cents per pound to a rock-bottom price of 5.5 cents per pound, making the sizable crop grown on the ten thousand acres of the Mileston Plantation worth a lot less than it was before. After paying its patchwork of day laborers to pick the crop, as well as tenant farmers and sharecroppers, there was not much profit left to sustain all the hands involved. By the 1930s, Mileston no longer had the resources to pay its white plantation manager, Mel Blake. Before his death in 2017, his son, also named Mel, a former State Department diplomat then in his nineties, remembered when his family left Mileston for nearby Lexington. Since he was only seven at the time, his father explained their move in the simplest terms he could. "He told me that there was a big difference between a planter and a farmer," Blake recalled to me one summer afternoon in Washington, DC, that seemed as hot and sticky as the Delta. "A farmer could survive a bad season without too much risk. A planter was taking a much bigger financial risk than a farmer, and now Mileston would be a place for farmers rather than planters." Blake remembered no discussion of its purchase by the government, which would be something he would not understand until he became an adult.

The government's plan, as outlined in a 1941 Department of Agriculture memo, was that these former sharecroppers "would develop an exemplary pattern of rural life for the Delta Negro. He has been given the security of tenure and a chance to take hold for himself on the right soil of the plantation county." Plans called for a school and community center, which served to anchor the Mileston Plantation's residents in spite of what might potentially go on around it: that is, white racists using intimidation to oppress the minds and bodies of African American men and women. Low-interest loans were provided to these farmers for the purchase of the land as well as housing and farm equipment. The Farm Security Administration (FSA) also established a farm cooperative so that these families, rather than being sharecroppers, would be shareholders in their own farming operation in addition to becoming landowners.

But there were elements of the old plantation structure left in place. The way the bureaucrats at the FSA saw things, it was best to maintain a system that mirrored the old: small farms operated by individual families and centrally managed by the cooperative. In the new system there were no white overseers, and the feeling was that if Black residents had a proprietary interest in the operation, they could become self-sustaining farmers.

Of course, there was some resistance to the Mileston plan from the descendants of the Delta's wealthy white settlers, those people Mississippi writer David Cohn tagged as "pioneers with means."[2] Many were opposed to a communal—some might argue socialist—farming culture populated with poor people. FDR's Resettlement Administration got its share of resistance from Mississippi politicians and residents. First, local governments worried that they would not be getting their fair share of tax receipts from resettlement communities like Mileston and appealed to Mississippi's segregationist members of Congress, especially Senator Theodore G. Bilbo and Congressman William Whittington. In response to queries from these politicians, in December 1936 the Resettlement Administration stated to local officials in Mississippi that "land bought by the Federal government for resettlement purposes will pay its pro rata share of all taxes." But once the issue of taxes was settled, Congressman Whittington, speaking of another resettlement project that same year, voiced what was the real concern: independent farming communities run by Black farmers would disrupt the longtime system of white paternalism in the Delta. Writing on behalf of "the citizens of the Delta" to the regional director of the Resettlement Administration, Whittington expressed alarm at "all aspects and the theory and practice of this project," noting that "thoughtful citizens now regard it as a hot-bed of radicalism and as a breeding place for agitation of discord between landlords and tenants," which might be "productive of trouble."

The worries of the political class in Mississippi began to filter down to ordinary people. Two years before my father's arrival in Mileston, a 1947 newspaper editorial warned, "At this time there is great talk about the Negroes getting power in this section. If anything hurries the day when the Negro takes a big hand in our financial and political affairs, it will be through the Co-op movement." The politics of intimidation would not be set in motion directly by the co-op movement, but instead by the US Supreme Court's 1954 *Brown* v. *Board of Education* decision mandating the desegregation of public schools, which bred discontent among whites in the Delta and across Mississippi.

It was in the mid-1950s that my father, employed at the time as Holmes County's Negro County Agent—an adviser to Black farmers through the county cooperative extension program—realized that it was time to leave. During this post-*Brown* stage of massive resistance—not just to integrated school education but to Black progress in general—the Delta no longer felt like a safe place for his growing family. The murder of Emmett Till served as one sign of looming hostility, but there were also others. In March 1955, Circuit Judge Tom Brady—who would later be appointed to Mississippi's Supreme Court at the height of the Civil Rights Movement—spoke to a packed high school auditorium in the town of Tchula, roughly six miles up the road from Mileston, calling the attack on segregation an "all-out war." "The question of segregation today is only a small segment in the plan to destroy Christianity and the world," Brady told the white citizens of Tchula, which at the time had a population of less than two thousand people, two-thirds of whom were Black. Men like Brady and Mississippi senator James O. Eastland incited scared whites to make life difficult for Black people in Holmes County, particularly the Black independent farmers in Mileston. Amid this environment of white hostility, my father believed that the work he came to do in the Delta would be diminished and his goals might never be accomplished. By 1956, he chose to be transferred to south Mississippi, which had a larger network of Black landowning farmers stretching back to right after the Civil War. It was there that my father thought his work could make a difference.

In spite of the dangers that existed in the Delta, my mother stayed behind until my father could find a place for the family to land. Then one day she received an unexpected phone call from her doctor over in the town of Lexington. He urged her to leave as soon as she could, never explaining why. "Trust me, please just go," the doctor later cautioned her while giving my sisters vaccinations. My mother took her children and left, never fully understanding the urgency, but eternally grateful for his insistence. In the last months of my mother's life, she told me that story over and over like a mantra. Until she died, she believed the doctor's push for her to leave may have saved her life and her family.

A year after moving south, my family bought a farm outside the town of Mount Olive, just two years after my birth in 1957. It was eighty acres, a parcel of land that was larger than anything we could have purchased in Mileston or anywhere in the Delta. In this region, Black landowning was rare and suspect. Rather than working to build a network of Black farmers—an effort that in the Delta, my parents realized, might cost my father his life—my family opted to leave. But I know leaving was something my father never wanted to do. And that is why I keep coming back to Mileston: I want to understand why.

Mileston survives today, but it seems just barely. Few of the tidy homes the resettlement commission built survive, replaced by now-rusting trailers. The town school sat empty for years, a victim of a declining population and consolidation. Now I find myself back on this spot of land frequently, confronting my memories and seeking to understand my family's connection to this land.

My first memories of coming to Mileston are from late springtime trips there with my father when I was around seven years old. In what I suspect was a sentimental journey for him, we'd make the trip from our home in south Mississippi, deep in the hills of the Piney Woods, up Highway 49 to Clarksdale to visit one of my father's college friends, stopping in Mileston along the way. Since it was just the two of us, rather than peering through the small backseat window of our Volkswagen Beetle, I was allowed the privilege of sitting in the front seat so that the road opened up in front of me. I always knew when the Delta was approaching, since it seemed as if everything changed when we reached Yazoo City. The kudzu-covered hills disappeared, and the land flattened out completely and became more expansive. By the time we arrived in Mileston, the horizon appeared so endless that it was as if my father and I had entered another world. As far as I was concerned, we had.

On our first trip in 1964, as dusk approached, a glow covered the two-lane blacktop and seemingly everything around us. I was mesmerized, as if under a spell. The light was a reddish yellow. It was the same color I witnessed in the sky on my south Mississippi farm, but the effect, the glow, was perhaps blocked by the contours of the landscape. In the Delta, the light covered everything like a canopy and the wide vista of the landscape made its luminance feel endless. Of course, night always approached before we arrived at our final destination of Clarksdale, but the memory of the light hovered around my dreams. Each year when my father asked me to make the trek with him again, I never hesitated.

The last trip I remember my father and I took together was right before I entered high school. By then, I was beginning to think about college and a way out of Mississippi. The wistful gaze that overcame my father's face each time we got to Mileston is forever seared in my memory. It comes back to me each time I visit.

The post office is long gone, as is the store I would visit with my father, replaced by the West Holmes Community Mart and Farmers Market. It is run by Anthony Givins, a retired teacher from Florida who is hoping to make a go of it in the Delta by working with a new version of a farm co-operative that has sprung up here. He's working with Calvin Head, who grew up in Mileston, to make the store a place where local people can buy fresh vegetables grown right in the fields of Mileston.

Despite nearly approaching the age of sixty, Calvin Head's face lights up in a boyish grin whenever he speaks about Mileston's history and its connection to his current project. He runs the West Holmes Community Development Organization, which seeks out high school students to plant and harvest vegetable crops on land donated by farmers in the area. Right now the land bears the bleak brown cast of winter, but when you look at the sprightly gleam in Head's eyes you can tell he is already thinking about spring planting. Fresh from a day of rabbit hunting in the upper Delta, Head tells me that he is trying to keep the spirit of the old Mileston farm cooperative alive, although he is growing vegetables rather than cotton. Each year he finds fifteen to twenty young people who work with him to sell vegetables to a broad market: residents enrolled in the USDA's Women, Infants, and Children program can redeem their vouchers for produce, plus the students sell at farmers' markets as well as to corporate clients like Walmart and Sysco. During the harvest season students earn about $700 each month; while not a living wage, it helps to supplement their family incomes, which are close to the poverty line. Some are even saving money for college.

"I would like to see this place growing enough food to feed itself," Head said, echoing the original goal of self-sufficiency outlined by the early re-settlement community. He's telling me all of this just outside the building that houses his cooperative, right next to what was once the local post office and town store. In the founding plans for the resettlement community, each house was set up with a barn, a smokehouse, a spot for a garden, and a small orchard of fruit trees. About a dozen of these houses remain. They all have a distinctive L-shape, even with modifications made over time.

Head's challenge is finding available land, and he has met some resistance in his efforts to persuade growers to devote more of their acreage to his vegetable crops. Soil healthy enough to grow vegetables is in short supply, due to the land's decades of growing cotton as well as its constant exposure to pesticides. Plus, pesticide drift from aerial spraying can obliterate vegetable crops. "We have land here from the old FSA project, but the people still making money in the Delta are white farmers," Head said with a hint of regret. "They get to put pesticides wherever they want, which makes it hard for me to grow the vegetables that can sustain this co-op."

Indeed, on several of my trips to Mileston I have seen crop-dusting planes flying overhead. On my visits here as a boy, fruit orchards—another victim of pesticides—used to be as much a part of the landscape as cotton fields. Because of the overwhelming presence of these chemicals on the landscape, Head can't even do his rabbit hunting nearby and has to head north to Quitman County. The grasses that once sustained the rabbit population are all gone, all because of the use of pesticides.

After talking with Head, I go to visit the site of the community center and the Mileston School where my mother once taught. Just a few years after this visit, the school and community center were torn down since they were already decaying and collapsing.

A woman walking by sees me looking at the school's abandoned set of steps and, with a bright smile, introduces herself as Lolvone Williams. I tell her of my connection to Mileston and explain that I am hoping to find some of my mother's former students, if any remain. The next thing I know, Lolvone has whipped out her phone and has me talking to a man by the name of Griffin McLaurin, whom my mother taught in tenth grade. His family moved to Mileston from my hometown of Mount Olive, the reverse of my family's migration.

A week later, I pay McLaurin a visit to the twenty-eight-acre plot of land his family purchased in the 1940s. When McLaurin greets me on his front porch, he tells me that the last time he saw me I was toddling across the lawn of my family's farm in south Mississippi. At the age of eighty, he lives in one of the original houses built by the resettlement project, the same one his family moved into in 1941. It even has the original wood stove.

I learn that McLaurin's uncle, B. F. McLaurin, was the administrator of the Mileston project. His uncle's wife, Sezzie, taught home economics at the school and also worked with local women to teach them how to cook, can vegetables, and keep house. As families were leaving during the Great Migration, his uncle saw an opportunity for his brother to own some profitable farmland, with richer soil than they had on the small plot they shared with their large extended family. So, the family pulled up stakes in the Piney Woods and headed to the Delta. "The key thing I have tried to instill into young Black people I meet is that there is nothing like owning a piece of God's great earth," McLaurin tells me. "For Black people in the Delta, Mileston was their forty acres and a mule. That is just what it was for my family."

To live in Mileston in the 1950s and 1960s you had to fight, and McLaurin was willing to go to battle. Along with twelve other men from Mileston, in April 1963 he went to register to vote with Hartman Turnbow, who, in a bizarre turn of phrase, famously said, "I came here to die to vote." Today, McLaurin is the only member of the group who survives. McLaurin was also there when Mileston became a command center for the Civil Rights Movement in Holmes County; he played a crucial role in the movement, doing everything from championing civil rights to getting Black public officials elected. In 1967, his work was critical in helping Robert Clark become the first Black person elected to the Mississippi State Legislature since Reconstruction.

McLaurin tells me that he knows my father never wanted to leave Mileston. "But he also knew that this project could have grown, but the state of Mississippi was never going to allow it," he said. While my father saw the promise of Mileston, he also understood the forces that in time would work to destroy that promise. So, it was the slow decline that he witnessed each time we visited that led to the wistful, somber expression I remember so well.

As McLaurin describes what his farm looked like when he moved there in 1941, with its garden and fruit orchard, I realize that what my father did when we left Mileston was to create a place that mirrored it in south Mississippi. The safe, rural Southern upbringing I had never could have happened in Mileston. After talking with McLaurin, I feel absolved of my guilt that my family left. But still, each time I visit I know the regretful expression of my father has now migrated to my own countenance. And I fear that I may be one of the last to visibly express that plaintive yearning I feel about this place.

CHAPTER 2

"IT'S GOING TO TAKE A MOSES"

God, the Lord, said:
"Go down, Moses
Way down in Egypt's land
Tell old Pharaoh to
Let my people go"

—"GO DOWN MOSES," traditional spiritual

Each year more land becomes available for Calvin Head's Mileston farm cooperative, which is not just a factor of Head's persistence but is also a factor of demographics. As the population has aged and older people give up farming, they are willing to lease Head land for his cooperative. Yet those young people working for him who are saving their money for college will most likely not return once they get their degrees unless they have something to come back to. Although I admire Head's optimism that the cooperative will be a reason for young people to return, I also know that in the Delta, the towns with the largest Black population are also the ones in the most economic trouble. Like the rest of Mississippi, the Delta has a brain drain problem. There is also the issue of population loss, since Holmes County, where Mileston is located, has lost more than 7 percent of its population in the last decade. But in the Delta the loss of people, combined with decades of disinvestment and dispossession, makes the loss of a generation of creative problem solvers more of a profound crisis.

One day when I visited Head, a group of prospective funders for his project were visiting as well, a sign that Head is ensuring that his project has a future. On another visit I learn that his fundraising prowess has allowed him to lease the abandoned gymnasium of the school in Mileston, a school that was closed because of the consolidation of Holmes County schools. Head now has a refrigerated storage unit as well as a greenhouse to grow hydroponic vegetables, so his operation is expanding. But the land that surrounds them is owned by white farmers who grow cotton, and their economic needs and desires seem to take precedence.

Mississippi had eight FSA resettlement communities created through an experimental poverty eradication program, but only one of them was designated for African Americans. In the National Archives, I found the plans for all the white resettlement communities, but not for the one at Mileston. After inquiring, I thought perhaps they might be held in the National Archives' Atlanta facility but was told in an email by the archivist that "the government chose to keep only a sampling of all the Farmers Home Administration [the agency that replaced the FSA] records. Unfortunately, in doing so they destroyed so many wonderful accounts of rural America in the 1940s."

When I related the news to Head, he seemed to take it well. He says that despite all the challenges he faces, it is nothing like what his grandparents went through or Mileston residents like Griffin McLaurin endured. And he believes that in the Delta, Mileston is a unique place because of its history. "Just down the road in Tchula, the way people think is completely different. We've been independent, landowning farmers here for more than seventy years. When you leave here, the old Delta mindset starts to kick in." When pressed, Head won't tell me exactly what he believes that mindset involves. Since he knows of my tie to Mileston, he is sure that I will be able to see a real difference just four miles down the road in Tchula.

The way Mileston stands apart from other Delta communities like Tchula is something the writer John Hersey recognized when he decided to embed himself in Mileston for a 1964 story published in the *Saturday Evening Post*, "A Life for a Vote." Although Hersey is most remembered for his 31,000-word *New Yorker* article "Hiroshima," which tells the survival story of six individuals who witnessed the nuclear destruction there, his reporting from Mileston captures the ways the community stood apart during the Civil Rights Movement with men and women who were brave enough to register to vote in Holmes County. Yet a likely explanation for why this article by Hersey is not as well-known is his choice to change names and geographic locations to protect the men and women he profiled. Rather than Holmes County, the location in Mississippi is Ittabala County, the county seat of Lexington is called Athens, and Mileston is referred to as Noonday. Hersey stresses to his readers that although he has changed names and locations, the reprisals, violence, and other events he documents occurred exactly as described. The only reason we know the identities of the people shielded by pseudonyms is through his reporting notebooks and the inclusion of their real names in early drafts.

"In Ittabala County, as elsewhere in the South ever since the 17th century, Negro labor has made possible a way of life the whites do not wish to give up," Hersey observed. Reading Hersey's reporting reminds me of stories Griffin McLaurin told me on his porch about his efforts to register to vote alongside Hartman Turnbow. Hersey's pseudonym for Turnbow is "Randoman Tort," whom he says people describe as a "broad-speaking man," much like how McLaurin described him to me. One of the primary figures in Hersey's article, Turnbow was one of the first men in Holmes County to register to vote.

On the morning of April 9, 1963, fourteen Black men arrived in the Holmes County town of Lexington to register to vote. Sheriff Andrew Smith was waiting on the courthouse steps with his deputies. Farmer Hartman Turnbow was among the men and, while not there in a leadership position, he found himself assuming that role when the sheriff asked the men what had brought them to the courthouse. Turnbow was the first to respond by noting, "We've come to register," meaning they came to register to vote. Then Sheriff Smith, with one hand on a blackjack and the other on his gun, asked who would be first. At that moment, most of the men were ready to run, but Turnbow told himself that he came there that day to die or vote. With little hesitation he said, "I'll be first," and the men settled in and stayed beside him.

After taking his stance at the courthouse steps, Turnbow's house was bombed and he was constantly threatened but never gave up, and Hersey captures that resilience in his description of "Randoman Tort." Although I am fairly certain about who the real people are behind the pseudonyms, I decided to look at Hersey's notebooks and drafts of the article at the Beinecke Library at Yale to make sure I had decoded his article accurately. But I also was interested in how Hersey chose Mileston to center his reporting and specifically who might have led him to Mileston. And even more important, how did Hersey spend months in the Mississippi Delta in the summer of 1964 undetected by agents of Mississippi's Sovereignty Commission? This group effectively served as a state-sanctioned spy agency that would have placed Hersey under surveillance had it known what he was doing.

When white college students arrived in Mileston during Freedom Summer in 1964, the place surprised them. Many of them were expecting subservient, beaten-down Black people but, as one Freedom Summer volunteer said after arriving there, Mileston was "not at all what I pictured Mississippi to be like." Here, plantations did not dominate the landscape and breed subservience. Further, Black farmers in Holmes County "are the backbone of the movement," the volunteer observed, since they owned their own land and "cower before no man." It made me wonder if it was a Freedom Summer volunteer who led Hersey to report in Mileston.

The clue was not in Hersey's drafts or his reporting notebooks but in the illustrations in the article itself. Illustrator Tracy Sugarman was Hersey's contemporary—and neighbor in Westport, Connecticut—who was an older Freedom Summer volunteer. Sugarman spent time in Mileston and must have suggested it as a place to center a story. When I met Sugarman years ago—he was donating a set of his drawings to the Library of Congress, where I worked at the time—I told him my family once lived in Mileston. He remembered the place fondly and said the Mississippi Delta was a place that stays with him always. Sugarman also recalled to me that he took numerous sketches that summer and more than a thousand photographs. As he wrote in his memoir, "The year 1964 was simply when my imagined Mississippi evaporated in the heat and passion of the struggle I witnessed in the Delta. For me, it was the very beginning of a journey of discovery that has continued to unfold for more than four decades. A place I had once only imagined has become a reality of flesh and bone and blood; of anguish and exhilaration; of courage I had never before witnessed; of hopes kindled, of hopes extinguished, of hopes incredibly reborn."[1]

As Hersey observes about the town of Tchula—which he names "Meeks"—it was a "mean little town" where people didn't feel as if they could challenge the county's white power structure because they lacked the independence of Mileston farmers. In Tchula, it was harder for a Black man to decide that without a vote his life was not his own. What I now wondered was how much of the past Hersey documented lives on in Tchula today.

Tchula sits on the other side of the muddy and slow-moving Big Black River and is a poor town with a population of just around 1,600 people. The town is majority Black and has always been. Nonetheless, throughout the era of slavery and segregation, the white population owned all the businesses and controlled all the wealth. The Black population existed largely to work for those whites who held the power. As in many Southern towns, the railroad tracks were once the dividing line between Black and white, and whites lived in their own section of this tiny hamlet, with a columned mansion at the center of that part of town.

It's hard to believe that in a town that now has an unemployment rate of 7.2 percent and a poverty rate of roughly 42 percent, there was once a mansion here that was filled with priceless art. Sara Virginia Jones, the daughter of a local plantation dynasty, owned this house, and its walls were lined with nearly four hundred works by artists as prominent as Paul Cézanne, Marc Chagall, Pierre-Auguste Renoir, Salvador Dalí, David Hockney, and Andy Warhol. The Jones family owned the Marcella Plantation, which was adjacent to the land that became the Mileston Resettlement community. Sara Jones began collecting art in 1968 after being given a book about the printmaker Stow Wengenroth, which inspired her to purchase a print of his. Over the next twenty years, she actively collected art through a dealer in New Orleans. The collection is incredibly diverse and is not focused on a particular period or artist. It seems that her only rule for her dealer was to buy what she liked.

Jones's collection of nearly four hundred works on paper was bequeathed to the Mississippi Museum of Art upon her death in 1990. As an indication of how valuable the collection was, the Mississippi Museum of Art posted security guards at her locked-up house immediately after her death. While families who owned cotton plantations are not necessarily known for philanthropy—the Delta has not produced a philanthropist of the likes of a Carnegie or Rockefeller—the Jones collection makes up roughly 5 percent of the holdings of the Mississippi Museum of Art, which makes it a significant act of philanthropy. Unlike many Delta cotton dynasties, the Jones family had diverse investments, including oil wells in Oklahoma. In addition to the prints, Jones also gave the museum an original James McNeill Whistler oil painting titled *Nocturne*, which Jones had purchased from her uncle's estate. It is one of the few documented philanthropic contributions from a cotton-industry magnate in the state of Mississippi.

The Joneses fled Tchula, as families like them have fled from many small Delta towns, taking their wealth with them. Today, Tchula does not look like a town with the level of wealth that would have allowed one of its residents to amass a significant art collection that includes old masters such as Rembrandt and contemporary masters such as Will Barnet. And while the art Sara Jones collected was donated to a Mississippi museum, it begs the question of why this town was never itself an object of the Jones family's largesse. The house was the site of an annual high school graduation party—for white Tchula residents only. In fairness, the Jones family was just following the social confines of Delta life. While white residents would be welcome in your home, Black residents in Tchula were viewed simply as part of the labor force. And there is the difference between Tchula and Mileston: Tchula residents were entirely dependent on the white minority for work and Mileston residents felt a measure of independence from whites.

In a strange twist of fate, today the once art-filled mansion is owned by Eddie Carthan, who grew up in Mileston and was Tchula's controversial first Black mayor. In another era, Carthan would not have been able to walk the street outside this house, much less think of owning it. But the house is now worth far less than even one of the paintings that once hung inside it, putting it in the realm of affordability for a man who now farms and owns a small hardware store. When Carthan took office as mayor of Tchula in 1977 at the age of twenty-seven, the town was completely segregated. The white population, comprising 15 percent of residents, lived on one side of the tracks—where he lives today—and the Black population, comprising 85 percent, lived on the other. The streets in the Black side were unpaved and had no sidewalks or streetlights. Many homes were without indoor plumbing and there were no social services. With some available federal funds, Carthan began work on public housing construction and infrastructure projects, such as water and sewer lines. The newly hired workers had spent half the year as low-paid labor on cotton plantations and the other half as welfare recipients, but now finally saw the possibility of doing something different.

In the 1970s, federal officials seemed eager to take on the cause of battling Black poverty in the South. With federal funds, Carthan built a public library and opened a child development center. But by the time he ran into problems with the white power structure of Tchula, Ronald Reagan was in the White House and the programs that had helped Tchula move forward were beginning to be dismantled. By the 1980s there were hardly any farm jobs to return to, so Tchula began to spiral backward again.

When Carthan was elected in 1977, four other Blacks were elected, providing the majority needed to back Carthan's agenda. But Tchula's white power structure pushed back. By 1981, Carthan was ousted from office, imprisoned on felony charges, and tried for the murder of one of his political rivals. Carthan says that Hartman Turnbow's example of defiance is what kept him going, particularly when his fortunes began to turn in 1978 with the resignation of one of his supporters on the board. Some say this was not a voluntary resignation and that the supervisor had been forced out by threats against his family, himself, and his home. The pro-Carthan alderman was replaced by another Black man, Roosevelt Granderson, a convenience store clerk and close ally of a wealthy white cotton farmer by the name of John Edgar Hays. Hays had always wielded a great deal of power in Tchula and still wanted to keep control of this racially divided small town. With Granderson's appointment, Hays had an alderman who tended to his interests, and the opposition was able to block Carthan at almost every turn.

Eventually, the board of aldermen installed Granderson as mayor. In 1981 Carthan's two remaining supporters on the board were defeated after an election that later was shown to be full of irregularities. To propel this small-town soap opera toward its climax, Granderson was then killed in his store by two men who in turn tried to frame Carthan for the murder, claiming he had hired them to knock off his old opponent. Granderson's death meant Carthan's white predecessor was returned to the mayor's seat. After a lengthy legal ordeal—actor Ossie Davis toured the country raising money for Carthan's legal defense—Carthan was acquitted of murder and thus avoided the electric chair, but after finishing a prison sentence for lesser charges, he sank from public view for about five years.

In the late 1980s and early 1990s, Carthan reentered the arena and led a struggle by Mississippi small farmers fighting to keep their land. He also fought cotton gin owners who refused to gin the cotton grown by Black farmers, forcing them to travel thirty or more miles to have it done at a higher cost, and he exposed the connections between the gin owners and local banks that discriminated against poor Black farmers. Today a member of the Holmes County Board of Supervisors, he's still involved in politics and trying to change the Delta, a place he sees as "a diamond in the rough." Now in his seventies, he feels his fighting days are winding down.

When I ask Carthan about whether there is a difference in mindset between Mileston and Tchula, he agrees that there is a difference, but there are exceptions. "The people of Tchula and the people of Mileston are somewhat similar. The dividing line comes about between those who were landowners and those who worked on the plantations. As Black people, we all had the same status, but the dividing line was that your life had a provisional status when you lived on the plantation. You lived life on the plantation knowing that everything could be taken away with a single misstep, but if you owned your land that could not be taken away." Owning land offered both protection and a defense against the white power structure.

Carthan tells me that he learned about civil rights, human rights, and the cost of freedom from a young age. His election as mayor in 1977 was the first significant manifestation of the strength of the Voting Rights Act in his community, but the political struggles he encountered also showed the limitations of Black political power. Still, he knows he never would have learned how to navigate those struggles had he not grown up in an independent Black community. "I went to every meeting and would hear men like Hartman Turnbow speak as well as young Mississippians like Hollis Watkins," who accompanied Turnbow the fateful day he registered to vote. In the summer of 1964 when he was just thirteen, during a protest in Jackson after the murder of civil rights activist Medgar Evers, Carthan, along with hundreds of other protesters, was thrown into a makeshift prison in a cattle stockade on the Mississippi State Fairgrounds. "When I was growing up, I did not have to deal with white racism since I lived in an all-Black community. Later, when I noticed the difference in the way Black people interacted with whites when they came to town in Tchula and saw how they deferred to white people about everything, I knew that I wanted to change that."

Carthan feels that growing up in Mileston gave him the perspective of independence, one that he tried to inject into the residents of Tchula after he became mayor. But he learned that trying to change the mindset of a people comes with a price. He may have gained political power as mayor, but economic power trumped whatever gains he made. Those who extracted what they could from Tchula have abandoned it, taking business and tax revenue with them. "Political power without economic power is meaningless," Carthan tells me one afternoon at his long dining room table. Rather than being filled with priceless art—art purchased on the backs of Black laborers—the walls are covered with pictures of Carthan and political figures from a wide spectrum, from Jimmy Carter to Louis Farrakhan. Carthan recognizes the strange twist of fate that has taken him across the tracks to the old white side of town, one that is now absent a single white face.

In spite of everything Carthan has been through, he still believes in the Delta. As he tells me, the Delta may still evoke the sound of the blues, but it has not lost its lyricism. That's why he has stayed and continues to do whatever he can to change the Delta. And what does he think can do that? He believes it is a mixture of community organizing and attention from the federal government, particularly in providing broadband internet access since the Delta is the least digitally connected region of the state. But the election of 2016 smothered any hope of federal intervention, whether for poverty reduction or broadband internet access. During the Biden years it seemed the infrastructure bill might tackle the issue through greater broadband access, but Carthan is still not sure if that will change the fortunes of Tchula. Now, with a second Trump administration and its "America First" policy, it is doubtful that the new political realities of the country will lead to alleviating Black rural poverty and helping places like Tchula. On the surface, that doesn't seem to be the intent of "America First" policies.

Carthan believes that the Delta may follow the lead of communities in the rest of Mississippi and other Southern states, with local leaders luring companies with large tax breaks as well as a promise to ignore union protections for workers and thus ensure a powerless and desperate workforce. Plus, with the forces of voter suppression also on the horizon, he also fears a loss of political power.

Based on his experience of growing up in Mileston and being mayor of Tchula, Carthan believes that had the landowning experiment of Mileston spread across the Delta, the fate of the region's Black population might have been different. Given the forces that sought to undermine places like Mileston, it's clear that the white population knew how transformative Black landownership would have been, since even members of Congress saw landownership as a "breeding place for the agitation of discord."

"It's going to take a Moses to change the Delta," Carthan tells me, "and this time Moses might actually be a white man or a white woman." As I leave the white columned porch of Carthan's house, I wonder where that Moses might be and where on my travels through the Delta I might find him or her. Moses was known for his patience in leading his stiff-necked people out of Egypt, but even he could be wrathful sometimes.

What occurs to me while processing Carthan's sense of yearning is that there have been so many times that a Moses has sought to come to the Delta to lead people out of the wilderness. Both John Hersey and Tracy Sugarman documented the people in their midst who worked to move the Delta forward into what Sugarman called a "remarkable work in progress." The men and women Hersey profiled were the leaders of their time, but there are few of them left, and many of their descendants have fled this land as well. Population loss and disinvestment in education are a formula for keeping rural places like the Delta from reaching the potential and promise many observed here during Freedom Summer. For those who remain in the Delta, living in this place demands that they come to terms with the ghosts that echo across the fields.

CHAPTER 3

"WE THOUGHT MISSISSIPPI WAS SAFER THAN ARKANSAS"

He was a poor sharecropper
Worked hard every day
To make an honest living
And his multiple accounts to pay

—JOHN HANDCOX, "Where Is the Man Frank Weems?"

The jagged slope of the Loess Bluffs marks the end of the Mississippi Delta and the beginning of Hill Country. On the edge of where these bluffs begin in Holmes County sits a portion of Delta land once called Providence Farm that during its existence represented hope, racial reconciliation, and a new way of life for former Southern sharecroppers. "We haven't got much here," farm manager A. E. Cox (familiarly known as Eugene) once remarked to a journalist about Providence Farm, "except maybe a few principles."[1] Now, there is not even evidence of those principles or what they were. In fact, today it is hard to believe that such a place ever existed. All that remains of Providence Farm are fields shrouded in the kudzu vines that create a curtain of green covering the ground and the bluffs that sit off in the distance. There are no ruins of a barn or abandoned farm dwellings that allow the imagination to resurrect the past and envision the rhythms of daily life here. The green and gold Mississippi historic marker that sits beside the road only tells part of the story, noting that the farm ceased operations "due to civil rights era tensions." The ambiguity of that description combined with the setting speaks to the ways tension in the Delta often leads to erasure.

If you're driving along the Delta's Highway 49, it would be easy to miss the road that leads to the place once known as Providence Farm. On the crisp fall day I tried to find it, I initially sought out help in uncovering where the farm was once located, yet everyone I encountered had no knowledge of its existence. Neither Eddie Carthan nor strangers I asked on the streets of Tchula knew where it was. The gas station at the intersection of Providence Road and Highway 49 was in operation, but there was no attendant inside to ask directions—although in this age of automation you could still buy gas at the pumps. Beyond the service station's rusty barred windows, the only thing around me were vast fields lush with dark freshly plowed earth, one sign that the cotton crop had already been harvested. The other sign was the pieces of cotton tangled in the roadside grass that the wind blew across the road like tiny ghosts. When I finally stumbled upon the historic marker—after driving closer and closer to the bluffs off in the distance—the only living being was an armadillo rustling along the edge of a stretch of dirt road. The leathery gray creature scampered away quickly once my footfalls announced a foreign presence.

Near the historic marker rests an unpaved road deeply rutted with tire marks that at one time must have led to the farm itself. Even after walking along the road for more than a mile, I still saw no signs of a farm, past or present.

Today the state of Mississippi owns part of the land, primarily because it holds a sacred Native American burial site. Yet for nearly twenty years the piece of land labeled Section Thirteen of Township Sixteen in Holmes County was one of intense personal connections between several families, both Black and white, as well as an oasis for medical care in a part of Mississippi that still has a shortage of physicians. When Providence was established, African Americans had to travel anywhere from fifty to two hundred miles to be treated at a hospital. Opening a desegregated medical clinic in segregated Mississippi undermined the status quo of the state's health care system, along with breaking other social taboos.

On this site, the ideals of the New Deal were paired with interracial cooperation and Christian ethics, which seemed benign at the time of the farm's founding in the late 1930s but in the aftermath of the Supreme Court's 1954 *Brown* decision proved to be unwelcome. No one should have feared the residents of Providence Farm, since its founders were largely idealistic theologians and Christian missionaries seeking to create the Kingdom of God on earth through a simple Christian theology of brotherhood and justice. This belief in the power of justice was intended to be Providence's protection. Yes, it was also a place constructed with an agrarian vision, but its ideals were completely at odds with the Delta's historical exploitation of tenant farmers and day laborers. Making the word of God become flesh in the work of a cooperative farm in the Mississippi Delta proved difficult in a place that leaves little room for the riches of grace.

Place is an essential part of human identity, even if, as in the case of the Delta, that place is one tarnished with despair and tainted by violence. The Mileston project was set up as a farm cooperative association under the statutes of the state of Mississippi, with its administrators at the Farm Security Administration recognizing the limitations defined by place. Although bureaucrats are often blamed for not understanding the local environment in which government programs are being instituted, the FSA studied and came to understand the Delta as a place, including its social and racial dynamic. In their summary of the Mileston project, FSA administrators acknowledged that "the Negro dominates the Delta population" while at the same time recognizing the need for their cooperative venture to match the mores of the plantation system in which they would be operating, one that, of course, was dominated by powerful white planters.[2] The strategy was to create change without it being recognizable or seem as if it broke the existing structure of Delta life. Yet the agrarian reform that Mileston brought about still represented a threat to individuals and groups whose interests were affected by any endeavor that moved sharecroppers out of the labor force. At the same time, its administrators worked diligently to assuage the fears of those who viewed the project with suspicion.

Providence Farm's founders believed they were creating their own space, place, and location rather than living within an existing locale bound by its own customs and traditions. "We are seeking to build a socialized economy of abundance in the midst of the 'collapse of cotton tenance,'" wrote cooperative farm supporter Sherwood Eddy in a fundraising letter in 1936 for what was then called the Delta Cooperative Farm and which led to the founding of Providence. Eddy even envisioned a "chain of Cooperative Farms Incorporated." Rather than seeing themselves as part of the Delta, Providence Farm and its predecessor, the Delta Cooperative Farm, sought to reinvent the Delta through a vision that operated outside of the region's institutionalized patterns of exploitation, segregation, and discrimination. These two farms were seeking to create a new idea of a place within the Delta that was radical in spirit and vision, free from the feudal legacy of sharecropping. What its founders failed to realize was how difficult that endeavor would be within a cultural landscape that had already determined its own intransigent idea of itself.

The idea of a cooperative community that took hold at Providence was one that attempted to create a kind of revolutionary economy in a place not known for accepting or encouraging economic revolution. The founders of Providence knew far more about theology than farming. Rooted firmly in theologian Reinhold Niebuhr's idea of translating faith into social action—Niebuhr called Providence America's "most important experiment in social Christianity"—the community remained true to its idea of itself even though it meant upsetting the status quo. In the end, its founders realized the path to Eden they were seeking to create was one built atop a road bound toward eternal perdition.

The story of Providence Farm begins not in the Mississippi Delta but across the Mississippi River in Arkansas with the formation of the Southern Tenant Farmers Union in 1934. The Southern Tenant Farmers Union was a multiracial group that organized sharecroppers to voice their grievances to plantation owners and even wage a strike if an agreement couldn't be brokered. At the time of the union's founding, sharecroppers and farm laborers in the Arkansas Delta made the equivalent of 50 to 75 cents per day, or about $100 per year. In principle, the organization believed that farmworkers should organize themselves into unions not only to gain higher wages but also to protect them from the threat of violence by plantation owners.

Organizing sharecroppers in the South was dangerous work, because it meant turning laborers against landowners who were at the top of the power hierarchy. It was so dangerous that Howard Kester, one of the white leaders of the union, wore a cyanide pellet around his neck given to him by his friend George Washington Carver, the famous scientist from Tuskegee Institute. Carver wanted Kester to have a way to end his miseries in case he was ever captured by a lynch mob intent on torturing him (Kester had already escaped a few). But Kester didn't just have to worry about angry lynch mobs. He also had to face the scorn of his own family, who might have preferred he put the pellet to use. As Kester once bluntly noted, "Our neighbors and our families . . . could not seem to understand why we associated with 'niggers and poor white trash.'"

Well acquainted with the kind of hostility that met Kester personally as well as professionally, the Southern Tenant Farmers Union came to be an organization dependent on dark nights, fast cars, and back roads for its survival. In 1936, as sharecroppers joined the union under Kester's leadership, new union members and their families were kicked off the land by planters and left homeless and hungry. Here is how folk singer and union activist John Handcox described the situation in a 1953 oral history:

> When the planters in East Arkansas saw that the people were joining the union they told them to get off the land. They didn't wait for them to go—they threw them off. It was a cold winter. The hungry people had no place to go. When they held union meetings the laws clubbed them till they lay like dead on the ground. It didn't make no difference if they was men or women. They killed some union members and threw some others in jail.[3]

One of the men who was clubbed was a sharecropper by the name of Frank Weems. After a white mob cornered him, beat him, and left him for dead, Weems disappeared and was thought by his family to be dead, leading Handcox to write a labor movement anthem whose chorus became a rallying cry: "Yes, I want somebody to tell me, where is the man Frank Weems?" A year later Handcox encountered Weems on the streets of Chicago, where he had landed after escaping Arkansas in fear. Even though he survived, Weems was never reunited with his family.

The threat of violence, imprisonment, and death across the river in Arkansas led to the founding of the Delta Cooperative Farm in February 1936 and its successor several years later, Providence Farm. Upset by the plight of the sharecroppers in Arkansas, within a month, Sherwood Eddy, a Christian missionary and elder statesman of the YMCA, rallied a group together to purchase an inexpensive 2,138-acre plot in Bolivar County, Mississippi, land bought on what Eddy described as "faith and a shoestring." Buying this land also gave the dispossessed sharecroppers from Arkansas a place to go. Among them was Vera Weems, the wife of Frank Weems, and her eight children. By August 1936, twelve white and nineteen Black families had moved to what became known as the Delta Cooperative Farm.

"We thought Mississippi was safer than Arkansas," the founders of the cooperative recalled years later to activist preacher Will Campbell. Like me, Campbell wondered why a ragtag group of Christian socialists who believed in racial integration felt they could bring such a radical social experiment to the Mississippi Delta, a place with the meanest of poverty often paired with the presence of garish opulence. In Arkansas, Paul Peacher, sheriff of the town of Earle, placed the striking Black tenant farmers inside a stockade and submitted several to public flogging. There were Delta sheriffs who committed similar acts of violence and intimidation, including those in Holmes County, where Providence Farm was located. The only viable explanation for thinking Mississippi was a safe place was that the glow of idealism often overshadows the realities of people and place. It took guts and a special type of blindness to imagine a place like the Delta Cooperative Farm.

The residents of the Delta Cooperative Farm were neither sharecroppers nor landowners, which meant they existed outside of the defined social structure of the Delta. As cooperative members, they had access to a nonprofit store, a credit union, and both a consumer and farming cooperative. A writer in the *New Republic* in 1937 called the project "one of the most daring, complex, highly civilized experiments in living that the Western Hemisphere has known."[4] While that sounds hyperbolic, keep in mind that this was the 1930s and the cooperative was interracial and based in Mississippi. Even in the 1930s, cotton brokers like Will Clayton of Anderson and Clayton—a firm that moved 15 percent of the world's cotton crop at the time—still thought of cotton as a "slave crop" with a revenue margin not large enough to support paying a workforce of men who were truly free.[5] The Delta Cooperative Farm stood as an outlier in the South for believing that "races should be separated until we are educated into a better social system."[6] Left unspoken in that statement was the farm's belief in interracial justice as being integral to that education into a new social system.

Although the cooperative still had to comply with Mississippi's strict segregation laws, there was equal access to community facilities, something unheard of in the Jim Crow South. Despite this bending of the racial rules of the Delta, whites and Blacks lived on opposite sides of the road and went to separate schools. The only thing that was equal about their education was that both Black and white children went to school for eight months, rather than the standard four months a year for most Black children in the Delta. Eugene Cox recalled that the white members of the cooperative board extended the time of school for Black children after an illiterate white sharecropper stated, "It ain't fair for black chillum to git only four months of school."[7]

But as a farming operation, the Delta Cooperative Farm was doomed from the start. The leadership was essentially a group of preachers without a pulpit rather than experienced farm managers. Sherwood Eddy placed his protégé Sam Franklin in charge of the farming operation. Franklin, like Eddy, was a missionary and had no idea of how to run a farming operation in the land where cotton was king. With the coming automation of cotton picking and mules being replaced by tractors, a cooperative model rooted in social Christianity and failing to keep up with technological advances was no match for its ruthless competitors operating in the plantation system.

In addition, despite being a cooperative led by well-meaning white Christian socialists, leaders like Franklin were unaware of their own racist paternalism. The cooperative's leaders imposed a top-down decision-making process, appointed only whites to management, and treated the cooperative's members not too differently than sharecroppers. Tensions rose and the Black farmers even threatened to walk off the farm.

After a few years of operating a cooperative farm rooted more in theological principles than those of productive agriculture, the Delta Cooperative Farm ceased operating in 1941. Created largely as a place of refuge, the farm was more a social act of heroism than it was a profitable farm. It was at this point the trustees of the Delta Cooperative Farm turned their energies to Providence Farm in neighboring Holmes County. This shift came about because of changes to the boards of the cooperative farms as well as a shift in the farms' original goals and mission. Board member Sam Franklin noted that the change was "directed to the concrete needs of thousands among us, victimized by racial prejudice and by economic injustice. We asked ourselves how we could make our little Farm community a center for social change in the whole locale."[8]

Established in 1938, Providence had a cooperative store much like the Delta Cooperative but also had a medical clinic and a dairy operation. Dr. David Minter ran the health clinic. In the summer, with volunteers from the Alpha Kappa Alpha sorority, Minter managed a mobile clinic that traveled through Holmes County treating as many as ten thousand patients. Eugene Cox, who came from the Delta Cooperative Farm, had a deep devotion to practical Christianity and saw his work as the farm manager—which involved organizing educational programs and operating the credit union—as a ministry.

Rather than seeing their work as transforming Southern race and class relations, Providence largely focused on serving the health and economic needs of the local community. At the same time, it quietly nurtured Black farmers for leadership roles that its leaders felt would need to be filled after World War II. Providence trustee Charles Spurgeon Johnson optimistically believed that World War II would make more Americans see Blacks as "fellow citizens in the world community," thus leading to increased opportunity in the postwar years. Yet the war changed race relations in the American South in a way counter to Johnson's idealistic calculation.[9]

Optimism was as much a part of the architecture of Providence Farm as it was at the Delta Cooperative Farm. Through its medical clinic and its summer camps run by Black educator and activist Fannye Booker, Providence Farm operated as a small community with a simple mission of doing good works rather than as a radical cooperative that challenged the power structure of the Delta. This work went largely unnoticed for nearly a decade.

Delta residents and politicians continued to view Providence with suspicion but largely left it alone. Although its economic influence was minimal, the question remained for Delta whites about what would happen if this group decided that it now deserved political power. Tensions built over the continuing efforts of Delta whites to whittle away at what little economic power the region's Black residents—particularly Black independent farmers—had gained. This was also the McCarthy era, when Mississippi politicians like Senator James Eastland believed Black citizens existed as an inferior underclass that could be easily swayed by the promises of communism. And civil rights and communism were viewed as being part of the same project. By the mid-1950s the tensions reached a peak, but rather than instilling fear in Black residents, the racist oppression emboldened them to push their efforts even further.

When Providence Farm finally captured the eye of Holmes County's white residents, everything quickly disintegrated.

"Well, 1934 looked like it was hopeless. 1954 gave us hope," remarked Howard Kester in an oral history when asked about the Supreme Court's overruling of the separate but equal doctrine in *Brown v. Board of Education*. "There was something of real significance that was going to occur then or so we thought."[10] A little more than a year after the *Brown* decision, on September 27, 1955, five hundred white citizens of Holmes County assembled at Tchula High School and demanded that David Minter and Eugene Cox leave Mississippi immediately, with a few random folks even calling for lynching both men. Cox and Minter had started working in Mississippi in the 1930s, survived the postwar period, and then suddenly everything changed in the 1950s. An incredible backlash just wiped out the work of a generation of Christian idealists. Something of significance was indeed happening, but just not the way Howard Kester expected.

Stepping into the wake of this racial backlash in post–*Brown v. Board* Mississippi in August 1955 was a fourteen-year-old boy from Chicago by the name of Emmett Louis Till. Although warned by relatives about the dangers of the Jim Crow South, Till was unaccustomed to the type of segregation he encountered there. In an innocent act of teenage daring, he is said to have whistled at the wife of a white store owner in Money, Mississippi.

Four days later, Till was abducted by two men in the middle of the night from his uncle's house, beaten, tortured, and murdered. His body was tied to a cotton gin fan and dumped in the nearby Tallahatchie River. Though his killers, store owner Roy Bryant and his half brother J. W. Milam, were arrested and brought to trial less than a month after Till's body was found, the pair were acquitted by an all-white, all-male jury that deliberated for just sixty-seven minutes. Later, one juror said to a *Time* magazine reporter, "If we hadn't stopped to drink pop, it wouldn't have taken that long." This travesty of justice effectively made Till's murder a lynching.

The push for closing Providence Farm came exactly a week after the acquittal of the two men who murdered Emmett Till and dumped his battered body in the Tallahatchie River. Till's murder took place nearly forty miles from Providence, but its aftershocks were felt across the Delta. In a place like the Delta—which already possesses a tenuous relationship with truth—memory and imagination hold more power than fact. During this time in the Delta, the rhetoric of anti-integrationists often equated integration with communism. Accusing racial progressive groups of communism was an efficient way for the white power structure to discredit their foes. Moreover, it is hard to underestimate the impact of the Till murder and the acquittal of Bryant and Milam on the social landscape of the Mississippi Delta. It seems the impact of those events, combined with the rise of the White Citizens' Council, its massive resistance to integration, and the incendiary accusations that accompanied that resistance, were all factors leading up to the farm's closing.

The details in the historical record are murky, since many of them are shrouded in rumor and innuendo, yet they mirror similar events in the

Delta. In an odd parallel to the Emmett Till case, the controversy about Providence Farm began with an accusation that four Black teenage boys were speaking obscenely to a white girl. Instead of being pursued by a lynch mob, the teenagers were arrested by the county sheriff, Richard Byrd, who then conducted a two-hour-long recorded interrogation of them. A nineteen-year-old Black man named Curtis Freeman was accused of flirting with Mary Ellen Henderson, a ten-year-old white resident of Providence Farm. Although Freeman swore to the sheriff that his comment, "You sure look good to me, Sugar," was directed at a Black girl named Sugar standing nearby, he was charged with "unlawful use of vulgar and obscene language" in the company of a white woman. Several weeks later, a Holmes County court sentenced Freeman to six months of hard labor on the county farm.[11]

During the interview, the sheriff, joined by three other men from the community, shifted the focus of the questioning from the alleged incident to Providence Farm—the sheriff linked them to the farm since Freeman's parents patronized the cooperative store and attended the educational institutes offered at Providence—and the questions turned to daily life at the farm: Did Eugene Cox promote or discuss integration? Did Dr. Minter encourage Black residents to register to vote? The questioning went further and accusations were made that Providence Farm held interracial parties at the farm's swimming hole. All of the interrogation was rooted in the racial fears of the time. The only crime committed was that four young Black men just happened to be in the wrong place at the wrong time. No legal counsel or parents were present, even though several of the boys were minors.

While the interrogation focused on Freeman's alleged crime, the sheriff also determined that the Providence Cooperative Farm was promoting integration and equality in violation of Mississippi's segregation laws, although there was no concrete evidence. At the September 27th meeting, Eugene Cox, Providence Farm's executive director, and David Minter were effectively put on trial, one that was presided over by state representative J. T. Love and attended by over five hundred locals. The tapes of the interview with the boys were played in their entirety, and Cox and Minter were accused of leading integrated social spaces. The meeting concluded with the order that the men and their families leave Holmes County as punishment for their "strange racial opinions."[12] Initially, Cox and Minter were determined to stay in Providence in spite of the order. But then they overheard a white man from Tchula tell a small group, "What we need for these S.O.B.s is a couple of grass ropes."[13] For many, that would have been the sign to immediately flee Holmes County, but at that moment Cox and Minter only committed to the idea of leaving. Despite the hovering threat of violence against their families, it took Cox and Minter several months to close the farm and leave the Delta.

It was essentially a kind of bloodless lynching that led to the end of Providence Farm and the distribution of the cooperative's assets. Cox and Minter invited activist Will Campbell to oversee the liquidation of the cooperative's property and the relocation of the residents. Campbell, like me, had a difficult time finding the place the first time he visited. "We knew the farm was located several miles off US Highway 49," he recalled about his first visit there in the fall of 1955, but because the phone lines had been cut after the mass meeting in Tchula, he could not reach the cooperative by telephone. To find the farm, Campbell decided to ask Black families for directions, since they would be less likely to send him in the wrong direction.[14] On the same day as Campbell's visit, by nightfall three carloads of men had appeared at the end of the road to the farm. They had come to intimidate the Cox and Minter families, building a campfire in the evening to indicate their continued presence. Several months later, the farm's assets were liquidated and the land was divided among former residents and local farmers. Today, Providence is just another abandoned Delta farm lost under the weight of Mississippi's historical memory.

Providence doesn't even live on in the minds of those who once lived there. Such is the case for Dr. Minter's son, William Minter. Minter was four years old when he arrived in Providence and fourteen when he left, yet he remembers very little of the decade he lived there, short of a recollection of finding arrowheads around the now preserved Indian mounds. "I remember the houses where we lived on Providence Farm and the houses of other people, but otherwise my memory is scattered," Minter told me. When I asked whether the events were wrapped in trauma, which might lead him to remember less, Minter told me "there was definitely trauma but it wasn't tied to what happened to us." Minter later sent me a copy of a December 1955 article by liberal Mississippi journalist Hodding Carter III from the *Saturday Evening Post* titled "Racial Crisis in the Deep South," which uses what happened to Minter's family as an example of the ways white Mississippians were seeking to erect a stronger racial barrier in the post-*Brown* years. "In the article there is a photo at the top of the page of my family outside the medical clinic, and several other photos telling the story of the Emmett Till murder," Minter recalled when we spoke about the article. "I have always seen this article as one of my first lessons in white privilege. Yes, we were threatened with lynching, we were attacked, but no one killed us. They killed Emmett Till."

Whereas the end of the Providence Cooperative Farm was spurred by organized massive resistance in Holmes County, Mileston's cooperative structure had begun to collapse ten years earlier in 1946, when Congress dissolved the Farm Security Administration and replaced it with the Farmers Home Administration. While the Farm Security Administration's resettlement program at least helped a small segment of Black farmers, the Farmers Home Administration effectively shut out all Black farmers. In 1940, Black farmers represented 35 percent of tenant farmers in the South but only received 21 percent of the loans allocated to tenant farmers to purchase land.[15] The Farmers Home Administration focused more on landowning farmers, which excluded most Black farmers in the Delta from its programs.

What I have come to realize is that the work my father did in his early days at Mileston was focused on trying to maintain momentum for the cooperative infrastructure that had been put in place during the New Deal. The frustrations he had with that work—stemming from farmers' lack of motivation—which, I recall, were similar to the frustrations he had trying to teach agriculture at the high school level, led him to work for the Extension Service, a part of the Department of Agriculture designed to help rural farmers. The aim was to make agricultural education available to farmers and to disseminate agricultural research through a network of extension agents. Of course, the Department of Agriculture felt that a segregated extension service would best serve Black farmers, so white agents in Holmes County worked with the owners and managers of big farms but not directly with Black tenant farmers and sharecroppers. As a Negro County Agent, my father was unable to help Black sharecroppers if white landowners objected to his presence on their land.[16] And the tensions that existed in Holmes County in the 1950s made the work with landowning Black farmers even more difficult.

Which brings me back to Providence Farm. As I dug through the papers of A. E. Cox at Mississippi State University one morning, I discovered that he had saved everything related to the White Citizens' Council and its activities, effectively documenting the growing power of the organization in Holmes County. Not only did Cox document the Citizens' Council's interference while he lived in Holmes County—actions that led to his departure—but he also kept track of its ongoing influence across Mississippi, up through the 1970s. It seemed as if his archive screamed out to pay attention to these materials, a fact that I noted to the archivist. When she asked why I was looking through this material on Providence, I casually mentioned that I was trying to understand the forces that led my father, the Negro county agent at the time, to leave Holmes County for south Mississippi. I knew that Providence's assets had been liquidated and the land was divided among former residents, including some Black farmers. As the county agent tasked with educating farmers on the most current agricultural research, my father more than likely would have had some contact with those farmers.

The archivist thought the best way to get the answer to my question was to check the county agent reports for Holmes County, which were also kept at Mississippi State, the home of the Agricultural Extension Service. But when she pulled the files, the archived reports ended before this period of turmoil, creating a gap in the record. The omission of those reports juxtaposed with the voluminous archival material from Eugene Cox stood in egregious contrast to each other. While I don't know the circumstances behind the omission, it felt purposeful, much like the absence of archival material on Mileston in the National Archives. It reminded me of how writers will often use an archive as a source for crafting a story, but won't consider the intentions behind that archive's construction and what may have been excluded or left out. And here I was, in an expansive wood-paneled room filled with echoes from the past, yet the voices I wanted to hear were silent. So, because of my personal connection to the story and the gaping silence from the archive regarding a piece of that story, I began to look for other clues.

One of those clues was a scrapbook from the Delta Cooperative Farm that included photographs of the family of Frank Weems, whose brutal beating led his family to Mississippi. When the archivist mentioned that another researcher had also expressed an interest in the scrapbook and had it digitized, I asked if they might tell me who that was. This information, I thought, might lead me toward another clue that might fill the silence of the archive. The researcher was photographer and video artist Carrie Mae Weems, who is the granddaughter of Frank Weems. Weems's photography and video work is known for interrogating dominant historical narratives as well as exploring the tension between romance and reality. Knowing that there were photographs of her family in that scrapbook, I confess that I envied Weems for a moment. I wanted to find my father's words in the archive to guide me. But maybe Weems's connection to this place in the Delta might lead me toward insights beyond what my father could have written in a bureaucratic report.

Weems, like me, was seeking to understand her family's time in the Mississippi Delta: the forces that brought them there as well as the forces that led her father to eventually leave and move to Portland, Oregon. Thinking of her grandfather's story, with his death and his eventual reappearance on the streets of Chicago, Weems told me, "I have come to realize that my grandfather was worth more dead to the Southern Tenant Farmers Union than he was alive. He forged an idea of what the union was attempting to do. When they discovered he was alive, there was no way they could use him."

Instead, they used his family to raise money for the Delta Cooperative Farm. During the time Weems's family was at the Delta Cooperative Farm, FSA photographer Dorothea Lange visited and took a portrait of Carrie Mae's uncle Clarence, which is among the files of the FSA at the Library of Congress. The picture's caption reads, "Clarence Weems, a young co-operator on the farm. He remembers the evictions in Arkansas, for his father was beaten and disappeared." But also, part of the file is a letter dated December 1, 1936, from Sherwood Eddy. It is clearly a fundraising letter, since it mentions Frank Weems and notes that his family is safe on the farm, but their safety would be improved if they secured donations of $1,000 to make the Delta Cooperative Farm debt free by the end of the year. So, the tragic story of Frank Weems became a fundraising calling card for the Delta Cooperative Farm.

In our conversation, Weems mentioned that her father's family had also been documented by FSA photographer John Vachon after they had been evicted in Arkansas and before her grandfather was beaten and left for dead. When I found the photograph in the Library of Congress, I realized that it was an image I had seen many times, one that had made me shudder. A sense of hopelessness and abandonment is embedded in the image. The caption only notes that the people are evicted tenant farmers in Arkansas surrounded by their meager possessions—but it captures their full vulnerability at a decisive moment. It is a photograph I always thought gave a voice to the trauma of the moment, yet I neglected to understand the ways the trauma captured in the photograph would echo across generations. Unlike the photograph of Weems's uncle, the family in this photograph is not named, their poverty and circumstances the likely reason for their anonymity in the archive. All that the photograph captured was their loss of a home, and it made them an artifact of what we like to think is a vanished past. It effectively erased their humanity.

Photographs are often a sign of history's injury, just as the absence of history from the archive reveals the ways we seek to hide hurt or misdeeds. When there is a gap in the archive, we seek to close the holes in our cultural narrative by turning to other forms of documentation. The scrapbook of the Delta Cooperative Farm reminded me not only of the possibility of that social experiment but also that erasure is part of the Delta's story. In the Delta, pieces of the story of a place are often discarded to tell a specific narrative with what remains. Yes, there may be a historic marker acknowledging that Providence Farm and the Delta Cooperative Farm once existed. The full story of Providence Farm and the Delta Cooperative Farm lives not in the archive, but on the land itself. And for people like Carrie Mae Weems, the legacy of the Delta Cooperative Farm is held inside them, echoing a vision of the past in the present and the future. It cannot be simply filed away in the dark corner of an archive.

But the history of the land that was once called Providence Farm runs deep. Nearly two hundred years ago it was designated Section Thirteen of Township Sixteen, North Range. As Will Campbell observed about this piece of land, "It has seen a lot. In a way its saga is the story of the nation."[17] Part of that saga is erasure. Another piece of the story is what Campbell described as the "era of domestic psychosis" that led to the dissolution of Providence Farm.

"The past is a foreign country: They do things differently there." That immortal first line from L. P. Hartley's *The Go-Between* succinctly summarizes the problems inherent to history and memory when thinking about the Mississippi Delta, even though it was written to describe early twentieth-century Britain, with its class system as rigid as that of the American South. It serves as a reminder of the ways the history of the Delta—both the place and its people—is often actively misrepresented and half remembered. In the Delta, the question is always, how do you make the past feel like it has not been lost?

CHAPTER 4

THE PAST IS A FOREIGN COUNTRY

Oh you know I'm homeless, homeless, might as well be dead
Hungry and disgusted, no place to lay my head

—BESSIE SMITH, "Homeless Blues"

When US senator Robert Kennedy arrived in Jackson, Mississippi, on April 9, 1967, just days before his visit to the Mississippi Delta—and more than a decade after Providence Farm closed—he was greeted at the airport of the capital city of the Magnolia State by a group of twenty men, women, and children carrying everything from the flag of the Ku Klux Klan to signs bearing hostile messages, including one scrawled with the words "Race Mixers Go Home." The sentiments that greeted Kennedy were much the same as those that residents of Providence Farm once confronted. Another group of demonstrators shouted for Kennedy to go to Vietnam rather than come to Mississippi.[1] But it was not just protesters who looked upon Kennedy's visit with hostility. The main newspaper of Mississippi's state capital, the *Clarion-Ledger*, reported the visit using a framing that, with the hindsight of history, seems just as menacing as the small group of protesters who encountered Kennedy upon his arrival.

In 1967, the Equal Opportunity Act of 1964 was up for renewal. That year Kennedy, along with other members of the US Senate Subcommittee on Employment, Manpower, and Poverty, held hearings around the country to assess the effectiveness of programs associated with the War on Poverty. Kennedy and his colleague, Democratic senator Joseph Clark of Pennsylvania, also wanted to increase national visibility for the issue of poverty. The subcommittee decided to hold the first of those hearings in Mississippi, not to agitate the public and the state political power structure but in recognition that Mississippi had become a focus for anti-poverty activism.

Although the *Clarion-Ledger* included several stories about the visit during Kennedy's time in Mississippi, the substance of these hearings and their focus on hunger in Mississippi were not part of its reporting.

To present-day readers, a caption to a front-page photograph of Kennedy while in Jackson during the Senate subcommittee hearings seems more mocking than serious: "Senator Robert Kennedy's haircut drew comments and rejoiners [*sic*] at the press conference Sunday afternoon." In response to those comments, Kennedy explained that he had not had time to get a haircut before the trip. Bear in mind that in the 1960s, long hair was a key cultural signifier. By paying attention to the length of his hair, the paper was indicating to its readers as well as the state's conservative political establishment that Kennedy was connected with the 1960s counterculture movement as well as a left-leaning agenda. The newspaper, owned by the powerful and influential Hederman family, was mercilessly adept at tuning its news coverage in a way that might not have matched reality, but certainly paired with the cultural mood of white Mississippians.

The photograph, positioned at the bottom of the page, was one of many published that week. Scenes from Kennedy's sojourn through the Delta were consistently nestled at the bottom of the page or buried inside the paper, as if the visit was of minor significance or studying hunger in the region was of little consequence. The captions to the photographs were the only text supplied by the *Clarion-Ledger* itself. The stories published about this historic visit in the *Clarion-Ledger* were assembled from Associated Press wire service reports rather than from one of the paper's own reporters—a way for the editors of the paper to signal their disdain for Kennedy's visit rather than using their own reporters to fully cover the work of a man who had been judged by many white citizens, like those who greeted him at the Jackson airport, to be notable only for interfering in the sovereign affairs of the state of Mississippi.

Kennedy had come to Mississippi at the urging of Marian Wright, who was then working as a civil rights attorney in the state. Along with Senator Joseph Clark, Kennedy was there to hear from the state's citizens about the effectiveness of the programs of Lyndon Johnson's War on Poverty. The trip brought into the national spotlight the economic, political, and social repression rendered by Jim Crow and exacerbated by the collapse of the farm labor system with the introduction of mechanical cotton pickers.

Wright testified before the committee that there were families in Mississippi, particularly in the Delta, who were starving and desperate. "There is nowhere to go," Wright said. "I wish the Senators would have a chance to go and just look at the empty cupboards in the Delta and the number of people who are going around begging just to feed their children." Wright also testified that "the poverty program has done nothing to change the basic economic structure that needs to be changed."[2] One of the witnesses Wright brought to Jackson to appear before the committee was a woman by the name of Ora Wilson of Greenville, who was told the only way she could get welfare benefits was to work in the fields chopping and picking cotton, although agricultural work had dried up in the area now that automation—and the introduction of pesticides for weed control—had taken away jobs in the fields.

Veteran Mississippi journalist Curtis Wilkie, who covered Kennedy's trip to the Delta for the locally owned *Clarksdale Register*, described the Southern media's framing of Kennedy's trip to the Delta as "nothing short of comic." Wilkie, a journalist who later covered presidential campaigns and the Middle East for the *Boston Globe*, made this statement from a place of historical authority. It's not just his gruff yet courtly Southern accent that makes him sound like someone you can believe. The photographs lining the walls of his house bear witness to the history he has encountered during his career, whether it is an image he took of Martin Luther King Jr. in Marks, Mississippi, two weeks before his assassination in 1968—"Were you ever frightened?" he asked King that day—or a shot of Wilkie colliding with then presidential candidate Jimmy Carter as both reach for a flyball during a softball game in Plains, Georgia, in July 1976.

Wilkie made the choice to cover Robert Kennedy's Delta trip since, as he remembered, "by that time I was essentially my own boss at the paper," even though he was only twenty-six years old at the time. But other than Hodding Carter from Greenville's *Delta Democrat-Times*, there were no other Mississippi journalists who covered Kennedy's trip seriously.

For its biased coverage of Mississippi's struggles during the Civil Rights Movement, the *Clarion-Ledger* was named by the *Columbia Journalism Review* "quite possibly the worst metropolitan daily in the United States." The paper's pattern of bias continued into the most heated days of the Civil Rights Movement and was on full display for the duration of Kennedy's trip. The front page of the *Clarion-Ledger* consistently presented stories, no matter how trivial, that provided a counternarrative to Kennedy's visit, albeit one not necessarily rooted in truth. The paper even gave space to former Mississippi governor Ross Barnett's false assertion that Kennedy had slandered him when he revealed in a speech at the University of Mississippi just a year before that Barnett had acquiesced to Kennedy's demand, in his previous role as attorney general, that the University of Mississippi admit James Meredith as the school's first Black student. Given the disdain many white Mississippians still felt toward the Kennedys, Barnett thought he might use this occasion to his political advantage. "He only came here to oppose my candidacy for the governorship of Mississippi," Barnett commented, who was running again for governor using the campaign slogan "Roll again with Ross." "In his typical left-wing fashion he [Kennedy] has again resorted to his same old trick of misrepresenting the facts to generate dissension among Mississippians," Barnett concluded. Now that the tapes of Kennedy's conversation with Barnett are part of the public record, we know that it was Barnett who was misrepresenting the facts.

Of course, Barnett had an inflated view of his importance to Mississippians and lost his bid to become governor. Mississippi did not "roll again with Ross," but the editors of the *Clarion-Ledger* still used a few items from Barnett's playbook of disinformation to diminish the importance of Kennedy's visit.

Just one month after Kennedy visited the region, my father and I made the trip through the Delta once again, driving the very same roads and seeing the same terrain. And like Kennedy, my nine-year-old self wondered about the lives of the people who lived in those tin-roofed structures that looked as if they could not survive a heavy wind. Before the national spotlight highlighted the conditions inside those weather-beaten buildings, they were merely an element of the natural landscape of the Delta, just part of the scenery. Both Black and white Mississippians outside the Delta were conditioned to pay little attention to the poverty that existed right before our eyes. The *Clarion-Ledger*, through its coverage and framing of Robert Kennedy's visit, was seeking to reinforce the idea that poverty—particularly Black poverty—was something Mississippians could ignore. Somehow, I ignored that coverage, since Kennedy's trip finally made real to me what life was like inside the shotgun houses that dotted the Delta, and it haunts me even today.

What stands out looking at the paper today is a story from April 9, 1967, featured at the top of the fold with the headline "Stennis Renews Attack on Activities of CDGM." "Stennis" was US senator John Stennis of

Mississippi, who signed the Southern Manifesto decrying the Supreme Court's 1954 *Brown* decision and voted against both the Civil Rights Act of 1964 and the Voting Rights Act of 1965. "CDGM" was the Child Development Group of Mississippi, which ran Head Start preschool programs in the state. Stennis's antipathy to racial equality and Black advancement was well-known. What was new this time was he had found an ostensibly race-neutral way of attacking a group that was benefiting poor Black children. "The Child Development Group of Mississippi has been inefficient and wasteful," Stennis was quoted as saying.

But it wasn't the actual wastefulness that Stennis resented about the CDGM. Labeling the organization as incompetent was a dog whistle, a way of saying it was being run largely by Black people. The federal leadership behind the Head Start program mandated that it be operated with the "maximum feasible participation" of the poor, which meant it bypassed local government to work directly with local Head Start groups, many of them operated by Black residents. The objection from Stennis was that this program was being run without white oversight, which automatically made it corrupt in his eyes.

Head Start had been launched in Mississippi in 1965 as part of President Lyndon Johnson's War on Poverty. It offered preschool training, two hot meals daily, and medical care. The newly formed Office of Economic Opportunity allotted $1.5 million for Mississippi to launch Head Start schools under the auspices of the CDGM, a group operated through a network of people who had been active in the Civil Rights Movement in the state.

Given Stennis's firm opposition to the Civil Rights Movement, it is not surprising that this powerful senator would oppose a program like Head Start, particularly since the way the program was being administered placed it under federal rather than state supervision. Placing the lens of history over these old newspapers reveals that as Robert Kennedy was seeking to help the poor of Mississippi by bringing attention to their plight, Stennis was undermining Kennedy's work to change food and welfare policies for the poor. As Kennedy aide Peter Edelman noted in an oral history published in 1974, "So, if you put all of these things together—the consequences of the Civil Rights Movement, of mechanization, of the minimum wage, of the switch over in the federal food program, there was probably more extensive hunger in Mississippi in the spring of 1967 than there had been in some time."[3] The *Clarion-Ledger*'s framing of Kennedy's trip reveals the ways that Mississippi was waging its own war on the War on Poverty. While Robert Kennedy was witnessing poverty in the Delta—people living in run-down shacks without running water—Mississippi senators James Eastland and John Stennis, along with Congressman Jamie Whitten, were denying it. Mississippi governor Paul Johnson also denied the existence of hunger in the Delta, sneering that "all the Negroes I've seen around here are so fat they shine!" For the governor, poverty not only did not exist, but the circumstances of those thought of as poor and Black were simply different.

As a nation, we like to think of the past as a place or region that we would prefer not to visit—as if confronting the realities of history could harm us—rather than acknowledging how much of the past lives on in the present. The Delta's past seems even more foreign, given that the social, cultural, and policy choices that could have transformed it have been routinely thwarted by Mississippi politicians as well as the media organizations that reinforced the narrative the state's political class wanted to promote.

Yet it is by peering into this foreign land of the past that one can see the ways that the inequality imprinted on the poor in one part of the country came to define the ways we as a nation would frame ideas about race and inequality. In both the negative attention the *Clarion-Ledger* paid to Head Start and Stennis's political rhetoric labeling the aid to poor children as wasteful, we see the origins of the sentiment that recipients of federal dollars are lazy, corrupt, and incompetent. By the 1970s, that sentiment comes to be applied to the entire welfare system and labels it a form of robbery, an unjust transfer of funds from hardworking Americans to undeserving and unproductive poor people.

Years of farm automation and the forces of big agriculture have changed the Delta since Kennedy's trip in 1967, yet the issues Kennedy sought to confront still are part of life in this region. Yes, Kennedy visited in the wake of the mechanization of agriculture, which had left so many Delta residents living perilously in poverty and unsure of where their next meal was coming from. Many of the families Kennedy encountered had no income at all but were required to pay $2 just to gain access to food stamps. Yet many of the same counties Kennedy visited continue to have high levels of food insecurity given the lack of steady employment, a legacy of the forces that brought Kennedy to the Delta. Modern industrial agriculture did not provide jobs for the people he visited, nor did it employ the generations after them.

Robert Kennedy was wounded by the poverty he encountered. But the oft-repeated denials of the existence of poverty seemed to drown him out. The question that remains today is how much of the poverty and food insecurity Kennedy encountered still exists on the route he traveled through the Delta, from the river town of Greenville up to Clarksdale.

In the springtime, the fields of the Mississippi Delta are freshly plowed and reveal the dark loamy soil that is shielded from view when the cotton crop is in full swing. When Robert Kennedy arrived on April 12, 1967, the fields were also freshly plowed, though not with the precision one encounters today. More than half a century later, as I retrace Kennedy's trip, a sometimes blinding, heavy rain fills the deep ruts between the symmetrically tilled rows until they appear like miniature rivers in these massive fields that stretch out for what seems like forever. Of course, the shacks perched on cinderblocks that Kennedy encountered along Highway 61 are now gone, most of them destroyed or completely in ruins. The road is also now four lanes rather than the simple two-lane blacktop that existed up until roughly a decade ago. To the untrained eye, poverty has been erased from this land; the expensive farm equipment would seem to indicate some measure of prosperity. But the Delta is a place that bears the thickness of memory on its landscape. Even with the sky hurtling rain, I can see the past manifested on top of this rich soil. Poverty exists as part of the blood memory this land bears, buried deep in the Delta's soil.

To encounter poverty in the Delta, Robert Kennedy headed toward the shacks that he saw surrounded by freshly plowed ground. As Kennedy once told a friend about poverty, "You don't know unless you see." Today it is easy to simply bypass the Delta's poverty on a speedy four-lane road. To see poverty, you must want to know about it in the Delta and know where it exists, which is often in the deepest parts of small Delta towns.

But if you exit that highway, into towns like Leland, three-room shotgun houses can be found in many of the Black neighborhoods. Or in the Baptist Town neighborhood of Greenwood, which is lined with shotgun houses much like those Kennedy visited. When I ask Errick D. Simmons, the mayor of the town of Greenville, where poverty exists today in the Delta, he agrees that the poor have been shuttered off into neighborhoods in small Delta towns that travelers through the region may never see. "The descendants of the people left stranded on the levee during the Great Flood are still out there on the levee," Simmons tells me. He is referring to the fact that Black citizens of Greenville were prohibited from leaving during the 1927 flood to ensure that white Greenville could keep its domestic servants. Those who have remained in Greenville today have been left behind just as they were in 1927, providing an odd historical parallel.

Greenville was once known as the "Queen of the Delta," and nearly a decade ago its downtown was listed on the National Register of Historic Places. Main and Washington Streets, both wide boulevards, bear the signs of the town's past grandeur, with a neoclassical bank and a Gothic Revival Catholic Church. Empty or boarded-up storefronts stand amid this past elegance today. Kennedy saw this once-grand part of Greenville but also the part that is poor and remains that way. He began with a visit to a job training program in Greenville and visited a nearby tent city—called Freedom City by its residents—established by striking farmworkers, including Ora Wilson, whom Marian Wright had called to testify at the committee hearings in Jackson.

Greenville and Washington County showed significant population loss in the 2020 census, with 6,215 residents leaving the county since 2010. In 1967 Greenville had about 40,000 residents; today the town's population is under 30,000 residents, 80.5 percent Black and 16.4 percent white. Poverty in the town is among the worst in the nation: 32.2 percent of Greenville residents live below the poverty line and 2022 Census data shows that the median annual household income is $35,148, with a median income for Black residents of $29,894 and a median income for white residents of $69,111. More than 75 percent of students in Greenville qualify for free and reduced school lunches. Whites have departed Greenville at a much faster rate than its Black residents, perhaps because they could afford to move. Industry is largely absent, with the exception of Ben's Original rice, which has produced rice in Greenville for more than forty years, and the port of Greenville, which largely serves agricultural interests. After the Mars Inc. corporation dropped the name "Uncle Ben's" from its rice—in recognition of the racial reckoning that was taking place in 2020 after the murder of George Floyd and other unarmed Black men—in July 2021 it also invested $2.5 million in nutritional and educational programs for the children of Greenville. While Mars's corporate philanthropy is admirable, it cannot solve the problems of historic and structural poverty that exist in Greenville.

Up the road from Greenville, Kennedy had a memorable encounter in the Delta town of Cleveland. Curtis Wilkie was there when Kennedy entered a house barren of any furniture, and a twenty-month-old boy sat beside his mother on the floor where his meal of cornbread and rice was scattered around him. "I'll never forget how the flies were swarming in that room," Wilkie recalled to me at his home in Oxford on a sun-dappled spring morning in 2022. Then, Kennedy knelt by the child and gently stroked his face for about two minutes without saying a word. As Marian Wright had warned ahead of the visit, the cupboards in the house were empty and the living conditions were intolerable. As they left the house, Cliff Langford, the editor of a weekly newspaper in Cleveland, complained that the sub-committee had picked the worst situations to observe and report on to the public. Langford added that he knew of no one in the Delta who was starving. "Step over here and I'll introduce you to some," Kennedy said to Langford, pointing to a group of children standing nearby.

In the 1960s, the United States government defined poverty as the absence of the basic material necessities needed to sustain a decent life. The house Kennedy entered in Cleveland was an impoverished household by government standards, one with little food or material goods that even had an open toilet without plumbing behind the house. But Cliff Langford's idea of poverty was rooted in the social context of white Mississippians, who had been taught that Black poverty was to be tolerated and ignored. Having been shaped by the culture and exploitative economy of the Mississippi Delta, Langford accepted the circumstances of the Black poor because in no way did their life ever overlap with his.

More than half a century after Kennedy's visit, Cleveland still looks like a sleepy Delta town, but with retail sprawl and some polish and gloss. Delta State University is the town's largest employer, and the retail establishments along Highway 61 are directly linked to the expansion of the university. Today Cleveland is also the home of the GRAMMY Museum, which has a Mississippi-centered gallery celebrating the contributions of the state and the Delta to American music. That is fitting given that just four miles outside Cleveland, musicians Charley Patton, Robert Johnson, Honeyboy Edwards, and Roebuck "Pops" Staples all worked at a plantation called Dockery Farms. Like the GRAMMY Museum and the town of Cleveland, Dockery glimmers on the landscape, free of the detritus of its sharecropping past. Established in 1895, its buildings, including its cotton gin, have been restored and preserved, with the names of its founders emblazoned on the side of a barn visible from the road. The freshly painted candy-cane stripes on Dockery's old service station and company store speak only of its historical connection to the blues and little of the exploitation and poverty associated with cotton farming and sharecropping in the Delta. The past is both preserved and erased at the same time.

While poverty still exists in the Delta town of Cleveland, it would be difficult to find circumstances like those encountered by Robert Kennedy. But as in every Delta town, poverty is tucked away in places not visible to the unaided eye. I have even had to train myself to seek it out in Cleveland rather than rely on the addition of the boutique Cotton House Hotel and the rest of the downtown's makeover to shield it from view. If you look at the economic standing of residents living in two of Cleveland's four census tracts, in 2022 a predominantly white census tract had a median income of $60,051, while the predominantly Black census tract had a median income of $18,093. While high school graduation rates are similar in both areas, the white area has a higher college completion rate. Incarceration rates are less than 1 percent in white Cleveland and 2.2 percent in Black Cleveland.

Yet there are still Clifford Langfords who will deny that any poverty exists, given the way Cleveland shines and appears prosperous in comparison to many Delta towns.

That fact led to my question to Curtis Wilkie, which I asked him just days before the anniversary date of Kennedy's trip to the Delta: Now that there are no longer shacks on the side of Highway 61, can politicians get off the hook by ignoring poverty? And how does ignoring poverty affect its invisibility? It's something I wanted Wilkie to talk about, since I know how much history he has witnessed in his long journalism career, both as an observer of Mississippi and the wider world beyond its borders. Wilkie felt that politicians, particularly Mississippi politicians, are not only denying the existence of poverty or never acknowledging it; they are basically encouraging it. "The political leadership of Mississippi is involved in a campaign to drive poor people out of this state. You see it with the way Mississippi refuses to accept nearly $2 billion a year in Medicaid expansion. We're one of a handful of states that won't expand Medicaid, and my only thought about why we won't is because it is designed to help poor people." If Mississippi would expand Medicaid, it would receive $1.6 billion in federal funds in the first year and $1.64 billion in the second year. Yet Mississippi's current governor, Tate Reeves, speaks of Medicaid expansion as "adding approximately 300,000 Mississippians to the welfare rolls," confirming Wilkie's thesis that the state does not want to help poor people.[4]

In the poorest state in the union, it is extremely difficult to qualify for benefits, with just under three thousand residents receiving cash welfare benefits each year. But money targeted for the poor in Mississippi has lined the pockets of the wealthy more than it has assisted the state's neediest residents. In 2021, more than $94 million in welfare money spending was "questioned" by auditors, who alleged either outright misspending or lack of documentation showing money was spent properly. Just in one year alone, $4 million in welfare funds designated for what is known as the Temporary Assistance for Needy Families program was embezzled. Much like the plantation system that once existed at Dockery Farms, Mississippi's welfare system today exists within an empire dominated by the white and powerful.

That means that we are not only ignoring the poverty we can see but also the poverty that is out of our view. It makes me wonder why we no longer follow Kennedy's advice about confronting what we see, which sadly seems idealistic from our twenty-first-century vantage point.

In looking back on his time as a Kennedy aide, Fred Dutton described Kennedy's interest in poverty as not quixotic or idealistic. "He was a power operator," Dutton said, noting that Kennedy was keenly aware of the political implications of his anti-poverty work in the Delta.[5] That may be true, but Kennedy was also guided by a communitarian idea of government that we have lost and can't seem to embrace as a society. When I asked Curtis Wilkie what had changed since 1967, he said, "There seems to be a self-satisfied sense among some people that, well, we had that problem with Black poverty at one point. Now that we are peacefully integrated there's a tendency to kind of try to put a lot of that into the past and no longer think about it." This is not just white people turning a blind eye to the past, Wilkie believes. "There's probably a conscious effort by certainly a lot of white people and probably a lot of upwardly mobile Blacks to just kind of say, 'That's in our past, we need to move on from that,' for different reasons. Whites seem to want to just sweep poverty and the past under the rug as though it never existed. And my sense is a lot of Blacks just are uncomfortable with the idea that they kind of came from this environment. It was wretched and there is some shame associated with having come from those circumstances and that they still exist."

Writer Linda Williams Jackson knows the shame associated with living in a three-room shack. Her life on a plantation not far from where Kennedy visited is "one of those sad memories I shoved to the back of my mind," she recalled to me one afternoon near her home in the Memphis suburb of Southaven, Mississippi. For her children's book *The Lucky Ones*, Jackson draws on her childhood memories of shotgun houses without running water and uses Robert Kennedy's trip as a backdrop to the story. Jackson, who was only ten months old at the time of Kennedy's visit, says her family's house was just the type of house he would have visited. There was little food in the home, and no one had work or any source of income. Her mother and older siblings worked in the cotton fields near the Delta town of Rosedale and ended up unemployed in 1967 because farm labor jobs had dried up. "It took me years to realize that my mother was not employable," Jackson told me. Learning of Bob Moses's prediction in 1965 that plantation workers "will be unemployed and unemployable" explained her mother and older siblings' circumstances. "It took me years to realize that my mother had no marketable skills that would make her employable. And I always assumed my older siblings chose not to go to high school. It took me years to realize that there was no one to encourage them to do things differently."

Jackson attributes her success to teachers who took an interest in her, much like the way the teacher in her book *The Lucky Ones* takes interest in her character Ellis Earl and allows him to dream of becoming a teacher or a lawyer. But Jackson also knows how poverty can keep children from dreaming. "I was very concerned about my family's welfare even at a young age," Jackson told me. "When I was ten, my mother was forty-eight, and I thought for sure that when she turned fifty, she would be old and disabled. So, at age ten, I began to worry that I would have to drop out of school at age twelve and find a job to take care of her. That was just the reality of my daily life."

When she thinks of the Delta of her childhood and Robert Kennedy's trip there, Jackson feels sadness. Kennedy brought a sense of hope to the people of the Delta, hope that she herself sometimes felt when her relatives talked about their memories of his visit. As the memory of that visit fades, so does the hope. "I had suppressed many sad memories of my Delta childhood, and writing *The Lucky Ones* brought them back to the surface. Anger comes into play when I look at the Delta today. Shouldn't we be past this by now? Shouldn't we be better people by now?"

Both Linda Williams Jackson and Curtis Wilkie express not just anger about the ways we have failed to learn from the Delta's past and present but also disappointment. What is unspoken and what I keep returning to in my mind is that when Robert Kennedy was assassinated in June 1968, his communitarian philosophy of government also died with him. Today it is rare to hear any politician even mention poverty. "Kennedy dwells on the tragedy of the poor," journalist Richard Harwood observed. Harwood even described Kennedy's speeches as a "catalogue of pain."[6] That same catalogue of pain exists in the Mississippi Delta today, but there is not a single politician paying attention to it. Today many politicians speak of poverty and poor people with an air of wanton cruelty rather than empathy or concern. Poverty is not a thing of the past, but talking about poverty is. Yes, the past is indeed a foreign country where they do things differently.

CHAPTER 5

"THE JEWEL OF THE DELTA"

You can shake it, you can break it you can hang it on the wall
Throw it out the window, catch it 'fore it fall

—CHARLEY PATTON, "Shake It & Break It"

Along the famed Highway 61 that Bob Dylan said was the road that can carry anything and everything—and one bluesman, Mississippi Fred McDowell, called "the longest road I know"—stands the town of Mound Bayou. If Highway 61 symbolizes the ability to travel and start a new life, Mound Bayou is the living embodiment of that sentiment, since it was founded by former slaves who were looking for a place to begin again. As a descendant of one of the founding families observed, this central Mississippi Delta town once stood out as an "example of cooperative efforts of Black people and a symbol of their ambitions and their determination, and what cooperation can do."[1] Founded in 1887, Mound Bayou was a safe space in a Mississippi Delta largely hostile to Black people and Black progress. The very idea of the town was revolutionary for that time and place: a self-reliant, autonomous, all-Black community amid a white-owned, plantation-based economy. This town built on independent spirit and drive gave birth to dozens of Black-owned businesses (including two sawmills, three cotton gins, and a cottonseed oil plant) and had its own train station, a Carnegie library, a few schools, a hospital, and even a bank.

As an independent town self-governed by Black people, Mound Bayou was one of the few places in the Delta where subservience was not the rule. Its residents did not have to wear the "mask that grins and lies," to quote poet Paul Laurence Dunbar's description of the dominant visage of Black men and women as they navigated a world in which they were deemed inferior. Mound Bayou's social structure and its everyday interactions existed in a realm relatively free of the subordinated racial status imposed in other places in the Mississippi Delta. Musician W. C. Handy, who experienced the specter of Jim Crow on his frequent sojourns through the South, recalled that in Mound Bayou "the boot was on the other foot."[2] The town was even renowned among white cotton merchants for the quality of its cotton, an important factor in a place where the crop known as "white gold" was king.

Yet even today, an all-Black town in the middle of an economic landscape largely controlled by the white planter class seems unimaginable, particularly one containing the multitudes of Mound Bayou. If the Mississippi Delta is a landscape haunted by the ghosts of its past, Mound Bayou seems to have once existed in a realm separate from the visible spirits that inhabit the rest of this alluvial plain. Its history and origin tell a compelling story of Black progress. But it is also a complicated story and reveals how even in a place where Black people of the Delta sought to make their own world, external forces bound up in the social determinants of race hampered their utopian vision.

This was a town that enjoyed the attention of many, including President Theodore Roosevelt, who called Mound Bayou the "Jewel of the Delta" and an "object lesson full of hope for the colored people." Tuskegee Institute founder and president Booker T. Washington was also a booster of Mound Bayou. Washington even described one of Mound Bayou's leading citizens, Charles Banks, as "the wealthiest, but I think I am safe in saying . . . the most influential, Negro businessman in the United States" and "the leading Negro banker in Mississippi."

Mound Bayou was also commemorated in song by British music critic and composer Leonard Feather. In 1942, RCA Victor recorded his song "Mound Bayou" with vocals by a white woman from Mississippi named Linda Keene, backed by British trumpeter Henry Levine and his Strictly from Dixie Jazz Band. Much like the song "(When It's) Darkness on the Delta," in "Mound Bayou" the composers and performers portrayed a sentimental image of the Delta, one free of the actual obstacles faced by the people of the town. The singer simply croons about missing "my Mississippi town," with the name "Mound Bayou" sung as if to evoke an idea rather than an actual place built by the sweat and toil of Black people. As a white woman from Mississippi, Linda Keene very likely never set foot in the town that she feels so blue about missing.

Today, however, a place that gained favor and support from the man known as the "Wizard of Tuskegee" and memorialized in song—in that seemingly endless tradition of romanticizing and mythologizing the Mississippi Delta—now resembles many other Delta towns whose glory days are not that far in the past yet seem distant. Integration and industrial farming made it virtually impossible for Mound Bayou to exist as a place outside the structures that shape the land that surrounds it. Now that its residents can shop anywhere, the businesses that were central to the town are gone. It no longer has a bank, and the town's sole ATM sits inside a dark corner of a dingy convenience store. Its once-acclaimed high school is now shuttered, a victim of the school consolidation trend that affects small towns with declining populations all over the Delta and the entire state of Mississippi. The recording artist Nanci Griffith once sang that "Delta towns wear satin gowns" in a song she wrote about leaving the Mississippi Delta in the evening rain. That vision of the Delta town of Mound Bayou is more fitting than the one described by Leonard Feather and Linda Keene. Yet today the satin gown Mound Bayou once wore is tattered, and no amount of evening rain can disguise its frayed fabric.

Residents who grew up here during the Civil Rights Movement—a time some describe as Mound Bayou's second renaissance—keep the glory days of this town alive and are proud of what the town represents, despite its visible decline. If you visit the Mound Bayou Museum, which is housed in the now-shuttered high school, the artifacts of that past are on display and well documented. Despite the careful curation, today it is hard to imagine the town was once dubbed the "Jewel of the Delta." As it grew and thrived, it seemed like a place that was impervious to outside forces. The great irony is that a place that once provided shelter from the sharp edges of a system of racial segregation has fallen so far now that the system has crumbled. Still, the question remains: How much did the vestiges of Jim Crow that haunt the entire Delta landscape also lead to Mound Bayou's decline?

When my father took me through here as a boy, he noted with pride what Mound Bayou represented. He had attended civil rights rallies here in the 1950s and saw his beloved queen of gospel, Mahalia Jackson, perform on stage here. The praise that the founder of his alma mater of Tuskegee gave to Mound Bayou engendered a special connection to the place. And most of all, he remembered it as a safe place for Black people to gather and to imagine how they could live a life of real freedom. In the 1950s and 1960s, it was filled with modern ranch-style houses—visible signs of post–World War II prosperity—many of which remain. While some are still well kept, many others are not. Despite the racial prominence, progress, and pride that Mound Bayou represents, today it is a town in which 38 percent of its residents live in poverty. This might account for the inconsistent upkeep of its houses, but others are abandoned, a sign of the population decline visible across the Delta. Back in the 1970s, the population was between three thousand and four thousand residents, while today the number of full-time residents is under fifteen hundred. As Minnie Fisher, a descendant of an original settler, remarked in a 1979 oral history conducted by Radcliffe College, "A lot of our children . . . are everywhere now in the colleges. . . . The only thing we are trying to do now is to have something for them to do when they get out of school."[3] As someone who grew up in small-town Mississippi and vowed to never return, I know those students Fisher spoke of made a life far from Mound Bayou, just as I did from my small hometown.

Mound Bayou was founded in 1887 by cousins Isaiah T. Montgomery, Joshua P. T. Montgomery, and Benjamin T. Green, all of whom had been slaves at the Davis Bend Plantation near the town of Vicksburg more than a hundred miles to the south. And the "Davis" in "Davis Bend Plantation" refers to the family of Jefferson Davis, the onetime president of the Confederate States of America. After the Civil War and the subsequent confiscation of the plantation by the Freedmen's Bureau, Isaiah Montgomery's father, Benjamin—who had once been enslaved by Jefferson Davis's brother Joseph—bought the estate. From 1868 to 1878, Davis Bend was a self-governing, Black-run plantation and the third-largest cotton producer in the South. But by 1878 relatives of Joseph Davis regained ownership of the plantation—some would even argue that they wrested control of the land through a deft legal strategy rooted in racism—and then forced Montgomery to leave and the community of formerly enslaved people of Davis Bend to disband.

After the Civil War, Joseph Davis had submitted an itemized list of claims of damage to the Freedmen's Bureau for damage to "people and property" totaling $176,800, the equivalent of over $5 million today. This, of course, irritated the army officers in charge of Davis Bend in the early days of Reconstruction. The *New York Times* referred to Davis Bend as "the nest in which the rebellion was hatched," noting with irony that it was now the dominion of freedmen.[4] Although Davis's demand was not met, the Freedmen's Bureau ruled that Davis and his family could not reclaim his property until the lease with the now-emancipated slaves ended. In 1867, Davis sold the property to Benjamin T. Montgomery. In 1874, a dispute in the Davis family placed the Montgomery family in a tough position: Jefferson Davis brought suit against the heirs of Joseph Davis, saying that the property at Davis Bend was legally his, and in 1878 the court ruled in his favor. By this time, Benjamin Montgomery was dead, Davis Bend had fallen on hard times, and their experiment in creating a community of co-operation on a former plantation was over.

Undeterred by this setback, Isaiah T. Montgomery built a relationship with the owners of the Louisville, New Orleans, and Texas (LNO&T) Railway and purchased 1,500 acres of forested, swampy, and malaria-ridden land along the railroad in the middle of the Yazoo-Mississippi Delta. This was not exactly choice Delta land; it was considered undesirable to the white settlers who were then clearing parts of the Delta. Clearing it would be backbreaking, yet Montgomery believed that with access to the railroad, the crops the land produced would have a way to be transported and sold. So, with twenty-five founding families, many of them from Davis Bend, the land was cleared, the acreage was divided into numerous cotton farms, and Mound Bayou was born.

Some argue that Mound Bayou, as an all-Black town, was sold to its residents using racial pride as merely a marketing technique, when the real beneficiary of the original settlers' hard work would be the railroad company. Of course, the LNO&T was thinking about creating rail traffic and the cotton it could transport. But if the railroad company was speculating, so was Isaiah T. Montgomery. As a teen, he had worked as the body servant and private secretary of Joseph Davis, having been educated on the Davis plantation even as the family defended slavery and secession, and he had observed and learned how dealmaking worked. Montgomery had also discerned how to ingratiate himself with powerful whites to get ahead. If you are going to survive on a plantation owned by the family of a man who once said, "You cannot transform the negro into anything one-tenth as useful or as good as what slavery enables them to be," you must develop a unique set of survival skills.[5]

Like many Black people in the post–Civil War South, Montgomery and his group of families from Davis Bend were searching for a utopia where they could create their own version of the Promised Land. By engaging with and embracing Montgomery's vision, the initial settlers of Mound

Bayou found a way to shape a productive and prosperous life as well as create a welcoming place for Black people in the middle of a landscape that would prove to be one of the most hostile places for Black people in the American South.

In 1907, Booker T. Washington published his account of Mound Bayou's founding, saying, "It was not the ordinary Negro farmer who was attracted to Mound Bayou. It was rather an earnest and ambitious class prepared to face the hardships of this sort of pioneer work." Washington saw Mound Bayou as an exemplar of his idea of racial uplift and bootstrap economics. Yet when you begin to explore its history, it seems to more closely embody W. E. B. Du Bois's idea of Black achievement, given the great strides in literacy, business, landownership, prosperity, and happiness in all forms to be found there.

Just a decade after Mound Bayou's founding, Du Bois went to the international Paris Exposition, where he brought an exhibit of Black American progress—photographs, charts, artifacts, and books—for the American Negro Exhibit. He called it "an honest, straightforward exhibit of a small nation of people, picturing their life and development without apology or gloss, and above all made by themselves."[6] While Du Bois never went to Mound Bayou, the images of the town at the time as well as those of Isaiah T. Montgomery's family in their prim Victorian dress would have fit in with the images Du Bois curated for the 1900 Paris Exposition. As photographic historian Deborah Willis observed, the photographs Du Bois commissioned for the Paris exposition "served as evidence that Black Americans were as multifaceted as anyone else." Mound Bayou sought to project a similarly multidimensional idea of Blackness and Black progress. Both Du Bois's exhibit and Montgomery's Mound Bayou desired to project an idea of the progress Black America was making despite the forces that sought to stall and resist that progress.

Had Du Bois visited Mound Bayou, he would have seen how the community used group economics to achieve collective success. A place Du Bois did visit that was somewhat analogous to Mound Bayou was Tulsa, Oklahoma's Greenwood district. After visiting there, Du Bois believed that Black people could achieve success by relying on a "closed economic circle." Montgomery's vision of creating a place where its residents could survive and thrive within a tightly defined boundary seems to have much in common with Du Bois's idea of an economic circle supported by and run by Black people.

But Mound Bayou's politics were much more aligned with those of Booker T. Washington. That became clear in 1890 when Montgomery was chosen as the only Black delegate to Mississippi's state constitutional convention, the same convention that would become the model for Black disenfranchisement for the entire South. Given his prominence as the founder of an all-Black town and his business acumen, whites in the Mississippi Delta viewed Montgomery as a "safe" and "sensible" Black leader and chose to seat him over his white rival.[7]

In a long speech delivered at the convention, Montgomery said he was willing to sacrifice Black voting rights—"a fearful sacrifice laid upon the burning altar of liberty"—if that would end racial tension and conflict, "to bridge a chasm that has been widening and deepening for a generation, while it promises no enduring prosperity to me and mine."[8] Five years later, Booker T. Washington would cement an accommodationist vision similar to Montgomery's in his Atlanta Compromise speech, in which Washington said, "In all things purely social we can be as separate as the five fingers, and yet one as the hand in all things essential to mutual progress." Du Bois criticized Washington's stand, noting that "his doctrine has tended to make whites, North and South, shift the burden of the Negro problem to the Negro's shoulders and stand aside as critical and rather pessimistic spectators; when in fact the burden belongs to the nation, and the hands of none of us are clean if we bend not our energies to righting these great wrongs."[9]

Like Washington's speech, Montgomery's alignment with Mississippi's white power structure was interpreted in different ways. Whites greeted Montgomery's proclamation with "surprised wonder" and enthusiasm. Black Mississippians who had fought the battles of Reconstruction were adamant in their opposition. Outside Mississippi, a Black editor in New York wrote that "no thoughtless, flippant fool could have inflicted such a wound as Mr. Montgomery has done in this address."[10] Famed abolitionist Frederick Douglass called Montgomery a traitor and thought he had been tricked into his stance.

When Montgomery's accommodationist actions were echoed in Washington's Atlanta Compromise, W. E. B. Du Bois said Washington was "the most distinguished Southerner since Jefferson Davis, and the one with the largest personal following."[11] It is reasonable for Montgomery to come to mind when reading this quote, given the connections he had with both Davis and the Wizard of Tuskegee. Though both Washington and Montgomery saw themselves as working for racial progress, they did so by unwittingly aligning themselves with the forces of white supremacy in the name of Black progress.

Montgomery's alliance with the forces of Black disenfranchisement in the South are rarely spoken of in Mound Bayou today. The focus is on the racial pride Montgomery instilled in the town, which he used to sell the town to powerful people all around the country. Racial pride was a central marketing technique for Mound Bayou during its founding, and remains so today. Markers noting the historic sites of Mound Bayou are scattered all around town, each one accompanied by a code that when scanned with your mobile phone takes you to a website that says, "Welcome to Mound Bayou, MS." On the day I followed these signs around town, I began at a historical marker for T. R. M. Howard, a town physician and civic leader who founded the Regional Council of Negro Leadership, a parallel organization to the white Delta Council. Across from Howard's marker stands Taborian Hospital, a hospital and medical clinic run by the fraternal society the Knights and Daughters of Tabor. It still stands in all its Art Deco glory even though it is now empty.

The marker for Howard is at the spot of what was once known as Friendship Clinic, established in 1948. After a donation of $40,000 in 1950 by Dr. John William Brown, it was renamed in honor of Dr. Brown's sister, Dr. Sara Winifred Brown, who was a longtime health care advocate for Black citizens of the Mississippi Delta. Howard proclaimed that this donation was "one of the largest philanthropic gifts ever made by a Negro in America to a Negro philanthropic cause."[12] The donation was also a testament to Howard's influence, which stretched beyond his work as a physician and surgeon. T. R. M. Howard held interests in banking, finance, and commercial agriculture, all of which helped him build a level of wealth that allowed him to fund civil rights causes and promote Black financial empowerment.

Taborian Hospital—where Howard worked before establishing his own hospital—may be well preserved, yet not all the structures that were symbols of the town's once-regal standing are in the same condition they were during its heyday, including the Sara Brown Hospital/Friendship Clinic. The location that was once Mound Bayou Bank is boarded up, even though it is on the National Register of Historic Places. Isaiah T. Montgomery's home, also a National Historic Landmark and listed on the National

Register of Historic Places, still stands even though its foundation is cracked and crumbling and appears to be held up by wooden supports. Although many of the buildings from the town's founding period are empty and in varying states of renovation and repair, the older buildings of Mound Bayou still remind a visitor that this place was at one time the largest and most self-sufficient African American town in the nation. It just takes some imagination to envision the world that was built and once existed here.

Although residents today remember the triumph of Mound Bayou over outside forces, strife and struggle have also been part of the town's story. Mound Bayou successfully defended itself from a group of marauding white men who sought to destroy it in the 1920s, a source of great pride in the Delta. The greater challenges the town faced have been economic, such as the decline in the price of cotton that led to the closure of the Bank of Mound Bayou in 1914. Given the town's dependence on the cotton economy—it was in fact built on and maintained by cotton—national and global history intersected in this town founded by former slaves. Consequently, as the economic situation of cotton growers around the world deteriorated, so did the fortunes of Mound Bayou.

By the 1920s Mound Bayou found itself caught up in indebtedness and credit scarcity and could not maintain its upward climb.[13] Next, the Great Depression hit the entire Delta hard, and Mound Bayou was not shielded from the economic devastation that spread across the country. Then, in 1941, a fire destroyed part of downtown. The Jewel of the Delta had to find a way to rise from those ashes.

If the late nineteenth and early twentieth centuries were Mound Bayou's glory days, the post-Depression 1940s marked a renaissance of sorts in the town, despite the devastating fire of 1941. On February 12, 1942, over seven thousand Black Delta residents gathered to celebrate the opening of Mound Bayou's Taborian Hospital. The Mississippi Jurisdiction of the International Order of the Knights and Daughters of Tabor funded the hospital, which was quite an achievement in one of the poorest counties in the United States. Much like today, health care options for Black Delta residents were limited. Sharecroppers in the area surrounding Mound Bayou had to depend on the largesse of their planter landlords for medical care, and sometimes that cost was deducted from their crop shares. Taborian

Hospital was a place where Black Delta residents could care for their own, as well as provide care to the surrounding communities.

Beginning in 1938, each member of the Knights and Daughters of Tabor paid an annual assessment into a hospital fund. People even contributed a single brick to the construction of the hospital, and a few nearby plantation owners saw fit to contribute to the fund. Of course, the planters welcomed this new hospital because it could relieve them of paying the medical costs of their tenant farmers. Within four years, the hospital had five thousand new members. When it opened, a yearly fee of $8.40 would cover the expenses of up to thirty-one days of hospitalization, including major and minor surgery.

Theodore Roosevelt Mason Howard was the chief surgeon at Taborian Hospital and became a major force in Mound Bayou's post–World War II revival. More commonly known by his initials, T. R. M. Howard was a Kentucky native but immersed himself in Mound Bayou and embraced its history of entrepreneurship. Howard purchased the Magnolia Mutual Life Insurance Company, a purely commercial venture that sold burial and hospitalization insurance to Black Delta residents. He became the chairman of the National Negro Business League and the president of the National Medical Association, the medical society for Black doctors. Howard shared his wealth with the people of Mound Bayou and built a park for the town as well as a zoo and the state's first public swimming pool for Black people. In 1952 he hired a young graduate of Alcorn College by the name of Medgar Evers as his insurance company's head salesman. In the course of visiting plantations to sell policies and collect premiums, Evers also began his work in promoting civil rights on these visits, with the full backing of Dr. Howard. Evers's wife, Myrlie, described T. R. M. Howard as someone you could tell was a leader with just one look—"kind, affluent, and intelligent, that rare Negro in Mississippi who has somehow beaten the system."

Medgar Evers eventually became an officer in Howard's Regional Council of Negro Leadership, a group Howard founded in 1951 as the parallel organization to the Delta Council, which was controlled by powerful white planters. Unlike the Delta Council, which sought to maintain white political and economic dominance in the region, Howard's group promoted an agenda of self-help, mutual aid, thrift, business ownership, and voter registration. When Evers left to become field secretary for the Mississippi NAACP in 1955, Howard hired another young college graduate, Hermon

Johnson. A recent graduate of Southern University in Baton Rouge, Louisiana, Johnson had visited Mound Bayou when he was in high school and it left an impression on him. When he graduated, Dr. Howard reached out to him and said, "I've got a job for you."

Johnson joined Magnolia Mutual and worked at the same desk as Medgar Evers had. Today that desk and the Underwood typewriter that sat on it stands in a corner of the Mound Bayou Museum, which is based in the old music room of what was once the town's high school. When I spoke with him in 2023, Hermon Johnson Sr. told me that he realizes the Mound Bayou of today seems to exist in a separate realm from the one he found when he arrived here in 1955. Then, Bolivar County, where Mound Bayou is located, had 5,167 Black farmers, of whom 494 owned their farmland, with total land valued around $4 million. Today there are only 160 Black farmers, a significant drop. Johnson remembers the period of postwar prosperity as he shows me the pages of the 1962 seventy-fifth anniversary program—one page even features a photograph of his house in a section called "Mound Bayouans Are Home Lovers," though the house is long gone. But he remembers the man who brought that prosperity to Mound Bayou, T. R. M. Howard, with fondness. "Dr. Howard was an awesome man," Johnson says. "Everyone who worked for him was treated with respect, regardless of their station, whether they were a cook or an officer in his company like me." The year Johnson arrived also marked a turning point in Mound Bayou, since it was the same year as the murder of Emmett Till. The aftermath of the murder reverberated further south at Providence Farm, but Mound Bayou was at the center of these events since it was the town that provided sanctuary to Till's mother, Mamie Till-Mobley, as she attended the murder trial in nearby Sumner. And it was T. R. M. Howard, Johnson's employer, who gave Till-Mobley a room in his home while she attended the trial.

During the trial, Mound Bayou became a place of safety for Emmett's mother and for members of the Black press who covered the case, including Simeon Booker of *Jet* magazine, who was present when the famous open casket photograph of Till's body was taken. Hermon Johnson Sr. remembers the guards around Dr. Howard's house but recalls little else about that period, acknowledging that as a young man right out of college he was just trying to make his way in the world. And given the dangers of that time, I believe his lack of memory may derive from the omnipresent sense of fear among Black Delta residents at the time. What does spring clearly from his memory bank is the sense of defiance that permeated Mound Bayou back in those days. His son, Hermon Jr., echoes his father's sentiments and notes that "if the blues is the music of resistance, Mound Bayou is the embodiment of the blues. Out of the resistance to oppression, we created something special here."

Hermon Jr. is one of those young people Minnie Fisher was hoping would return to Mound Bayou. After living in California for forty-three years, he is back in the Delta and is trying to restore the prominence of Mound Bayou to the story of the Delta as well as to the national narrative of American history. "Mound Bayou is not only just a distinct place in the Delta. It sits apart from other places in the country, since there are few towns that are governed and owned by Black people like Mound Bayou." While what Johnson says is true, he speaks of something else that is also true: Mound Bayou gave its life for integration. When its residents and other Black people in the Delta finally could shop and travel anywhere thanks to the passage of the Civil Rights Act of 1964—that is to say, by the mid-1970s, since it took time to break through the old customs of Jim Crow—Mound Bayou became more a relic of the past than an oasis in the present.

The core mission of the museum, as Johnson sees it, is to keep the spirit and history of Mound Bayou alive as well as make the town a stop for civil rights tourists. Outside of town there is a sign announcing a proposed new hotel for Mound Bayou, one that they hope will house tourists. Johnson gives me a selection of material, including the brochures for the town's fiftieth and seventy-fifth anniversary celebrations and a copy of *The Negro at Mound Bayou*, a history of the first twenty-three years of the town published in 1910. Later, as I read the book, I am taken by a section that looks at the future of the town. It is full of hopefulness but also caution. Charles Banks, a cashier at the Bank of Mound Bayou, made this observation:

The Negroes who shape and control the destiny of Mound Bayou understand conditions too well to allow any radical, nonsensical, and indiscreet policy to prevail here, on the one hand, and there are too many white men around us or in easy reach, who are our friends and willing to see that no impediment is thrown our way or undue advantage is taken of us by irresponsible parties, on the other. This has been demonstrated on several occasions. Verily, the future holds much in store for Mound Bayou.

It was a rather earnest and ambitious group of people who went through great hardships to settle and establish Mound Bayou. But the idea of equality with the white Delta residents who lived in surrounding communities was lost on them. In 1955 and throughout the Civil Rights Movement, the Till murder was processed as the last gasp of white supremacy. But T. R. M. Howard witnessed firsthand the penalties of challenging white supremacy in Mississippi. When he got involved in advocating for civil rights both before and after the Till trial, the forces of white supremacy rose in resistance and the threats became unbearable, forcing him to leave the state in 1956. He relocated to Chicago, a city that many Black Mississippi Delta residents had made their home, and thus in certain ways the distance from the state was not that great. What Howard came to realize, and perhaps the rest of Mound Bayou ignored at their peril, is that white supremacy has a vast reach. Integration may have changed where people could shop, but it was white supremacy that kept Mound Bayou from continuing its progress. Mound Bayou residents had a difficult time seeing that, since they felt they existed in a world unto themselves.

The Civil Rights Movement did not change the structures that Black Americans took to the streets to stand up against. And today, as voting rights and civil rights fall in importance in twenty-first-century American society, the past seems perilously close to the present. That means this is a moment to build social structures free of the forces of white supremacy as well as structures that challenge those forces. As I look at the complicated history of Mound Bayou, I can see some of that defiant spirit wrapped up in the story of this place. Hermon Johnson Jr. is right when he says this place embraces the radical spirit of Black people in the Delta. The Delta has always been a radical space. But in choosing the path of accommodation, its founders also helped keep some of the structures of white supremacy in place. Telling the story of Mound Bayou, then, is going to take soul-searching and a deep look into the past to make sure we tell a story free of the mythology of the place, one that is far from the way the town was captured in popular song. Imagining Mound Bayou's future first requires making a radical interpretation of its past. As the song says, "When you see me walking with my head way down, it's because I miss my Mississippi town." Yet the question remains, can the future of places like Mound Bayou be imagined free of the romanticized version of their past?

In his novel *Wolf Whistle*, Mississippi Delta writer Lewis Nordan portrays the Emmett Till murder from a fictional perspective and through the darkness of that event. "The Mississippi Delta is not always dark with rain," he writes. "Some autumn mornings, the sun rises over Moon Lake, or Eagle, or Choctaw, or Blue, or Roebuck, all the wide, deep waters of the state, and when it does, its dawn is as rosy with promise and hope as any other." When I look at images of Mound Bayou in its infancy, or in its second flowering in the 1950s and 1960s, I feel a similar kind of hope. I even remember feeling some of that hope when my father told me the story of the town. But when I look at how far Mound Bayou has fallen, I am gripped by a feeling of hopelessness that this town will ever rise up from its current crumbling state.

What I feel more profoundly in Mound Bayou, particularly in talking with the Johnson family, is a sense of exile. Like a people in exile, many in Mound Bayou exhibit a profound need to look back at the past and have difficulty looking forward. They can't imagine a future brighter than their past. And that is understandable, given how far Mound Bayou has fallen.

Although Mound Bayou may be crumbling, some of the ideas that had their origin within its borders live on at the edge of town in a large brick and glass building called the Delta Community Health Center. It's a building I began to pay a great deal of attention to when I moved to the Delta in May 2023. Each day I drove past the building, I noticed that there were more cars in the Delta Community Health Center's parking lot than I see anywhere else in downtown Mound Bayou. It serves as a profound contrast to the empty parking lot outside the well-preserved edifice of Taborian Hospital. And the existence of this health center makes me wonder if it is the place that truly embraces the spirit of the founding of Mound Bayou, one free of the ways its founders learned from their former masters. Yet I also know the descendants of the founders of Mound Bayou fought against the establishment of the Delta Health Center. This makes me wonder if resistance to a changing landscape of needs played as much a role in the decline of Mound Bayou as the forces of integration. Nostalgia for a storied past can subvert progress in the present.

CHAPTER 6

RACE, HEALTH, AND POVERTY IN A SANCTUARY FROM SEGREGATION

Well, the blues, is a achin' old heart disease
Do it now, you gon' do it? Tell me all about it
The blues, is a low-down achin' heart disease
Like consumption, killing me by degrees

—ROBERT JOHNSON,
"Preaching Blues (Up Jumped the Devil)"

A s the poet June Jordan observed on a visit in 1970, the Mississippi Delta is a place that exists as a beautiful and long blues song with its people bravely moving forward each day. When I moved to the Delta for four months to write and observe the people and the place, I encountered this spirit every day as I walked the streets of Clarksdale in the early morning or wandered through now-empty towns, where the blues was more of an echo than a resounding presence. For many who visit the Delta, particularly those who come to seek the origins of the blues, the realities of life here are more an abstraction than anything else. But I watched closely, and like June Jordan I came to see how the people who occupy this land keep moving despite every obstacle that might lead them to stumble.

Jordan immersed herself in Mississippi while she was here, particularly in the Delta. While she rarely explicitly mentions the blues in her writing about Mississippi, her tone and observations about the Delta make it clear she connected with the ways the spirit of that music reflected the life of the place and served as an intensely personal way of expressing pain. She saw the blues as a salve that healed the wounds associated with that pain. And I share that idea of the blues with Jordan.

If the blues is simply poetry wrapped in a struggle for survival, Jordan sought out people in the Delta who demonstrated that spirit of struggle. One of those people was civil rights activist Fannie Lou Hamer, whose heart-wrenching account of life in Mississippi delivered at the 1964 Democratic

National Convention echoed across the nation. In her testimony, after describing the savage treatment she faced when she fought to register to vote, Hamer concluded by saying, with the combined cadence of a preacher and a blues singer, "All of this is on account of we want to register, to become first-class citizens. And if the Freedom Democratic Party is not seated now, I question America. Is this America, the land of the free and the home of the brave, where we have to sleep with our telephones off the hooks because our lives be threatened daily, because we want to live as decent human beings, in America?"[1]

What Hamer did not reveal to the nation that day in 1964 is the brutality she also suffered at the hands of white doctors, people who she thought had a principal duty to first, do no harm. "People do some dirty, low-down things," Hamer told June Jordan in 1970, "and yet, and still, they suppose to be human beings. And God is perfect. Sometimes I wonder about that. I don't understand it, really. But maybe I'm not suppose to understand."[2]

The two women visited Mound Bayou together. Jordan was enamored of the town's history of Black self-governance and determination. She quickly learned that Hamer's attraction to this town founded by former slaves was grounded in the medical care that she received here, care that she could trust by doctors who treated her as a human being. "The reason I would rather go to Mound Bayou if I take sick, is that women go up to that hospital [the white hospital in Ruleville] and be sterilized, without signing anything," Fannie Lou Hamer confessed to Jordan with a mixture of sadness and shame. "And to be perfectly honest, see, I can give you medical proof: It happened to me."[3]

The story of Mound Bayou's Taborian Hospital and its founding is rooted in the ways that race, health, and poverty are tied together in the Delta. When June Jordan realized the problems that confronted the poor of the Delta also affected the place that in her mind existed as an Eden for Black America—or, as she put it, "a black Israel for black refugees from Northern poverty and its humiliations"—she grew angry. There was visible decay in the town, much like what I witness each time I visit Mound Bayou today. Yet in the time since Jordan's visit, this Eden of the Delta has slid further away. In 1970 the town had a pharmacy in its main business district but, as Jordan described it, a decrepit one. "My feelings of bitterness increase," Jordan noted, "as I consider that here, where there really is black control of black American life, it is only second-hand responsibility for problems created by racist America: problems of black illiteracy, unemployment and the physical illness that accompanies deprivation." Jordan's anger, combined with sorrow and a sense of collective tragedy, hits like another round of blues.

Poor Black people in the Mississippi Delta have historically had little autonomy when they became ill, as Fannie Lou Hamer's sterilization illustrates. This was particularly true for Black women, since between 1958 and 1964, the state legislature of Mississippi tried to pass several pieces of legislation aimed at the forced sterilization of Black women. "This is the only way to stop this black tide that threatens to engulf us," one state legislator proclaimed on the floor in favor of one of the sterilization bills.[4] The hostility ran just as deep for poor Black patients who needed routine medical assistance. Those who could not pay for their care were at the mercy of local white doctors. As one white Delta doctor told the *Boston Globe* in 1967, "If there is a nigger in my waiting room that doesn't have $3 in cash, he can sit there and die."[5]

When bluesman Robert Johnson sings of consumption killing him by degrees, he's not just using illness as a metaphor. He is speaking with profound honesty of the hopelessness that visited Black people in places like Mound Bayou and across the Delta no matter what sickness came knocking at their door. Although Taborian Hospital served Black people in the Delta, its model was one of membership, much like what we would today call a "health maintenance organization," or HMO. And while it served the poor and indigent, its financial model meant that it was established to preferentially serve those with the ability to pay. Racism may not have influenced the medical care provided at Taborian Hospital, but class played a role in limiting the type of care available to those who could not afford membership.

Beginning in the 1940s, Taborian Hospital provided community-based health care inspired by the model of the mutual aid societies that Black Americans formed across the nation and their mission to provide dignity in the undignified system of Jim Crow. Changes to the geography of health care in the Delta began with the civil rights struggle that began in Mound Bayou after the murder of Emmett Till. The movement forced Americans to examine not only racial structures but also the economic structures that were entwined with racism.

While Fannie Lou Hamer was testifying in Atlantic City about the political sickness that infected the Delta, a group called the Medical Committee for Human Rights (MCHR) had doctors across the state providing medical care to civil rights activists like her, as well as the thousands of white college volunteers who came to register Black voters during what became known as Freedom Summer. The MCHR was not just limited to providing triage care for this new crop of activists in Mississippi; it was also working to desegregate Southern hospitals and end the exclusion of Black doctors from the American Medical Association. Black doctors in the South could not be members of the AMA without being admitted to a local affiliate, and since those affiliates would not admit Black doctors—and the national AMA looked the other way as Southern affiliates discriminated against Black doctors—they weren't part of the broader professional network of doctors. Although Black doctors had their own National Medical Association, once headed by Taborian Hospital's T. R. M. Howard, white hospitals could still exclude Black physicians who lacked AMA membership.

As the MCHR doctors did their work during Freedom Summer and learned of the conditions under which many Black Mississippians lived, their goals began to change. Not only was there medical neglect, there was also rampant malnutrition. Thirty to 40 percent of Black children in the state had intestinal parasites. The infant mortality rate in Mississippi and the Delta was comparable to that of a developing country. In the 1960s, the Black infant mortality in Mississippi and the Delta—a region, it should be noted, located in the richest country in the world—was greater than 60 per 1,000 live births, twice that of whites.

One of the places the MCHR doctors worked was in the Mileston community, where my family lived in the late 1940s and through the mid-1950s. The MCHR clinic in Mileston survived for only two years and was plagued with financial difficulties. It was established less than ten years after a similar clinic at Providence Farm had been shuttered because of its perceived alliance with Black equality and civil rights. Of course, the Mileston clinic was not well received in Holmes County either because of its direct association with the Civil Rights Movement. The work the MCHR did in Holmes County made it clear that the need the clinic at Providence Farm sought to fill still existed. That was true not just in Holmes County but across the Delta.

A doctor at the MCHR by the name of H. Jack Geiger wanted to look for a more permanent solution to the health care problems affecting the poor Black community of the rural South. Geiger had worked in a community health center in apartheid-era South Africa and thought a similar model would work in the American South. He worked with other members of the MCHR, including Dr. Count Gibson of the Tufts University Medical School. In 1965, a year after Freedom Summer, the group received a grant from the War on Poverty program's new Office of Economic Opportunity to create two "demonstration community health centers": one in the urban North in Boston and the other in the rural South near Mound Bayou. The facility in Boston opened first and by 1967 the Southern center had opened its first permanent facility.

Mound Bayou's Taborian Hospital might have been more of a historical footnote if not for the establishment of the Delta Health Center by Tufts University. Although Mound Bayou had a long history of providing medical services to Black residents of the Delta, by 1966 Taborian Hospital was near bankruptcy. For nearly thirty years, Taborian Hospital provided the town of Mound Bayou and Black Delta residents a sense of dignity when they became ill—that is, until it could no longer keep pace with changes in the health care landscape. The Hill-Burton Hospital Construction Act of 1946 allowed for increases in federal aid to public hospitals nationwide, which included hospitals found in the counties surrounding Mound Bayou—$4.6 million between 1948 and 1965—and made it possible to modernize their facilities and expand the number of hospital beds. Because it was a private hospital, Taborian Hospital did not receive any of these funds. Although the act required that hospitals use a portion of their funds for indigent care "without discrimination on account of race, creed, or color," Southern states like Mississippi were allowed to maintain hospital segregation as long as there was care "of like quality." The establishment of Medicare and Medicaid in 1965, however, helped chip away at segregation in health care. The new programs accelerated the trend toward reliance on third-party payers of health care in the Delta, leading a few white doctors to seek low-income Black patients they once shunned. Hospital boards also realized that remaining segregated would now keep them from getting federal funds that would help their bottom lines and keep them in business.

A key development affecting health care in the Delta was the region's shift in population during the 1950s and 1960s. In Bolivar County, the mechanization of farming led to a 75 percent unemployment rate followed by a drop in population, since many agricultural workers left to find employment. By 1960 the combined membership of the United Order of

Friendship—which ran a competing hospital across the street from Taborian—and the Knights and Daughters of Tabor had dwindled to barely twenty-two thousand members, down from forty-seven thousand members in 1945. This led to a sharp increase in dues to be a member of the hospital. Yet despite the increased fees, both hospitals began to run a budget deficit. By this point, founder T. R. M. Howard of Sara Brown Hospital—the hospital of the United Order of Friendship—had left Mississippi and begun a new medical practice in Chicago. The Friendship Medical Center, its name an echo of his Friendship Medical Clinic in the Delta, began in 1973 to focus on providing legal abortions, showing an awareness of the concerns about female bodily autonomy held by Delta women leaders like Fannie Lou Hamer. Before the legalization of abortion that year, Howard had provided safe clandestine abortions through the Chicago group known as Jane as well as the Clergy Consultation Service.

Violence related to his civil rights activism certainly played a role in Howard's departure, since his attacks on the FBI's inaction in the Emmett Till case had angered the agency's director, J. Edgar Hoover, as well as many of Mississippi's prominent politicians. On the Ku Klux Klan's death list, Howard had armed bodyguards for his protection. The segregationist *Clarion-Ledger* newspaper in Jackson had even labeled him a "dangerous agitator" who was "hell bent on stirring up strife between the races."[6] Yet his move to Chicago also seemed to be following the lead of his medical clients. As more Black Delta residents migrated north, Howard recognized that the membership base for his hospital was shrinking. As he was a savvy businessman—though sometimes loose with his financial planning—and never known to be restricted by limits, it seems Howard recognized the model under which he had conducted his medical practice had a limited life.

The founders of the Delta Health Center also realized changes were needed in the way health care was delivered. Rather than simply seeking to treat sick patients, the center's philosophy was to look at what the founders called the social determinants of health, which included dilapidated housing, poor sanitation, malnutrition, and inadequate social welfare services. Unlike Mound Bayou's fraternal hospitals, the Delta Health Center encouraged poor people to participate in decision-making and recruited them for training and jobs at the center. Given the organization's origins in the Civil Rights Movement, it met opposition from the state's white power structure, which maintained the paternalistic view that Black and poor people in the Delta should have health care decisions made for them, much like they had been made for Fannie Lou Hamer in that hospital in Ruleville.

The response to the establishment of the Delta Health Center also exposed a similarly paternalistic view, but here the vocal pushback was from Mound Bayou's Black establishment, who had long been in charge of the Delta's two fraternal hospitals. Mound Bayou was a town that was proud of its accomplishments, leading its mayor, Benjamin A. Green—the son of the town's co-founder Benjamin T. Green—to declare at the 1942 opening of Taborian Hospital that Mound Bayou was "this law-abiding, God-fearing and jail-less city, an All-Negro city if you please, where you can sense freedom and safety as nowhere else in the mid-South." Green and the town establishment felt that they were the ones who knew what its poorer citizens needed, since they also boasted that there was not a loafer or vagrant to be found on Mound Bayou's streets. This boast failed to recognize that there were people living in impoverished circumstances in Mound Bayou. When these same people learned there were social circumstances affecting their health that only Mound Bayou's Black establishment wanted to address, it disrupted the social order of the town. For years the two fraternal hospitals had provided for the social welfare needs of the community, in line with what the founding families had determined were the needs of the town's residents. Now the poor people of Mound Bayou, those who might have been labeled as loafers, wanted to take charge of their own destiny rather than have it defined by the town fathers. The new Delta Health Center sought to empower the poor; the leadership of the fraternal hospitals only wanted to maintain the status quo.

What the organizers of the Delta Health Center had not anticipated was the opposition of the Black middle class to the improved circumstances of the Black poor. "They resented the fact that we were putting in screen doors and windows and patching up houses for people who lived on plantations," observed then Delta Health Center project director L. C. Dorsey. "They resented the fact that we had taken women who were working for them for 12 and 15 dollars a week and had given them jobs."[7] So, the Black middle class disliked losing a hold on their inexpensive domestic help.

The ongoing struggle for social justice in the Mississippi Delta, then, cannot be understood without considering class oppression as well as the racism that characterizes the region. As sociologist John Dollard observed about the Delta in 1938, "caste and class show the relations in which people stand to one another."

In his January 1964 State of the Union address, then president Lyndon Johnson announced an "unconditional war on poverty." At the time, 19 percent of all Americans lived in poverty. What Johnson sought to do with the War on Poverty and other programs that later became part of his "Great Society" agenda was to frame poverty for the American public not as a moral failing by poor people but a societal failing.

When Johnson traveled to Kentucky in April 1964 to sell his War on Poverty to the American public, he was not just seeking to put a face on that segment of the country social activist Michael Harrington called "the other America," the one that many Americans rarely see or encounter. The face of poverty that dominated the media in the aftermath of Johnson's State of the Union speech was largely white and Appalachian. *Life* magazine, then the most influential news weekly in the country, even published a twelve-page photographic essay in January 1964 after the State of the Union address called "The Valley of Poverty" that focused on Appalachian poverty. "Unless the grim chain [of unemployment and lack of education] can be broken," the essay noted, "a second generation coming of age in Appalachia will fall into the same dismal life—a life that protects them from starvation but deprives them of self-respect and hope."[8]

Although Black poverty in the Mississippi Delta mirrored the poverty of Appalachia, the public face of the 1960s War on Poverty constructed by policymakers was white. This choice illustrates how race has rarely been central to the ways we as Americans think about rural poverty and its lasting impact on the health and well-being of people from places like the Mississippi Delta. Although the patterns of poverty in the Delta today mirror national trends with respect to race and poverty in rural America, even back when public policy was paying attention to issues of poverty and social mobility, race has rarely been central to those policies. The institutional structures of Appalachia—with its legacy of coal mining and exploitation of workers—have always been easier for Americans to see than the equally destructive and dehumanizing structures of slavery, sharecropping, and Jim Crow segregation. And those structures kept Black people in the Delta poor, just as they did for white coal miners in Appalachia.

With the Civil Rights Movement in the center of the media spotlight in 1964, one could argue that Johnson politically could not afford to align the image of his anti-poverty programs with those of Black America, because then the faces of the scourge of poverty and the Black faces fighting for civil rights would be seen as one and the same. Despite Johnson's best efforts, in Mississippi that happened nonetheless, particularly in the Delta. In the Mississippi Delta, civil rights activism directly correlated poverty with the region's power structure, which was rooted in white supremacy. And those in power—many of them Mississippi politicians who were also Delta land-owners—did whatever they could to continue to mask the racism of these structures. They knew that disrupting the institutional structures that had existed for generations would benefit Black people and potentially shift the power dynamic. And they did whatever they could to stop programs that would change the fortunes of Black Delta residents in any way. In doing so, they affected the ways those programs would work on a national scale.

From his time working in the MCHR health clinic in Mileston, Jack Geiger understood the power structure of the Delta and knew that estab-lishing a medical clinic in the region would generate white hostility. So did his colleague Count Gibson. Both men knew that their proposed health center threatened the white medical establishment by virtue of their out-sider status as well as the organization's desire to empower Black Delta residents by educating them about the causes of their health issues. First, they threw the opposition off-balance by promoting an alternate site on the edge of the Delta in the town of Batesville. Of course, local white doc-tors opposed the project. Geiger and Gibson next suggested Mound Bayou, which they felt would get the least opposition out of all possible sites. Their hunch was correct: the opposition was minimal since the white doctors perceived Mound Bayou to be outside their realm of power and influence.

The local white medical establishment had to accept this new clinic because of the particularities of its funding and organizational affiliation. In all fifty states, governors could ordinarily veto program funding by the Office of Economic Opportunity (OEO), which was the Delta Health Cen-ter's funder. But there was an exception if the grant was made to an insti-tution of higher learning—in that case, the governor had no veto power. Since the Delta Health Center was affiliated with Tufts University and not a university in Mississippi, the funding was protected from the powers in Mississippi hostile to the center.

Although the white medical establishment had resigned itself to the new Delta Health Center, the leaders associated with Taborian Hospital and the other fraternal hospital, the Sara Brown Hospital (originally the Friendship Clinic), were not as accepting. Both facilities were in poor financial condition. Geiger was horrified by both hospitals, calling them "physically deteriorating and fiscally unsound." John Hatch, a Black man from the South who had been hired to build relationships and trust in the Black community—he even worked in the cotton fields to get a sense of the local people's labor conditions—was equally concerned about the condition of the two hospitals. In the end, Geiger and his colleagues suggested that the OEO merge the two ailing facilities into a new Mound Bayou Community Hospital and provide this new entity adequate resources.

By the time the Delta Health Center's building was completed, at the end of 1968, the clinic was seeing between 150 and 175 people per day at the facility, and another 30 to 40 people in their homes. One of the people making home visits was Sister Mary Stella Simpson, a nurse-midwife who joined the center soon after it opened. A member of the Daughters of Charity, Sister Mary Stella was a commanding presence in Mound Bayou, with her starched, snow-white swooping cornet perched on her head and her matching habit. Her letters to the sisters in her home convent back in Indiana reveal the conditions she encountered in the community. On April 4, 1968, she wrote to her sisters, "I saw an 11-month-old baby who was almost dead from starvation at clinic yesterday. I have seen pictures of these little starved ones from India and Viet Nam, but the actual face-to-face encounter is really an experience. . . . The little one doesn't know how to eat." In another letter she wrote, "Poor Mississippi will never be the same with all these health center people occupying the Delta area. Things really are a-changing."[9]

Today, when you take that same journey south on Highway 61 to Mound Bayou, there is a new health center there, one much larger than the one that opened in 1968, as well as a medical center that is named for one of its founders, Jack Geiger. The Delta Health Center now has seventeen locations across the Mississippi Delta. Today, roughly sixty years after the creation of the DHC and its sister health center in Boston, the Columbia Point Health Center, both established in the 1960s, there are more than 1,400 community health centers around the country—one in every congressional district in the United States—all part of a movement to provide health care to poor people, a movement that began in the Mississippi Delta.

While the Delta Health Center has grown and thrived and become a model for the nation, health outcomes in the Delta remain grim. Sister Mary Stella Simpson would be troubled to learn that Mississippi still has one of the highest infant mortality rates in the nation, and the highest rates in the state are recorded in the Delta in and around this health center. Malnutrition is no longer rampant, but it has been replaced by obesity and the diet-related plague of type 2 diabetes. There may be more access to food, but the health problems of many in the Delta today relate to the lack of access to healthy food, since many Delta towns are so-called food deserts that lack access to fresh fruits and vegetables. The gleaming presence of the Delta Health Center is a sign of change, but it led me to wonder how much had changed as well as how the battle against the social determinants of poor health has evolved over the past half century.

Before Taborian Hospital and the Delta Health Center, the women of the Alpha Kappa Alpha sorority—one of the "Divine Nine" Black fraternal organizations—identified the Mississippi Delta as an area in acute need of medical care. From the mid-1930s until 1942, the AKA-sponsored Mississippi Health Project collaborated with the Delta Cooperative Farm in Bolivar County and its successor organization, Providence Farm in Holmes County, to serve what its leader, Dr. Dorothy Ferebee of Howard University Medical School, deemed the "social welfare needs of the poor." Outside the DHC building is a marble marker noting the service of AKA and acknowledging that during its time in the Delta, the sorority served over fifteen thousand people. The marker stands beside a brass placard that reads:

DELTA HEALTH CENTER
1967
First rural community health center in the United States
Opened by Tufts University as Tufts Delta Health Center
Third health care facility in Mound Bayou
Serves as a much needed health resource for the poor
and disenfranchised in the Mississippi Delta

Since this is the first rural health center in the United States, the history lesson continues upon entering the Delta Health Center. An exhibition of photographs and documents illustrates the history and struggle to establish the center, including documents from the Mississippi State Sovereignty Commission that reveal how the state of Mississippi put the center, its founders, and employees under routine surveillance. Any outside entity coming to Mississippi, particularly one associated with a university in Massachusetts, was suspect for "stirring up civil rights activities." In 1968, several employees of the DHC who lived in the town of Rosedale demanded that the town provide sewers, clean water, and paved streets in the Black section of town. The commission felt that the Delta Health Center was conspiring to force Rosedale's Black citizens to make these demands—it even suspected the DHC was paying people to ask for these improvements—rather than recognizing that the people were simply demanding to be granted basic human rights. The full complexities involved in establishing the center makes you wonder how it even exists at all. Whether considering the conflicts with the state of Mississippi or with those who ran Taborian Hospital, or even with the federal authorities from the Office of Economic Opportunity who originally funded the center, the story of the Delta Health Center reveals how the struggle to achieve equity and justice for poor people in the Delta shifted from the needs of poor people to the desires of the powerful.

John Fairman, the current director of the Delta Health Center, understands both the origins and history of the center and the push and pull between the poor and the powerful in the Mississippi Delta. Fairman is a tall and courtly man who speaks with passion about his work in the Delta as well as his years in public health in cities across the country. "It is the poor who tell us what the world is and what our service to the world should be," Fairman tells me in his office early one morning before he conducts a meeting with his staff. As we begin our talk, he hands a stack of documents to an assistant to copy, all of them letters and notes from DHC founder Jack Geiger, to make sure I understand the history. But he also wants me to know about the unsung figures in the struggle to provide health care to the poor people of the Mississippi Delta. "There is a little-known guy in the history and that is Dr. Robert Smith," Fairman begins. Smith, a graduate of Howard University College of Medicine, was the founder of the Medical Committee for Human Rights. The grandson of a Delta sharecropper, Smith had provided medical care to the Freedom Riders as well as to others who were battered and beaten during civil rights protests. Smith issued the call for doctors to come to Mississippi for Freedom Summer, and Jack Geiger and Count Gibson answered the call. What all these men had in common was not just their activism, but the shared understanding that rethinking health care meant having people rethink their social situations as well, to understand the forces that lead to poor health outcomes. They understood Martin Luther King Jr.'s statement that "of all the forms of inequality, injustice in health is the most shocking and inhuman." It follows, then, that once the residents of Rosedale learned that lack of water and sewer service were affecting their health in ways that were both shocking and inhuman, they began to take an active role in changing their circumstances.

John Fairman grew up in the Delta town of Cleveland, just a few miles down the road from Mound Bayou. Like me, when he left Mississippi forty years ago, he never planned to come back. Fate landed him back in the place of his birth to run the Delta Health Center after decades of working in public health all around the country, mostly in urban settings like Boston, Houston, Denver, and Chicago. But being a Delta native has made him keenly aware of how rural health care is different from the issues he confronted in urban settings. His personal history shapes how he views the realities of the present. "I am well aware of the historical forces I am confronting every day here in the Delta," he tells me in a matter-of-fact tone that echoes his years of experience.

One of those historical forces is the legacy of the Jim Crow era. Fairman is aware of the ways the remnants of the era of segregated health care still affect life in the Delta. The way he combats that is with data. The DHC has a data scientist who looks at information provided by patients and tracks who they are providing health care to in granular detail at the zip codes level, as well as how the health of the patients they treat tracks with access to healthy food and with the history of sharecropping and poverty in the region. Fairman realizes that those in power in Mississippi may not want to think as much about the ways the health care past affects the health care present, but they can't argue with data that reveals current inequities.

He also realizes that outside of the DHC, there are few other health care providers in the Delta focused on the social determinants of health, particularly as they relate to Black residents. Just as the counties of the Delta that have the largest concentration of poverty also had large numbers of enslaved people, the descendants of those people also ended up as sharecroppers. And in the nearly two generations since the end of sharecropping, its legacy can be found in the lives of the people, even though the physical evidence of sharecropping no longer can be found on the landscape.

Hospitals are closing all around the Delta, and those that remain are dominated by a white medical establishment that may not be inherently racist but that denies the linkage between race and health. Fairman tells me that there is unconscious bias in these hospitals. "How can you have a hospital in a place that is more than 60 percent Black and not have any Black hospital administrators or leaders?" he asks. He also tells me a story of a white man who visited the DHC and asked a janitor nearby who was in charge. When he told him that Fairman, a Black man, was in charge, the visitor turned to the janitor, who was also Black, and said, "Well, I guess if you play your cards right, one day you can be in charge of this place like him."

History is very much on Fairman's mind as he gives me copies of the chronology of the Delta Health Center's founding, which was compiled by Jack Geiger. When I leave, I apologize to his staff, since it is clear that our talk has delayed their meeting. I am taken by how the staff's demographics mirror the population of the Delta, unlike the hospitals Fairman and I have just talked about.

Later, when I read the documents, I notice that the chronology covers more than fifty years, from the DHC's founding up through the early 2000s when Fairman became director and CEO. After Geiger left in 1971, the DHC was turned over to Black middle-class leaders in Mound Bayou, who persuaded the Office of Economic Opportunity to turn over the center's operation and ownership to a local board. Eventually, federal authorities demanded a new governing board after the DHC developed problems in terms of funding, mismanagement, and political cronyism.

What captivates me in the documents Fairman shared is the resistance to change, not just by the white power structure but also by the leaders of the town of Mound Bayou. As Fannie Lou Hamer noted, Taborian Hospital did fill a void left by white health care providers who either abused Black patients or refused to treat them. But that was not nearly enough, since by the late 1960s and early 1970s, Taborian was plagued by overcrowding, inadequate medical equipment, and poor funding. The DHC, by contrast, offered poor Delta residents thorough examinations and effective treatment that contrasted with the indifference shown by Taborian and white doctors in the area. Even more important, the DHC provided jobs and opportunity to people in the community. As Mound Bayou resident Barbara

Brooks told historian Tom Ward, the center educated people. "They set up programs for the illiterate and to tell them they had nothing to be ashamed of," she recalled in a 2011 interview.[10] Somehow, Taborian Hospital thought it could survive on the pride people felt in its homegrown origins rather than the quality of the care it provided. And it also thought it could ignore the larger problems that affected the community it served.

The Delta Health Center's parking lot is still full on the day that I visit. What permeates the ethos of the place is its link to the Civil Rights Movement and the way it sought to empower the people of the Delta, despite resistance from the powerful. As doctor and civil rights activist Aaron Shirley observed, the strength of the resistance to the Delta Health Center came from the way it threated the establishment: "The medical piece threatened the establishment to the degree that it would expose the traditional system for what it was, and it really wasn't making a difference, and it really did nothing to narrow the gap between health stats. The exposure of all of these medical conditions at a time where they should not have existed but did. But the other piece was more threatening in terms of change, social change."[11] Shirley knew a lot about threatening the establishment, since in the late 1960s he encountered resistance to creating a similar health center to serve the state capital of Jackson and surrounding Hinds County. Because his proposed center was not affiliated with a university outside the state, the governor had the power to veto the project. Shirley sought out Donald Rumsfeld, then president Richard Nixon's ambitious head of the Office of Economic Opportunity, to persuade him to overturn the governor's veto. Shirley succeeded, and the Jackson-Hinds Comprehensive Health Center was established.[12]

Aaron Shirley's story reminds me of something he said to June Jordan back in 1970: "I honestly believe that Mississippi, Georgia and Alabama will save this country. Because we are facing problems that Northern states will face 10 years from now. We have real hit-to-hit confrontation. The white man says, 'I hate you.' And we say, 'I ain' scared no more.' When this problem is solved, I honestly believe there will be a true partnership."

But the problem is still not solved. In the Delta, there is not the partnership Shirley envisioned. Shirley's words remind me that the Mississippi Delta mirrors our national story about race, health, and poverty because it is a story we as a nation are still working to resolve. But maybe we should approach race, health, and poverty as an ongoing struggle rather than problems to be neatly solved.

CHAPTER 7

"HUNGER HAS NO COLOR LINE"

Starvation in my kitchen
Rent sign's on my door
And if my luck don't change
I can't stay at my home no more

—BIG BILL BROONZY, "Starvation Blues"

In places of great poverty, hunger is a disease. When Jack Geiger and John Hatch began their work at the Delta Health Clinic, it didn't take them long to recognize the depths of the Mississippi Delta's malnutrition crisis. Hunger seemed to manifest itself like a fast-spreading virus. Public health nurses who made home visits often observed that people had little more than grits and beans to eat. One wrote that many children "live on a diet of cornbread, grits, and Kool-aid" and that "the effects of malnutrition are staggering." The inadequate diet of Delta residents materialized on the skin of children who were suffering from rashes, boils, dryness, and a protein deficiency that caused many of their bodies to consume their own protein tissue.[1]

To combat rampant hunger, the two men decided to do something radical: they began to write prescriptions for food. These prescriptions for food—meat, eggs, vegetables, and milk—could be filled by a network of grocery stores in the Black community of Bolivar County, where the clinic was located, and the bill was sent to what was then called the Tufts-Delta Health Center for reimbursement. It was something Geiger learned from his time in South Africa, where dried skim milk was provided to starving children. In the South African townships where Geiger once worked, powdered milk came to be classified as medicine since—like a strong antibiotic used to fight an infection—it saved children's lives.

Geiger and Hatch's approach did not sit well with officials at the Office of Economic Opportunity, the agency that helped fund the clinic. They saw a doctor's prescription only as a note authorizing the dispensing of pharmaceuticals for the treatment of an actual disease, not as a directive to put food in the mouths of poor people. But Geiger didn't budge. "If mothers and babies don't eat, all the medicine in the world won't work," Geiger responded.[2] What Geiger realized was that people in the Delta were hungry both out of extreme poverty and failed government policies regarding food.

In the Mississippi Delta's past and in its present, hunger is still a disease. As Robert Kennedy's 1967 trip to the Delta revealed, as farming in the region became mechanized, people were left without work and were hungry—some of them displaced from the plantations where they once worked, but all without any real economic future. Ignoring this change in economic conditions was a failure of public policy. Yet the bigger lesson of what Kennedy witnessed is not just what happened to the people of the Delta when farm mechanization took over. As historian Greta de Jong has written, "The black plantation workers who were pushed off the land by the modernization of southern agriculture were not to join the industrial working class in the post–civil rights era. Instead, they were the first to experience the transition from free labor to displaced persons that awaited millions of other workers in this new era of economic restructuring."[3] Kennedy may have been focused on the Delta, but he was also thinking about similar situations in other parts of the country. He witnessed how the economic restructuring of the Delta and the hunger that came with it would spread to other regions where economic shifts were also occurring, whether it was in the coal mines of Appalachia, or later in the industrial belt of the Midwest, or even in New York City's Bedford-Stuyvesant neighborhood, a place that as US senator from New York he had personally observed as experiencing similar patterns of poverty.

Robert Kennedy believed in government action to confront mass unemployment, poverty, and hunger, but that political ideology died with him when he was assassinated during his run for president in 1968. What replaced Kennedy's idea of government intervention was belief in unfettered free enterprise. In the end, a blind belief in the power of market forces replaced Jim Crow laws as a way for whites to maintain economic power. Politicians like Ronald Reagan linked government social programs with economic decline rather than social justice. Government action to combat hunger and poverty came to be thought of as wasteful, and anti-poverty policies as creating an indolent class of people who would not work. Yet in the Delta and places like it, the reality was that there was little work and the work that existed could not sustain a family. The idea that people in places like the Delta were not hungry and just lazy is rooted in a myth of American individualism that only perpetuates poverty and hunger. Consequently, a new Jim Crow was born, but one that was visible only to those affected by it.

Over time, as the country moved from agricultural and industrial capitalism to financial capitalism in the late twentieth century and into the twenty-first, the push toward market forces expanded from places like the Delta and spurred massive layoffs in other rural communities as well as places like the midwestern Rust Belt. Understanding what happened in the Delta helps us understand other economic developments in the post–civil rights era: the region's economic circumstances may be particularly entwined with its long history of racial oppression, but what followed across the country links the circumstances there with structural economic changes on a national level. This happened without regard to the race of the people affected. As Delta civil rights activist Fannie Lou Hamer told novelist Paule Marshall in 1970, "hunger has no color line." Hamer worked tirelessly to develop her Freedom Farm Cooperative to feed poor people in the Delta through grassroots participation. "All the qualifications that you have to have to become part of the co-op is to be poor," Hamer proclaimed.[4] Hamer knew the emphasis on market forces and the movement away from government intervention also knew no color line with respect to the people on whom it had an impact.

Although much has changed in the Mississippi Delta since Kennedy's visit and the Delta Health Center's prescriptions for food, food insecurity continues to be an issue, and food is still a political weapon. The people of the Delta may have more political power, but that power is diminished since they cannot use it to put food on their tables. Political power is concentrated at the local level, not the state or national level. Food and agricultural policies are set at the national level, and much of that power is in the hands of those who use the Delta's rich farmland for the industrial farming of corn, cotton, and soybeans. Those with power have little interest or incentive to grow food to feed the region's residents. The children and grandchildren of many of the families Kennedy visited continue to struggle to get food on the table—and the food that they can get is largely processed and high in fat.

In the years since the beginning of farm automation in the mid-1960s, the communities of the Mississippi Delta have experienced health inequities intertwined with discrimination, poverty, and racial exclusion. In three Mississippi Delta counties that Kennedy visited—Bolivar, Washington, and Sunflower, whose aggregate population is roughly a hundred thousand—over 65 percent of residents identify as Black or African American and about 30 percent live at or below the poverty level, more than 50 percent of women and 40 percent of men living in these counties have obesity, and the rate of diabetes is 13.5 percent. All eighteen of the counties that comprise the Mississippi Delta are characterized by high levels of poverty, high prevalence of chronic disease, and mortality rates that significantly exceed the national average. In addition, mortality rates in the Delta have increased over the past forty years while the national rate has decreased. In 2017 the death rate in the Delta from heart disease was the highest in the country, and it remains one of the highest today.[5]

President Lyndon Johnson's War on Poverty promised to end hunger in America by making issues related to poverty and hunger the "urgent business of all men and women of every race and every religion and every region."[6] But in the Mississippi Delta, with its legacy of a plantation economy rooted in white supremacy, the eradication of hunger threated the region's politics. What the Delta reveals is not the failure of Johnson's War on Poverty, but the ways farm policy—particularly farm subsidies—undermined those War on Poverty policies that could have had a long-term impact on the health of Delta residents and all poor Americans.

The biggest political battle of the War on Poverty that affected the Delta was indirectly related to food, and that was the battle over the preschool program Head Start. One Head Start program that received considerable attention was the Child Development Group of Mississippi (CDGM), which received a grant to set up a center in rural Mississippi to bring preschool to impoverished communities as well as to feed poor children who attended the program. As Head Start centers began opening, they hired Black women of the Delta in large numbers—and, in smaller numbers, men—thus removing them from the white-dominated labor force. Most white Mississippians opposed the CDGM and the War on Poverty in general, since they viewed programs like Head Start as seeking to not only decrease their labor force but also to bring integration to their communities. Several of the employees of the CDGM had ties to former civil rights activists such as Nola Mae Coleman, the daughter of an activist who testified to Congress that Senator James Eastland had used convict labor on his farm, which was an established fact and common knowledge in the Delta. Five miles outside the town of Leland, a place called Strike City had its own Head Start center. The community of Strike City was founded by former sharecroppers who demanded a minimum wage, health insurance, and the end of plantation work for children under the age of sixteen. The children from this community and its Head Start center were also the first to integrate local schools in this part of Mississippi, proving to local whites the direct connection between Head Start, school integration, and civil rights activism.

As economists Martha Bailey and Nicolas Duquette have found in their analysis of the War on Poverty, the programs of Lyndon Johnson's plan to end poverty, discrimination, and hunger were successful at "increasing human capital, improving health, and reducing racial inequality over the long term."[7] Where the War on Poverty did fail was in its architects' and planners' inability to predict changes in the economy that lowered employment and distributed economic growth unevenly. If economic growth had continued from the 1970s on, poverty rates would be much lower today. Consequently, there would have been fewer hungry people in the Delta. The failure narrative that blamed poverty on the poor in Mississippi—and across the United States—only reflects the success of politicians at rewriting history. Had more programs been allowed to begin and flourish in the Delta, the War on Poverty might have rattled some of the structures that created the region's poverty and kept its citizens poor and hungry. Resistance was in the air, and that was exactly why Mississippi did not want the programs in place. White Mississippians did not want to disrupt the status quo. Once again, the Delta was left behind, along with poor people across America. And the mythology that some of the neediest people in the nation were lazy and just needed to get to work began to take shape and flourish. Ronald Reagan famously noted that America "fought a war on poverty and poverty won."[8] But a close look at the history of the enactment of Great Society programs in the Delta reveals that the Mississippi political power structure fought against the very changes those programs sought to confront.

The War on Poverty is often thought of as a program that tripled federal expenditures on health, education, employment and training, and economic security programs, all important to the Delta and other impoverished regions of the country. What is less well known is that the War on Poverty was also linked with the 1964 Civil Rights Act and leveraged federal funds to push for desegregation. This gave the government the ability to pressure local governments to reduce racial discrimination and segregation, turning them into pocketbook issues rather than social ones. That is why Mississippi's congressional delegation fought so hard against the War on Poverty, including access to food.

Three powerful Mississippi legislators—John Stennis, James Eastland, and Jamie Whitten—manipulated policies and programs at the intersection of agriculture, food, health, and welfare to maintain white supremacy and to thwart any efforts toward Black advancement in the Delta. The intense desire these men had to maintain white supremacy in the Delta led to policies that affected people far beyond it. But it is through the actions of Congressman Jamie Whitten that this desire to imprint white supremacy on public policy can be seen most profoundly.

Even before the Civil Rights Movement, Whitten had worked against the progress of Black Mississippians, particularly Delta residents. Beginning in the 1940s, Congressman Whitten used his legislative power to block several US Department of Agriculture studies that attempted to identify social and economic problems facing Black army veterans returning from World War II to the South. The impact of Whitten's legislative maneuvers also helped keep Department of Agriculture farm policy from considering the impact of its programs on sharecroppers or farmworkers. In the 1960s, Whitten used his power to ensure his district received $23.5 million in individual farm subsidies to reduce cotton productions. These subsidies went to 0.3 percent of the population, yet in the same district, the 59 percent of the population living in poverty received only $4 million in federal food relief. This imbalance perpetuated poverty, food insecurity, and hunger.[9]

Whitten also killed a federal program designed to teach displaced Black sharecroppers and farmworkers how to drive tractors and use the tools of farm automation that were displacing them. Rather than training people for the jobs that were part of the new agricultural economy of the Delta, Whitten effectively barred an entire group of people from those jobs. When Mississippi was placed on a Department of Agriculture list in 1967 that would have surveyed hunger in the state, particularly in the Delta, he got Mississippi removed from the list, which prevented millions of dollars of food aid from coming to the state and, thus, made living conditions in the Delta worse. The domination of politicians like Whitten supported the protection of wealthy white rural farmers in the South and fueled the resistance to civil rights and anti-poverty projects that could have changed the fortunes of the poor in the Delta and across the country. He was critical of programs like food stamps and opposed lowering their cost—on the basis of their income, recipients of food stamps purchased a monthly allotment sufficient to feed their family—arguing that "when you start giving people something for nothing . . . I wonder if you don't destroy character more than you might improve nutrition."[10] Never did Whitten acknowledge that farm subsidy checks for Delta planters were their own form of welfare, but only for the rich. Whitten's legacy was to inextricably link federal farm, food, and welfare policy in ways that harmed poor people everywhere and not just in the Mississippi Delta.

Whitten's power to control food policy persisted into the 1970s, which meant that Mississippi was excluded from any government-based intervention plans related to hunger and food insecurity even after Lyndon Johnson's Great Society programs were being dismantled. Whitten's drive to control national and state food policy contributed to the failure of the War on Poverty in the Delta. It also reveals the overlooked connections between food, white supremacy, hunger, and poverty during the civil rights era. The logic of politicians like Whitten seems to have been that the only way to stop Black progress was to starve Black people. But the full story of the Delta's lack of access to food and anti-poverty programs is about the efforts of more than one politician. A chorus of other policies endorsed by other politicians contributed to the Delta's current state with respect to food insecurity.

Richard Nixon's New Federalism reduced funding for Johnson-era anti-poverty programs and left the poor of Mississippi without advocates in government or adequate assistance during periods of economic distress. Jimmy Carter did not make adjustments to Nixon's New Federalism and even tried to create what he deemed "pro-work and pro-family rules" for welfare recipients, but they were never enacted. The Reagan administration's approaches to rural poverty and hunger and its emphasis on market forces and private enterprise only made things worse. Finally, Bill Clinton's welfare reform left standards for cash payments of welfare to the states.

Today, in the poorest state in the union, just under 1,600 families receive cash payments, even though over 100,000 families live under the federal poverty line. Cash assistance reaches only 4 percent of poor families in Mississippi who qualify for aid. Through a historical lens, the story of the

Mississippi Delta begins to come into focus as a story of how we as a nation have failed the poor and allowed them to descend even deeper into poverty. The Mississippi Delta is not the poorest place in Mississippi or perhaps the entire nation because of the failures of its residents. It is poor by the design of its political leaders at the state and national level.

Why do we Americans see the War on Poverty as a failure and fail to see that there were people like Congressman Jamie Whitten—who did not work alone—fighting a war on the War on Poverty? To answer this question, I approached sociologist Bobby J. Smith, who has written extensively on the topic. "The first reason is because narratives of the movement almost exclusively focus on proponents of the movement and less on the opponents, specifically, white political and economic actors in the Delta," Smith explained. When focusing on opponents, we can learn more about their maneuverings and how they saw the War on Poverty as a threat to their power over the region—unless they were able to control how the War on Poverty was administered, as they did with the federal food stamp program. Another reason is because we rarely look at access to food and its connection with poverty. "When food is at the center," Smith explains, "we learn more about how the War on Poverty impacted the Delta and identify potential blind spots that may not necessarily be seen outside the prism of food." But the real reason we don't think about the impact of the War on Poverty is the myth that the program was entirely a failure. A decade after the War on Poverty began, the number of Americans living in poverty was half of what it was in 1960.[11] Of course, there is the persistent myth that Black residents of the Delta don't want to work and that government assistance leads to dependency. And there is also the belief that communities in the Delta gained power from the War on Poverty program. As Smith sees it, the War on Poverty was not designed to permanently shift power dynamics in rural Black communities of the Delta, which was the fear of politicians like Jamie Whitten, James Eastland, and John Stennis. In fact, Black Delta residents were never given full power or control over the War on Poverty programs that could have had a real impact on their lives. Instead, politicians had that power.

The people of the Mississippi Delta understood that the War on Poverty offered some innovative ways to confront the social problems that plagued the region and that could have placed it—and the nation as a whole—on a different trajectory. The political resistance in the Delta and the rest of the country was too strong, and the myths that arose from the ashes of the War on Poverty kept average Americans from seeing the ways anti-poverty programs worked. Instead, American public policy has institutionalized poverty in the Mississippi Delta and the country in general and has numbed us from really seeing poverty by creating the mythology that it is a moral failing rather than a failure of morals in our public policy. Poverty is a policy choice.

It would be a tremendous lie for me to say that I have always had an intense awareness of poverty and hunger in the Mississippi Delta. Even as someone who grew up in Mississippi and traveled to the Delta my entire life, I have experienced the ways mythology holds the power to overshadow the realities of the past. On my trips to the Delta with my father, I knew the tin-roofed plank houses by the side of the road were inhabited by poor people. I knew that, because there were houses like them near where I grew up, ones that I sometimes visited with my father. But poverty was distant from my comfortable middle-class existence and not very real to me. I never questioned why it existed in the Delta. I just saw the Delta as part of my family's origin story as Mississippi residents. And the shacks were merely part of the scenery of that story.

That is the power of myth: it keeps the mind from engaging with unwelcome truths. Today when I look at poverty in the Delta in places like, say, the Baptist Town neighborhood in Greenwood, I see a history of exploitation and pain. But I know others see a romanticized past when they look at that same place—perhaps they see its connection to Robert Johnson and the blues, and are completely disconnected from the painful history of poverty and exploitation. Growing up in Mississippi Black and middle class, I had the luxury of living in a realm that separated me to some degree from that history, although I experienced racial discrimination, particularly growing up in a segregated public school system. But I did not experience racial discrimination paired with poverty and hunger.

It was nearly forty years ago that I had to confront my own blindness to poverty in the Mississippi Delta. In 1987 my then girlfriend—now my wife—was on a business trip that took her from Memphis to Vicksburg, Mississippi. She had never been to Mississippi, and I thought this was a perfect opportunity for her to see a place I loved and had told her about, the Mississippi Delta. Instead of wasting time on interstate highways, I insisted that she take the famed Highway 61 from Memphis to Vicksburg and travel through the heart of the Delta. Though I have little memory of what I told my wife about the region, I know I mostly extolled the beauty of the landscape, its intense flatness, and the unique light that seems to envelop the land at sunset. I probably even sang to her, in a bad imitation of Bob Dylan's voice, "Yes, I think it can be easily done, just take everything down Highway 61." But I do know this: I said nothing about what an impoverished place the Delta was.

In the late 1980s, sharecropper shacks were still a common part of the Delta landscape. Many of these buildings had not yet been cleared from the fields or tumbled down to the ground, and my wife saw lots of them, some of them still occupied by tenants. As she drove down Highway 61 in her shiny rental car, she saw the people who lived in the shacks, including children in tattered dirty clothing, which gave a shock to her system. When she arrived in Vicksburg, she called me and expressed some anger about the route I insisted she take. I remember her telling me, "Why did you send me that way? All I could see was poor people and flat land. I couldn't see anything else, and now I feel really depressed."

During that conversation, I was dumbfounded and practically mute after hearing that. It was then that I realized something about myself I didn't want to admit: poverty had simply become so ingrained into my idea of the landscape of the Mississippi Delta that I didn't even see it. I saw only the beauty of the place and none of the pain that shaped the land. I felt intense shame when I recognized that the myth of American individualism that I decried while living in Washington during the Reagan years was a part of the very way I saw the place I was from.

To change the way we all see the Delta—and impoverished places like it—the quantitative and the qualitative must inform each other. It is important to know the size and scale of the problems faced in the lives of poor people in the Delta, both historically and today. And to change our way of seeing, we must also understand the ways public policy has institutionalized poverty in ways that keep us from seeing it even when the reality is right before our eyes.

But how do we change our way of seeing? To change what we see, we must also change what we know, which means we must first understand the ways the Delta was shaped by economic, political, and emotional forces that are American at their core, not merely Southern. And we must also recognize that the same forces that created inequality in the Delta have led to many of the same inequities across this nation.

One of those national forces that shaped the modern-day Delta and its inequities is the use of pesticides. Those pesticides keep crops like cotton, soybeans, and corn free of grasses and weeds. But it is the rampant use of those pesticides that keeps some of the richest soil in America from being a resource in which food can be grown that is safe to eat, in a place where people need healthy food and have limited access to it.

Anna Lew Spears grew up in Greenville, Mississippi, as the daughter of the owner of a Chinese grocer. For years, Chinese-owned grocery stores kept Black communities from being food deserts, as many in the Delta are today. Chinese grocery stores were clustered in the Delta towns where cotton plantations, sharecroppers, and Black laborers were concentrated, and Greenville was one of those towns. The Lew family was a relative late-comer to owning a grocery store, since they arrived in the Delta in 1970 after a brief period running a restaurant in New York. As many Chinese families did at that time, they purchased their store from a family leaving the grocery business.

One thing Spears remembers is that her mother grew a garden outside their store, which was the source of all the family's fresh vegetables. "My mother always made traditional Chinese meals; we never ate processed foods. And the vegetables we ate we grew ourselves." But at age seventy-seven, after years of her doctor saying she was aging in reverse, her mother was diagnosed with cancer. "The cancer progressed quickly. She was diagnosed at the end of October and was dead by the end of November." Spears has always questioned whether her mother's cancer was caused in part by the region's widespread use of pesticides. "I've always wondered if my mother's death is connected with the environment of the Delta, particularly the use of all of the defoliates."

Like most things related to farming in the Delta, the use of pesticides is wrapped up in politics. In 1966, Congressman Whitten published a book titled *That We May Live*, a pro-pesticides rejoinder to Rachel Carson's *Silent Spring*, a book that raised questions about the long-term impact of pesticides on the environment. Carson challenged the reckless devotion to profit, productivity, and the "control of nature" that helped proliferate the use of pesticides as well as the ways pesticides affected people, animals, and the environment. Whitten saw things differently. In his view, chemicals released "hands" from mundane agricultural work like chopping cotton— that is, weeding the cotton—thus liberating them to enjoy the conveniences of modern abundance and serving as an instrumental part of preserving what Whitten described as "our way of life" and a "high standard of living." The hands Whitten is ostensibly seeking to liberate are Black hands, but the way of life and high standard of living he is seeking to preserve is that of the white planter class.

In *That We May Live*, Whitten wrote, "We must use all our known weapons . . . if we are to enable man to keep that important one step ahead in his continuing contest with insects and disease, with pest and pestilence. To this end, we need public understanding, that we may continue to add to the years of our lives, indeed, THAT WE MAY LIVE!"[12] *That We May Live* is a national policy statement, one that on the surface is free of Whitten's views on race. At the state level, however, race and agricultural policy were always linked. Although there is nothing explicitly racist in Whitten's book, race is a subtext, particularly when you think of the ways his views on pesticides came to be applied in the Delta. At the time the book was written, Whitten's political power was being challenged by the Civil Rights Movement. The very pesticides he supported and defended affected Black Delta residents and led to their being dispossessed from the land they had worked for so many years. Once the "hands" that Whitten refers to were free from mundane agricultural work, they had to leave the land and were left hungry. Still, Whitten insisted that his position on chemical pesticides was right and that Rachel Carson was wrong. Whitten wrote, "Let us move [*Silent Spring*] over from the non-fiction section of the library to the science fiction section, while we review the facts in order that we may continue to enjoy the abundant life."[13]

The long shadow of Jamie Whitten's advocacy of pesticides was part of a conversation I had with Watson Turnipseed, a young redheaded farmer under the age of thirty who is the fifth generation in his family to enter that profession. After graduating from the University of Mississippi, Turnipseed worked for a brief time as a mechanic on cooling towers in New York City. He wanted to live in New York yet was not inclined to enter the financial industry like many of his friends. He wanted to work with his hands.

Given the pay inequity between his work and that of his friends, as well as the ways his working-class wages limited the type of life he could lead in New York, he decided to move home, work his family's land, and attend law school. While he would like to grow fruits and vegetables instead of work in commodity farming, he recognizes that there is no way to do that profitably since there is no central exchange in the Delta to sell the food. Plus, there are the chemicals that pervade agriculture in the Delta. You can see their impact on the land itself—dotting the landscape are brown grasses killed by pesticides.

Turnipseed talks with me before he has to get on his tractor to plant his corn crop, and in his truck, he drives me around the more than four hundred acres of farmland he rents from his grandfather, Frank Mitchener. The farm is just outside the town of Sumner in a community called Brazil. The barn that once housed the mules still sits on the land, evidence that this land has been farmed well before tractors, combines, and cotton pickers. One day he would like to farm all 3,500 acres of his grandfather's land, but today he supplements his work as a farmer with his work as a trial lawyer. "That is what keeps me afloat," he tells me with a sly youthful grin.

As we drive his land, Turnipseed takes me to one field where he thinks growing vegetables might be possible because it is surrounded by trees. "The trees would help prevent chemical drift," he says, meaning it would keep the pesticides that would kill the vegetables from getting into the field. Turnipseed makes it clear to me: he may be a commodities farmer—corn, soybeans, and, this year, his first cotton crop—but he is worried about the long-term impact of chemicals on the land that he speaks of with a great deal of personal affection. Then he quickly turns from talking like a farmer to talking like an attorney. "The jury's not out on the impact of chemicals," he tells me. "The jury has already returned a verdict: this stuff causes cancer."

Turnipseed's wife, Sydney Bush, works for a group that advocates to get locally grown fruits and vegetables into school cafeterias, focusing on minority farmers. When I point out that the two of them work on seemingly opposite teams of agriculture in Mississippi, they both laugh. "It's very difficult," she says. "We talk about it all the time and Watson always tells me, 'I'll grow vegetables if you show me the numbers that would make it profitable.'" And then there are the herbicides, of which dicamba is the main one used in the Delta today. When I ask them to tell me what dicamba is and what it does, Bush quickly responds that it "gives people cancer."

Dicamba is an herbicide that kills broadleaf weeds in grain crops, even killing them before they sprout up out of the soil. The problem is that when it drifts across a field, dicamba can cause damage to non-dicamba-tolerant soybeans, sensitive crops, non-crop plants, and endangered species. And that drift of dicamba can also kill vegetables. It is a problem for farmers like Watson Turnipseed because if you don't use the dicamba-resistant genetically modified corn, cotton, or soybeans from the manufacturer of dicamba, Bayer-Monsanto, your crop will die. "If you don't plant Bayer-Monsanto's variety of genetically modified seed, you're going to suffer yield loss and crop damage," Turnipseed explains emphatically.

When Bush turns to talking about issues of food sovereignty—the idea that people have a right to food grown by ecologically sustainable methods and the right to define their food and agricultural systems—her body language becomes animated, and I can hear the passion in her voice. But soon I remind her that all the examples of people who are doing the type of farming that aligns with her beliefs are in the eastern part of Mississippi, not the Delta. Some are even on the Choctaw Reservation. Yet Bush still wishes that sustainable agriculture might one day come to the Delta. The two stumbling blocks are pesticides and farm subsidies. "The price of corn is much lower than the price of a tomato," she tells me, "but it's still not profitable to grow tomatoes here."

Watson Turnipseed can't use his acres to grow food on a large scale, but he does want to see the end to the use of pesticides. Instead, he thinks technology is the solution: drones and lasers that kill weeds. "Everything's going to move toward precision," he announces to me with a big smile on his face and a great degree of certainty. "No one wants to keep spending a fortune blanket-applicating anything anymore because you realize you don't have to. And they're already doing it with, like, small drones to spray, where the drones have infrared technology that can kill the weeds."

It is probably a long time before this drone technology can be used toward growing enough food to feed the Delta. When I ask the couple if they know of anyone farming vegetables in the Delta, they mention the name Marquitrice Mangham. Just a year ago, Mangham opened a grocery store in the town of Webb called the Farmacy Marketplace. Located in what was once a furniture store, the Farmacy is a place Mangham started not just to provide fresh food to people in her hometown—before the Farmacy, the nearest grocery store was eighteen miles away—but also to bolster the Delta's food system by working with small farmers and providing a market for their produce.

Farmacy Marketplace operates under a nonprofit called In Her Shoes, whose mission is to increase the viability of small-scale, minority-owned farms in the Delta. "We want to see more thriving farms and to serve as a role model for young people who want to go into farming or would probably go into farming if they saw it as a viable career option," Mangham tells me one morning in her office in Webb. Her organization has an eight-acre farm near the Delta town of Marks, a place free of biological agents and chemical drift associated with pesticides. The farm provides hands-on training to three young apprentices from the agricultural training program at a local high school. "We try to give our young people a holistic view of farming to help them determine whether they want to go into farming," she tells me, but these apprentices also provide labor to help the farmers they work with plant and harvest the vegetables.

Farmacy Marketplace is clean, well-stocked, and looks like an independent grocery store you would find in a place more populated and affluent than Webb. The town has just over four hundred people, with 29.7 percent of the population living at or below the poverty line, much higher than the national average of 11.5 percent. Mangham's organization has a three-year plan to address food access as well as enhance or develop markets for small farm businesses. One of the ways she is expanding is by establishing a mobile grocery store that will eventually serve five Delta communities. Several towns have asked Mangham to open a grocery store, but the overhead costs of a network of brick-and-mortar stores are not sustainable. The model of a mobile grocery store makes it possible to serve more people and to expand the markets where her farmers can sell their produce. "In the long term, I think a mobile market is going to be more sustainable," Mangham tells me. "If we come together as communities as part of a cooperative, we can work together to be independent in providing food to our families and in our own communities."

The idea of food sovereignty is the foundation of the network of farmers and workers she is creating through the Farmacy Marketplace. Mangham is a third-generation farmer in the Delta, and the land she farms has been owned by women. Although they farmed cotton, soybeans, and corn, they also grew their own vegetables. "We used our vegetable garden not just to feed ourselves, but to help the community as well." But when they became aware of the impact of pesticides on health, they eliminated the use of it in the family garden. Her current work is a way of reclaiming a piece of her family's history. She is also a staunch believer in supporting Black farmers and landowners in the Delta and through her work does what she can to support those farmers.

In addition to facilitating the produce supply for the grocery store, she works with farmers to get to new markets. Although she likes to keep her operation independent of government funding, Mangham does help her farmers work with USDA programs that allow them to sell to local food banks. "We rely on programs that help build our programs, but the idea is not to be reliant on them or to be dependent on them long term."

An urban planner and lawyer, Mangham divides her time between Atlanta and Webb. For many years she was a transportation planner with the Atlanta Regional Commission, but when she inherited her family farm, she felt the pull of the Delta. Now she is applying her twenty years of experience in planning to farming and helping the community where she grew up.

The spirit of the Farmacy Marketplace, with its farm cooperative and work with local food pantries, reminds me of the work of another woman who moved toward farming, activist Fannie Lou Hamer. When I tell Mangham that what she is seeking to do with her cooperative has parallels to Hamer's Freedom Farm Cooperative, she smiles. "Like Mrs. Hamer, I believe in independence and reducing our dependency on others. One of my biggest sayings is that 'you have got to help yourself before anybody else helps you.'" Mangham started In Her Shoes without federal funds or money from anyone else, and she is proud of that. "If I didn't invest in this place, I don't think anyone else would think it worth investing in."

A few weeks after meeting with Mangham, I am in Fannie Lou Hamer's hometown of Ruleville. I head toward downtown, hoping to find the memorial to her I have read about, a statue that stands at five feet four inches, Hamer's precise height. Yet the statue seems taller, since it stands on a marble pedestal and has her holding a microphone, speaking out for the disenfranchised. The foundation of Hamer's brand of activism was to have no fear of the powerful and to use whatever means she had to stand up for the rights of poor people. As I drive through downtown, I can't find the statue. Then I drive past a boarded-up Piggly Wiggly grocery store, a sign that access to fresh food is limited in this town. As I gaze at the store, I wonder if this is a place where maybe she once shopped. I can imagine Hamer walking down the street with her head held high, but see no sign of the statue in the center of town. When I finally look up directions, the digital breadcrumbs lead me to the Black section of Ruleville, a reminder that segregated cultural memory has been imprinted on this little Delta town and others like it. Hamer has been deemed important to Black Ruleville, but not to the entire town.

At the foot of the statue is a photograph of Hamer in front of the US Capitol building with her fellow activists Victoria Gray and Annie Devine. Underneath the photo, Hamer is quoted: "Whether you have a Ph.D. or no D., we are in this bag together. Whether you're from Morehouse or Nohouse, we're still in this bag together." Then I think, the people of the Delta are all in this bag together, like Hamer says, but not enough of them realize it. If they did, there would not still be hungry people living here who could use prescriptions for food. And Fannie Lou Hamer's memorial would be in the center of Ruleville, since hunger has no color line.

CHAPTER 8

SAVING AN OPPORTUNITY DESERT

'Baby an I sho' don't wanna go'
I say, 'I'll do anything in the world for ya
But I don't wanna go down to that welfare sto'

—SONNY BOY WILLIAMSON, "Welfare Store Blues"

When Bessie Smith sang "Nobody Knows You When You're Down and Out," she could have been singing a song about the contemporary Delta rather than the Great Depression. For decades, attempts to break the cycle of poverty in the Mississippi Delta have contained a narrative that matches a suite of blues songs: a long line of pain that connects every attempt to create a form of measurable change. When my father arrived in 1949, he was full of hope for the Delta's future, yet the volatile anti-Black violence of the mid-1950s tempered the post–World War II optimism that accompanied him on his migration from Alabama. During the Great Depression, more than a decade before my family's arrival, the Black people of the Delta were without even a grain of optimism. The exception was the resettlement community at Mileston, but there was little else that looked like a glimmer of hope or progress.

The blues music of the Depression era often reveals the sordid details of the challenges of breaking out of poverty—or simply just surviving impoverished circumstances. Songs had titles like "Broke Man Blues," "No Dough Blues," "Welfare Store Blues," and Floyd Council's "Don't Want No Hungry Woman," which served as a commentary on how neither welfare nor the government could solve the impoverished circumstances of a place that was poor before the Great Depression hit.

This was also a period of migration out of the Delta to Northern cities like Chicago, which meant the music of the time not only mirrored the situation in the Delta but also revealed that the North was not the paradise it seemed. Job opportunities in Chicago diminished in the wake of the Great Depression. Welfare departments, much like the plantation owners left behind back in Mississippi, paid former Delta residents no mind in Chicago. Yet those who chose to remain in the Delta as part of the plantation welfare system lived a life that matched the rhythm and spirit of the music that migrated to Chicago, albeit a life without the freedom of movement of their Northern brethren. The blues that evolved during that time still reflected the quest for equality, freedom, and, especially, prosperity that Delta residents had long been seeking.

Since the 1960s, there have been numerous plans to end the economic exhaustion and desperation of the Mississippi Delta. Some were big, like the War on Poverty, and others were small, such as the Box Project. The Box Project began as an idea of three activists: Virginia Naeve, Clarie Collins Harvey, and Coretta Scott King, the wife of Martin Luther King Jr. During their journey to the Geneva Peace Conference in 1962, the three women discussed possible ways to help impoverished people in the Mississippi Delta. Coretta Scott King knew the name of a particular family that needed help and what they needed. Thus was born the Box Project, which provided families in need with boxes tailored to their respective needs. It is still in operation today.

The women who started the Box Project knew the operation was small, but they hoped their efforts would catch the eye of others who could bring systemic reform. In the 1990s, it seemed as if a new era was dawning in the Delta, one that would move beyond boxes targeted toward needy families. In 1988, the Lower Mississippi Delta Development Commission (LMDDC) was created with the goal of establishing a ten-year regional development plan with an eye toward creating sustainable social and economic change. "The LMDDC was part of a new international movement led by numerous regional alliances to respond to the devastating consequences of global economic restructuring," observed sociologist Clyde Woods in his book *Development Arrested.*[1] In December 1995, President Bill Clinton proclaimed a portion of the Mississippi Delta an economic empowerment zone, which included towns like Greenwood, Greenville, and Clarksdale. Just as with the War on Poverty, there is little evidence that the initiative led to any measurable degree of change when you look at those towns today. The blame for the failure lies not with the local governments or the people of the Delta, but with the way the initiatives were put in place and administered. Once again, the economically dominant planter class of the Delta exerted its power and affected the outcome.

Two organizations were chosen to co-manage the Mid-Delta Empowerment Zone. The first was the Delta Foundation, an African American nonprofit chartered in 1969 through an alliance of civil rights and community organizations. The other, the Delta Council, had long advocated for the interests of the Delta planter class. As a US Commission on Civil Rights report on the Mississippi Delta notes in 2001, "Among the latest strategies for improving economic conditions and promoting equality of opportunity for blacks are those being utilized by numerous community, nonprofit, and self-help organizations. These organizations typically are created and organized by coalitions of white and black residents."[2] The coalition between the Delta Foundation and the Delta Council in 1995 was that idea at work. But what it did not consider was the imbalance of power between the two organizations as well as the historic antipathy the Delta Council had to any organization allied with civil rights activism.

Formed in the aftermath of the Great Flood of 1927, the Delta Council was established to lobby for the interests of Delta planters, which by this time had grown into a multibillion-dollar agricultural industrial complex. As late as the 1960s, the Delta Council had opposed limits on child labor and a minimum wage for agricultural workers.[3] In this David-versus-Goliath scenario, it was the Goliath Delta Council who won out in the end. Just as it had in the past, the interest of the Delta planter class came to dominate the work of the LMDDC in the Mississippi Delta. With respect to environmental and development issues, it was the concerns of the Delta Council that set policy. Just a few years before the establishment of the LMDDC, when a member of the Delta Council was asked his view of the future of the Delta, he said, "Ten years down the pike, I see beautiful fields of cotton and soybeans, the growth of industry, and a program to encourage out-migration, which will solve a lot of problems."[4] The migration referred to here is the exodus of the poor and underemployed, and that is the vision that has come to pass. The agricultural industry has grown in the Delta, with beautiful fields all around, and the most recent census shows yet another wave of out-migration. The Delta has consistently lost population in the 2010 and 2020 censuses. What began as a program that would remedy what the War on Poverty was not allowed to do in the Delta became a war on the poor as the social safety net grew bigger holes after the institution of welfare reform by Bill Clinton, who had championed the LMDDC.

Soon after the Lower Mississippi Delta Development Commission closed its doors in 1997, the W. K. Kellogg Foundation, based in Battle Creek, Michigan, arrived in the Delta. Two years later, the foundation pledged to give grassroots leaders technical support and to invest between $10 million and $15 million over the next five to eight years through what it called its Mid South Delta Initiative. This was to be a partnership of Delta communities, leaders, and residents with a goal of creating and increasing economic opportunities in the area. The then senior vice president for programs for the Kellogg Foundation, Anne Petersen, said the foundation chose the Delta as a place to invest financial and technical resources because the region has untapped natural resources, and the citizens are willing to make advances. "There seemed to be an interest to move forward," Petersen said. "There are a lot of resources here and the best resource is the people."[5]

The Kellogg Foundation's ultimate goal, according to its vision statement for the Delta, is "Safe Delta communities, in which the majority of the residents are healthy, educated, and have incomes which allow them to adequately provide for their families and prepare for their economic self-sufficiency and a positive future for their children."[6] The programs that the foundation supported seem on the surface to match the goal of the foundation's grantmaking scope, which appeared to be intentionally broad so that it could meet the needs of local communities. The $20 million invested in the Hope Community Credit Union helped Delta residents who had no access to a bank and also helped provide access to capital to local communities—capital that has been invested in community improvements.

But while the investment in the Hope Credit Union held quantifiable results, that was not true for all of the Kellogg Foundation's grants. The Kellogg Foundation made grants large and small to combat everything from childhood obesity and teenage pregnancy in the Delta to a grant to the Delta Foundation to "promote youth-focused community dialogue and action that leads to dismantling the cradle to prison pipeline." But by early 2009, after spending over $40 million on the Mid South Delta Initiative, the Kellogg Foundation ended its program. The foundation felt there was not enough noticeable change in the circumstances of the Delta and its people. Plus, the officers of the foundation—as well as other grant-giving organizations—felt that the mindset of Delta residents was impervious to embracing and creating sufficient change to merit continuing the same level of support and investment.[7] At the outset of their Mid South Delta

Initiative, the foundation's officers saw the people of the Delta as their greatest asset. As they ended their focus on the Delta, they saw the people as their greatest hinderance.

There is a great danger of investing in a region through what might be called "social change philanthropy"—grantmaking to address root causes of social and economic inequity. Groups like the Kellogg Foundation that engage in social change philanthropy must offer a clear explanation of what exactly the goals are and how they can be achieved. Even more important, a foundation can only go so far in creating social change without the co-operation of state and local government. The local communities of the Delta seemed to embrace the work of Kellogg, but the state of Mississippi did not engage any of the initiatives in a substantive and meaningful way to see if there was sufficient "proof of concept" to grow any of the initiatives beyond the places and organizations where they began. Perhaps state government didn't get involved because it had its own funds it was using for its own form of social change philanthropy.

From 2017 to 2022, Mississippi redirected $77 million from its fund for Temporary Assistance to Needy Families, the fund that provides cash welfare benefits. Rather than providing funds directly to families, Mississippi chose to fight poverty through programs that help develop parenting skills among the poor, sponsor a "wrestling ministry," or start questionable initiatives for school-dropout prevention and job readiness. Instead of creating real change, these funds also filled the pockets of wealthy donors to the state's governor at the time, Phil Bryant. Millions of dollars were fraudulently diverted to celebrities, like former professional football star Bret Favre, and the politically connected. Some of the money taken from welfare funds even helped fund a volleyball stadium at the University of Southern Mississippi, Favre's alma mater. Although this scandal happened after the Kellogg Foundation began to pull back on its work in the Delta, it shows that in a state that has long condemned anti-poverty programs, there is little interest in working with a real grantmaking foundation to see what may create real change in the Delta, or, for that matter, any other impoverished region of the state.

What the Kellogg Foundation perhaps neglected to factor into its strategy in the Delta is that it is not a one-size-fits-all kind of place. Within every town and county lays a unique history that must be considered for a program to work. In addition to the aforementioned challenge of finding clarity on the meaning of success and a strategy for how to achieve it, there also needs to be people embedded in many of these Delta communities to discern what is needed to create quantifiable change.

The bright line of truth about the Mississippi Delta is that the long years of neglect for the health and economic well-being of its residents are rooted in harmful dynamics regarding race, politics, and economics. In the Delta, and in America more broadly, the prevailing thinking about race is an enduring and odd conflation of things that are absolutely political. The strategy for blocking programs to help Black people in the Delta—from the Great Depression to the Lower Mississippi Delta Development Commission—was rooted in politics that favored the powerful and influential over the poor and the Black. In all these cases, the political was married with the economic, which means that the policies that evolved—or didn't evolve—cleaved along racial lines, since in the Delta, and America, that is the dominant way of defining economic policy. And those policies rarely favor the Black and the poor.

In any strategy to create social change, the qualitative and the quantitative must inform each other, and that is a difficult calculus to create when those who have power are unwilling to share power with the poor or give them the tools that they can use for their own self-empowerment. In the Delta, as in all of America, race is an economic construct. Until we as a nation come to terms with that fact, the Delta and places like it can never move forward.

The question that remains is, what does effective social change philanthropy look like? The best example comes from the first half of the twentieth century. Rather than being directly connected to poverty, the example relates to public health. Between 1909 and 1914 the Rockefeller Sanitary Commission worked to eliminate hookworm infections, which affected more than 40 percent of school-age children in the American South. With the aid of a $1 million donation from John D. Rockefeller, the Rockefeller Sanitary Commission traveled the South providing deworming medication as well as educating doctors and the public about prevention. Though it was rarely fatal, hookworm affected the digestive system and led to anemia and listlessness, which affected children's ability to learn. After the eradication of hookworm, school enrollment, regular attendance, and literacy increased in the South. This improvement to public health—through a foundation's investment and the cooperation of state and local governments—translated into economic benefits in the region.[8] This effort was undertaken during a time when local government was neither thinking about the issue nor had the resources to tackle it if it had wanted to do so. And it was place-based policy.

Lawrence Katz, an economist at Harvard who studies the economics of social problems, pointed out the example of hookworm eradication when I asked him about examples of effective social change philanthropy. "Philanthropy is highly heterogeneous and very idiosyncratic because of the individual leaders and donors associated with a foundation," Katz reminded me. Yet sometimes a foundation can be nimbler and more innovative than government and less constrained by politics. Nonetheless, as Katz also noted, a foundation "can't do things with the scope of Congress passing an extended child tax credit," which Congress did during the COVID-19 pandemic—the result of which was a 46 percent decline in the child poverty rate. This expanded child tax credit reached over 61 million children in more than 36 million households. Funds were primarily used for childcare, food, housing, and other basic needs. The end of the child tax credit in 2022 led to the child poverty rate returning to pre-pandemic levels.

When I mention to Katz that the prevailing narrative among Mississippi's conservative politicians is that private-sector philanthropy should work to transform the Delta rather than government, he reminds me that "if the narrative is that it's all going to be philanthropy, that leads to not believing that government action can play a role. The work of philanthropy can be a pilot project that leads to larger government action. Much of what philanthropy does is advocacy to try to scale things up, because most philanthropic organizations know they themselves are not going to be able to tackle problems at scale."

Then there is the issue of race, which stands at the center of any discussion of poverty in the Mississippi Delta. Trevon Logan, an economist at Ohio State University, understands the intersection of race and poverty well, since his father grew up in a family of sharecroppers in Yalobusha County, Mississippi, right on the edge of the Delta. Logan used his own family's records of cotton-crop yields to estimate the productivity of manual cotton picking nearly a century after emancipation. His work shows that economic roles in the South were deeply intertwined with racial identity.

"Philanthropy is basically filling the gap in our rearview in these racialized states like Mississippi that have abandoned public goods, simply because any public good still must be accessed by African American people," Logan explained to me. "This idea has become totally welded to the idea of being against government, not believing in government, because what you really want to have are publicly financed private goods that can exclude members of the population. And that is the historical pattern in these parts of the country." In Logan's view, race is not just a social construct; it is an economic one as well: "The reason why race is such an enduring part of American life is because it is this odd conflation of things. It is absolutely political, which means that all these policies we see in all these various avenues of life will stick to racial lines because that is a way of defining redistribution."

The Kellogg Foundation's initiative in the Delta acknowledged that race was an issue, as well as the region's racial history regarding its connection with sharecropping. But it is hard to call out race as an issue in a place like Mississippi—current politicians emphasize "colorblind policies" as if race has never been an issue in the state—and expect that the state's political leadership will see the work of a foundation like Kellogg as worthwhile. It didn't happen during the War on Poverty and the state government is sticking to patterns rooted in its past. What becomes clear to me is that philanthropy alone cannot change the Delta. It must be philanthropy, the public sector, local governments, state government, and monetary policy, all of which are key to a strong regional economy.

Sydney Diavua at the St. Louis Federal Reserve Bank is a Memphis native, so she grew up in the city where some say the Mississippi Delta begins and is not a stranger to the region. She believes two steps are necessary in making change happen in the Delta: First, understand the community and especially communities that have been systematically disenfranchised. Next, work to transform the flow of capital. "We have to look at robust data that gives us an honest landscape of the type of capital that is flowing into the Delta," Diavua tells me from her office in St. Louis.

"Philanthropic organizations seem to be saying, 'We're looking for big impact. Why aren't we seeing it?' Well, what they don't understand is that the impact is pocketed." By that, Diavua means if you are putting money into some of the poorest areas in the Delta, it is going to be difficult to see real impact since the hole that needs to be filled is so deep. Essentially, for years the Mississippi Delta has been "philanthropy bombed." A group like Kellogg comes in, says it is going to get its programmatic results, and then pulls out of the Delta. That is why it would have been much better for Kellogg to have been hyperlocal in its approach in the Delta and much more targeted in what it wanted to accomplish. Perhaps with a more local approach that targeted specific needs and goals, the foundation's funding could have had some measurable impact.

Diavua reminds me that there must be coordinated efforts between federal, state, and local governments as well as with philanthropy. Again, the eradication of hookworms comes to mind as a successful model: it had all these components. What the past reveals is that a foundation cannot be a sole agent for change. That is especially true when there are serious infrastructure issues in the Delta, like access to broadband. The Delta has spotty-at-best broadband internet service, in a state where 19.7 percent of the population lacks access to broadband. "These aren't new issues in the Delta we're confronting at the Federal Reserve," Diavua says. "We're redis-covering them and finding new ways to confront them, particularly since there are digital equity issues as well. We have to find ways to deepen the impact of our policies on the Delta as much as possible."

That is true since, as the work of Kellogg in the Mississippi Delta dem-onstrates, the work of the philanthropic sector is cyclical. And the Delta cannot simply wait for a new cycle of philanthropy to make progress.

Although cotton farming is a speculative business, the Delta has built great wealth for many members of its planter class for more than a century. As I learned in the town of Tchula, there was sufficient wealth for one woman to amass a valuable art collection. Others in the Delta had similar levels of prosperity. Many of the "pioneers with means" who settled the Delta after the Civil War lived lavish lifestyles supported by cotton wealth, and they were reluctant to part with that wealth. As historian James Cobb points out, "Regardless of race, region, nation, or hemisphere, when reform proceeds under safeguards against redistribution of wealth or power, social and po-litical rights will prove difficult to extend and dangerous to exercise."[9] The political and social status quo in the Delta was built through a top-down approach, with those at the top of the economic ladder dictating how it would help those at the bottom. This principle had governed the econom-ics of the Delta long before the Reagan-era idea of trickle-down economics was applied to the rest of the country. Rarely was that wealth given back to the people of the Delta in any meaningful way; it never trickled down, except to other wealthy people in the form of lavish and extravagant alcohol-soaked balls and cotillions.

Further, despite the wealth generated by cotton, there are no philanthropists of the standing of the Carnegies or Mellons in the Mississippi Delta, because the laws of the state of Mississippi restricted how assets could be left to begin foundations or philanthropic organizations: the state's 1890 constitution prevented "one who would not be charitable at his own expense to be so at the expense of his heirs."[10] The initial funding for one of Mississippi's most prominent foundations, the Phil Hardin Foundation, was established through the wealth Hardin accumulated from a statewide bakery business. Since Mr. Hardin was a bachelor, it was not a problem to leave his assets to a foundation, one that now supports education initiatives throughout the state. The state constitution has since been amended, but not until 1988—well after the boom years of cotton wealth in the Delta.

I learned about Mississippi's longtime stumbling blocks to local philanthropy from Keith Fulcher and Tom Pittman of the Community Foundation of Northwest Mississippi. Focusing on local needs, including those in parts of the Delta, is a key part of their mission. During the pandemic, their foundation turned their focus to feeding people in the Delta. "Our research showed that 25,000 public school children in the counties we serve were going to be without breakfast or lunch," Pittman told me one afternoon in his office. When a tornado hit the Delta town of Rolling Fork in 2023—flattening much of a town that already suffered from a poverty rate of 18.9 percent—the foundation stepped in to help relief efforts, whether it was providing water or funds for temporary shelter. "We see ourselves as a group that's closer to what's going on. We can be the watchdog and we can be the talent," explains Pittman, the chair emeritus of the foundation. Fulcher, the current chair, agrees. "Somebody has got to be there when there are immediate needs, and I see that as our role."

The Community Foundation of Northwest Mississippi is also now the home of another program that focuses on immediate needs: the Box Project, a philanthropic group that was formed in 1962 to combat poverty in the Delta "one box at a time." "It's a program with a great story and great leaders who founded it," Fulcher tells me, referring to the founding role of Coretta Scott King. The foundation took it over in 2009, when the project was looking for a long-term home. Since its founding, the Box Project has reached over twenty thousand families in the Delta.

While Fulcher and Pittman are proud of the work their foundation does, they see themselves as part of the philanthropic landscape of the region and not as the solution to the region's problems. They have helped begin an early childhood coalition that helps run a program called "Excel by 5," which makes sure children are prepared for kindergarten. But they are emphatic that while they focus on local causes and needs, particularly in the Delta, larger players are needed, including the state and federal governments. This is how Pittman sees it: "Government has sources of permanent funding. And I don't care how big a foundation is, it is going to run out of money if it tries to work in one place forever. It just can't. And a foundation can't run a public school system. So, when we are talking about solving structural inequities, it has to be government, foundations, and communities all working together."

It's not that foundations, whether local or national, are finding new problems in the Delta to solve. Foundations are confronting old problems—hunger, poverty, educational inequity—problems that go back to the late nineteenth century, are ingrained in the culture, and have endured for decades. But what happens if those problems continue to be overlooked, forgotten, or simply ignored? Of course, no single foundation is going to solve the Delta's deeply ingrained social inequities nor should it expect that it can. What I worry about is whether foundations will simply give up on the Delta and places like it because the legacies of the past are so difficult to disrupt and change. And I worry that the Delta will continue to move in a pattern that perpetuates the abusive power of the few and the exploitation of many.

That is what I think about as I drive in and around Rolling Fork, one year after the tornado that destroyed much of the town. Although much of the rubble has been hauled away, destruction still marks the landscape. Two tornado-mangled trees frame the south side of the courthouse in the center of town, which is surrounded by a construction fence. The Classical Revival–style courthouse, built in 1902, is patched and boarded up, with trailers behind it serving as offices. The town library is boarded up as well. Beyond the courthouse are an assortment of empty concrete slabs, including one that was formerly the site of a funeral home, with a sign reminding residents that they are serving the community from their location in Vicksburg, forty-four miles away. A few houses are being rebuilt, but as I know from my conversation with Tom Pittman and Keith Fulcher, only people who had sufficient insurance before the tornado are able to rebuild. In a town with a high poverty rate, few people had sufficient insurance.

More than 70 percent of the people displaced by the tornado were renters. The Community Foundation of Northwest Mississippi has helped with housing assistance for these displaced people, but as Pittman and Fulcher point out, it cannot address the town's more systemic needs. Delta towns like Rolling Fork have small tax bases and fewer economic resources that will allow them to respond to such a massive disaster. Steady work was a problem even before the tornado; now, just over 10 percent of residents of the town are unemployed, three times the jobless rate of the entire state. This is a town in need of some source of permanent funding, but nothing like that seems to be coming this way.

The day I visited Rolling Fork, a heavy wind was blowing that moved the limbs of the trees that remained in the town. It seemed as if a dark cloud sat over Rolling Fork, on a day that had only a few moments of sunshine before I arrived. Yet, despite the rubble all around, one element of the town's story remains: the wooden statues that memorialize it as a spot Theodore Roosevelt visited on his famous Mississippi Delta bear hunt, one that led to the popularity of "Teddy Bears," the state toy of Mississippi. For many in this town, restoring the statues was a way to bring a sense of normalcy back despite so much destruction. The town barely survives, but the story of its brush with history remains.

As I drive north leaving town, off in the distance I see Mont Helena, a Colonial Revival mansion. Beautifully restored, it is now primarily used as a venue for weddings, though the couple who originally built it, in 1896, called it their retirement home. They built it atop a sacred Indian burial site in the middle of a cotton field—erasing and diminishing the presence of the Native people who were removed from this land to enable the owners to build wealth on the backs of poor, Black, disenfranchised people. This shining white house stands in shocking contrast to the destruction that still hangs over Rolling Fork. I stop my car, get out, and begin to walk across the field toward the house to take in its grandeur. The dark clouds in the sky serve as a backdrop that perfectly frames the gleaming white building and its columns.

Mont Helena also stands in contrast to that other symbol of Rolling Fork, blues legend Muddy Waters, who once sang these words:

You know I was born to lose
For me there ain't no escape from the blues

Though I know very little about the people who built Mont Helena or how they ran their vast plantation, I do know this: the building is a reminder of the way this entire region was built on spectacle and rooted in unfettered wealth and power. Philanthropic organizations cannot give enough money to overcome the structures of power that were put in place by what Mont Helena symbolizes and that remain despite wars on poverty and commissions that give merely the illusion of shared power and authority. There will be no escape from the blues that sprang from this land until the Delta's shadowy past and its legacy are confronted.

CHAPTER 9

A CRUEL AND INTOLERABLE BURDEN

I don't do nobody nothin'
But they hates me just the same

—C. W. "PREACHER" SMITH,
"I Don't Do Nobody Nothin'"

Back when the Mississippi Delta was considered a cotton kingdom, the story goes that the town of Drew had more cotton gins than anywhere in America. Though I can find no records to confirm that boast, manifestations of the cotton-driven past dot the landscape. Numerous metal structures loom over the fields in and around Drew and seem to loom over the roadsides.

Back in 1938, *Mississippi: The WPA Guide to the Magnolia State* described Drew as "a pleasant town typical of the new Delta in its lack of provincialism. Drawing a wealthy planter trade, the shops cater to expensive tastes for smart frocks, shoes, hats, and the latest novelties."[1] The empty storefronts of downtown are evidence that the wealthy planter trade left Drew long ago. As for the gins that would have been used by the wealthy planter class, many of them are now rusted and closed, a reminder that the ebb and flow of cotton production over the years contributed to these closures. Yet vast fields of cotton still surround the town today, bearing witness to the town's past and the present.

There is no doubt that Drew is a town whose history is linked with cotton and plantation-based power. Without cotton, it is doubtful the town would ever have come into existence. It sits in the middle of the northern section of Sunflower County, just south of the state penitentiary at Parchman, which was not just a prison but also a huge sprawling plantation that maintained a cotton crop until automation came onto the landscape in the mid-1960s. Former US senator James Eastland, who served in the US

Senate from 1943 until 1978, also once called Sunflower County home and owned a 5,800-acre plantation in nearby Doddsville that not only served as a basis of his wealth but also drove the agricultural and food policies he created; those policies conveniently subsidized his cotton crop and kept those who worked his land poor and disenfranchised.

The influence of Eastland's family and planters like them served as the backdrop of classic sociological studies by Hortense Powdermaker and John Dollard. Both studied Sunflower County as an example of how racial power dynamics shaped the Mississippi Delta and, in their thinking, the entire American South. Looking back on those studies provide clues into what life was once like in Drew as well as the forces that shaped the mindset of its citizens, both then and now.

In his book *Caste and Class in a Southern Town*—that small Southern town being the Sunflower County town of Indianola—Dollard describes the social structures he observed during his five-month stay in the Delta in the 1930s, noting that "caste defines a superior and inferior group and regulates the behavior of the members of each group."[2] In her 1939 book *After Freedom*, Powdermaker, for her part, observed, "'After freedom' there was still the cotton to be planted, cultivated, and picked. There were still the plantations. And there was a set of mores so strongly entrenched that not even a war could dislodge them."[3] Both studies observed how the Mississippi Delta constructed racial hierarchies as a means of social control and consequently kept a common ideology rooted in those hierarchies in place.

Dollard and Powdermaker captured the pervasive and oppressive nature of legal racial segregation and white supremacy in the Delta. But if you read their studies today, it is clear much of what they wrote also contributed to the mythology of the Delta as a world unto itself, a place influenced exclusively by the culture of the South rather than a broader American social policy. Both were Northeasterners who experienced profound culture shock during their time in the South. Seeing the Delta almost as if it were a foreign culture certainly influenced the way they perceived the place and its people. Plus, the Delta has always been more than the world of plantation elites and sharecroppers. Even during my family's time in the Delta in the 1950s, there was a small Black professional class that played an influential role in the social structure of small Delta towns. Dollard and Powdermaker also failed to see how there were strains within the elite white society that would eventually force it to surrender its hold on the social order.

Yet there is much they got right. Reading their work today, I am taken by not only what has changed but what has not. In the 1930s, Black Delta residents had no political power and felt they were not able to demand what they wanted. Today they have political power, yet no real economic power, and, owing to that lack of economic capital and influence, they feel as if they cannot demand changes to the social structure. When I encounter a feeling of learned helplessness among Delta residents that makes them perceive the world as if they are powerless to change their circumstances—or observe acts of deference by Blacks toward whites that echo the past—I am reminded that remnants of the world Dollard and Powdermaker described still exist. Caste may no longer divide the Delta's people into perceived superior and inferior groups, but race still regulates the behavior of each group. The plantation system is gone, but the remnants of that system still wield power.

It is, for example, painfully visible in Delta schools. The racial separation in the school systems, with whites attending private academies and Blacks attending under-resourced public schools, is the most glaring example of how the racial lines as they were drawn in the past determine the behavior, actions, and circumstances of each group. As Powdermaker observed about the racial hierarchy of the Delta, public sentiment was committed to the system of segregation, and a common ideology supported it. This social separation created separate and unequal social realms in Powdermaker's day, and unfortunately, a version of that inequality persists. If history influences culture, then the culture of the Delta has been influenced by this long history of social segregation.

As Dollard would likely observe of the Delta were he alive today, it is still a place that deliberately and unwittingly ignores ongoing racial segregation. Of course, cultural change is always slow and gradual, and these two sociologists were right in their prediction that change would happen at a glacial pace. As Dollard told folklorist William Ferris, change in the Delta "is going to be pretty slow because it's going to have to be a cultural change, and that has to be, in the end, a willing change, change with the consent of the participants."[4]

Drew native Gloria Carter Dickerson recognized long ago that social and cultural change can only be accomplished through the changing of individual habits. Her family's story of activism provided lifelong lessons in how change comes about because of individual choices that are both quiet and subversive. She also knows that sometimes change can come about by shifting the conversation away from what can't be achieved to what can realistically be accomplished.

Dickerson's organization, We2Gether Creating Change, developed a community-wide strategic plan that outlined a vision and mission for the town of Drew's future through a group called the "Drew Collective." Like many small Delta towns, Drew lacks a grocery store, but its small population makes establishing and sustaining such an enterprise difficult. "It was important to be rigorous and to find a solution," Dickerson told me. "The solution had to involve business acumen combined with understanding a community's history," something that Dickerson knows very well. Rather than letting the town's lack of a retail grocer be a reason for giving up, a few years ago the Drew Collective developed an online grocery store that delivers to a local location to provide healthy food in the town. The collective has also worked to remove abandoned and dilapidated homes that make the town appear shabby. Through a foundation grant secured by We2Gether, the town put a roof on its library rather than close it. I have noticed discernible change in Drew over the years since I first visited the town, much of it related to signs of visible pride, such as banners greeting visitors to the town and the removal of abandoned buildings. And this change is all being created with the cooperation of the residents of the town. Gloria Dickerson is heading this effort but, as she is quick to point out, she does not do this alone and works to build consensus in the community about the projects she believes are moving Drew forward. She is, as she often describes her work to me, trying "to create community spirit."

Dickerson has firsthand knowledge of the culture of hardship in the Delta. Although some might be inclined to characterize her outlook as overly optimistic, I would say her optimism is tempered by realism. What shapes that outlook is her memory of the caste-driven world Dollard and Powdermaker documented, which was still in existence when Dickerson was born on the Pemble Plantation in 1953. In those days, a set of racial mores were established and persisted even after the Supreme Court's *Brown v. Board of Education* decision. They were so strongly entrenched that no one dared defy them. That is, until Dickerson's parents, Matthew and Mae Bertha, decided to integrate the school system. They did it because they began to see cracks in the system of white supremacy that shaped the world of Pemble Plantation and the rest of Sunflower County and decided to confront it directly.

The Carters may have been poor and seemingly powerless sharecroppers, but they longed for a better life for their children. In an act of defiance and as a means of working toward that better life, they joined the NAACP in 1955. Yet they knew transforming the lives of their children also meant getting them the best education possible, which was not going to happen as long as they were part of the Delta's segregated system. Under that system, Black schools only received outdated, discarded books and dilapidated buses from white schools. The facilities were also inferior and there was not much in the course offerings that would be considered sufficient for preparing students for college. This combination of neglect and lack of educational substance was designed to keep the Delta's young people working in the fields.

Unlike white children in the Delta, who attended school from September to June, Black children started in mid-November, after the cotton was harvested, and stopped in March or April, in time for them to tend the cotton. Plantation owners not only determined the course of the lives of adult sharecroppers, they also acted as if they owned the bodies and souls of the sharecroppers' children, whom they viewed as a crucial part of the labor force. Delta planters kept alive the idea promoted by Mississippi governor James K. Vardaman in 1903, when he denounced the education of African Americans as "a positive unkindness that renders [the Black man] unfit for the work which the white man has prescribed him and which he will be forced to perform." Vardaman died in 1930, yet his attitude about education and a racialized class of farm laborers persisted well into the 1960s.

In the fall of 1965, to keep their children's education from being subordinate to the demands of the cotton fields and the forces of white supremacy that kept Black children in the fields, the Carters enrolled the youngest eight of their thirteen children in the formerly all-white public schools of Drew under a system called "freedom of choice." The decision was made not at the parents' insistence, but mostly in response to the children's desire for a change in their circumstances. They knew that integrating the schools would get them out of the cotton fields, since they regularly saw shiny yellow buses filled with white children driving past while they continued to pick cotton. The older children thought it might also create broader change in the community, particularly Ruth, who had been arrested in 1964 while demonstrating for voting rights during a trip to Jackson. Although the family knew there would be some pushback from whites, their idealism kept them from imagining the severity of the resistance they would face. The family's decision led first to night riders shooting up their house, and then, when the Carters did not submit to the request from the plantation overseer to withdraw the children from school, to getting kicked off the Pemble Plantation.

When "freedom of choice" became the Mississippi desegregation plan, it was an open secret that it was nothing more than a tactic to delay school integration. The Civil Rights Act of 1964 required that schools that received federal aid be desegregated. To follow the law and subvert it at the same time, Mississippi enacted what it called a "freedom of choice" system that operated under the idea that all parents could send their children to the school of their choice. But how many Black families felt as if they had the freedom to challenge segregation by acting on the promise of choice purportedly offered by this new system? What the segregationists knew was that Black folks who were dependent on white folks for their livelihood and a place to live would never choose the all-white schools for their children. Black folks knew that "freedom of choice" was nothing but the proverbial trick bag that would trap them. The power of inertia would keep schools segregated.

The Carter family understood the trap that had been set and still made the choice to integrate the schools. Consequently, the town of Drew made their lives difficult. Not only were they pariahs among the town's white residents; even some Black Drew residents shunned the Carters, fearful that an association with them would lead to the same type of violence and harassment the Carters received. Eventually, with the help of the American Friends Service Committee, they were able to find housing and given sufficient resources to feed their family. Wilmer and Mildred Young of Philadelphia, Pennsylvania, who, during the Southern Tenant Farmers Union strike in 1936, helped relocate Arkansas sharecroppers to the Delta Cooperative Farm in Bolivar County—which later became Providence Farm further south in Holmes County—also helped the Carters purchase a house. A young lawyer by the name of Marian Wright (later Marian Wright Edelman) provided legal advice and the Carter family filed a lawsuit against the Drew School District that stated the "fear of white retaliation, firmly grounded in fact, has deterred other Negroes from choosing the formerly white schools pursuant to the district's freedom of choice plan." The lawsuit asked for relief against the freedom of choice system, noting that it placed a "cruel and intolerable burden" on Black parents and students. The Carters won the lawsuit in 1969, freedom of choice ended, and Mississippi's public school systems were ordered by the courts to integrate immediately, which began in January 1970.

Since 1965, the year the Carters challenged school segregation, Drew has seen a shift in its demographics. Drew's population of 1,852, as of a 2022 census estimate, is nearly 30 percent lower than its population when the schools integrated in 1970. Its poverty rate has stayed constant at 43 to 44 percent, but the racial demographics have flipped from 53 percent white and 46 percent Black in 1970, to 11 percent white, about 85 percent Black, and 2 percent multiracial. Schools have consolidated and lack the resources they possessed during Dickerson's childhood, which means that the quality of education is not much better than before school desegregation in 1970. Because of these changes, which effectively constitute a lack of change, Gloria Dickerson decided to carry on her family's legacy of creating radical change in the Delta through her current work in her hometown. That meant returning to a town she thought she had left forever.

When you arrive in the town of Drew on Highway 49, the welcome sign proclaims that it is the home of Mae Bertha Carter as well as Pop Staples of the Staples Singers. Back in the 1970s, the sign outside of town announced that the town was the "home of [football great] Archie Manning of the Ole Miss Rebels," with those words framed by the stars and bars of a Confederate flag. The stretch of road outside of town is still called Manning Boulevard, but the old sign is gone, a reflection of changing times.

The old sign greeted visitors back when Gloria Carter left Drew after her graduation in 1971. At the time, Dickerson felt like she was carrying more burdens than the average high school graduate. She was only twelve years old when her family defied the town, and up until her senior year, she had been the lone Black student in her class and was regularly harassed by her classmates. That changed when court-ordered integration opened Drew High School to both Black and white students. Until a few years ago, she had nightmares about being taunted and threatened at school during integration, which she tells me took years of therapy to overcome. She would wake up in the middle of the night sobbing about the memories of her harsh treatment. Yet she never thought about quitting, since she knew that she had a right to the same education as the white children who called her racial epithets. Her parents fostered that intense belief that integrating the schools was the right thing to do. It even drives the work she does today. But there were other things haunting her.

On the night of Dickerson's graduation from high school in 1971, one of her classmates, Joetha Collier, was shot on a corner in the town of Drew while wearing a bright yellow dress. Local lore says that she was still holding her high school diploma when she was murdered. Three white men were arrested and charged but only one served time for the killing. And after only a few years in prison, he was given an early release. The shooting echoed the harassment Dickerson endured during integration as well as the historical violence against Black people in the Delta.[5]

All of this meant that when Dickerson left Drew to attend the University of Mississippi, she wanted to believe she was leaving a great deal of pain behind. Ole Miss did not have a reputation as a welcoming place for Black students, but she felt she could make it there because her two brothers were also studying there. Like them, she chose to major in accounting, and she eventually became the comptroller for the W. K. Kellogg Foundation, which was then doing work in her native Mississippi Delta. Between 1992 and 2021, the Kellogg Foundation invested over $63 million in the Mississippi Delta.

But being comptroller distanced Dickerson from working directly with the people the foundation was helping. Eventually, she asked to be reassigned to an office in Jackson, Mississippi, as a program officer for Kellogg's Mid South Delta Initiative, an economic and community development initiative. When the foundation decided to wind down its work in the Delta in 2009, Dickerson decided to retire. One of the reasons the funders gave for deciding to stop investing in rural areas, including Mississippi and the Delta, was they felt they were not having any impact.

When Dickerson heard the news that Kellogg's Delta initiative was ending, she was incredulous about the decision. As she tells me the story in her office on Main Street in Drew, she is calm and measured, yet her delivery is firm. "So I asked them, 'What's the major problem? What do you think is the issue?' What they said to me—and they heard this from several funders—is that until the people of the Mississippi Delta change their mindset, things are not going to change." Ever the problem solver, Dickerson's response was, "'Well, who's working on that? If that is the root cause of the Delta's problems, someone should be working on that.' So, that's when I decided that after the end of the initiative, I was going to work on the way people think, how much hope they have, examine the source of their ambition, and discern whether they even think about the Delta as a place where certain things are possible." I realized that what Dickerson was saying is that the future, like the past, is built by human beings. No one is coming to be a savior for the little town of Drew. The people themselves have to provide the agency for change. What Dickerson also recognizes is that people in rural Black communities have been denied access to the tools that can change them and their communities. These are pieces of public policy that by design exclude small, mostly Black Mississippi Delta towns as well as towns across rural America.

Dickerson's organization, We2Gether Creating Change, came about to fill a void and to bring Dickerson's idea to the Delta that change needed to come from inside communities rather than outside them. Instead of seeing Kellogg's decision as a defeat, Dickerson chose to examine what the foundation did in the Delta that did work, which happened to be community-based problem-solving. On the basis of the strength of Dickerson's analysis, the Kellogg Foundation even helped We2Gether to get started with a seed grant, which the foundation awarded to "enable the organization to achieve its mission of being a change agent in the transformation of the Mississippi Delta."

While some would think that the work Dickerson has taken on is too hard, that is not the way she sees it. As she said to me once, "What if Fannie Lou Hamer had given up during the Civil Rights Movement? Where would we all be today?" That reminds me of a 1964 quote by Hamer herself, words she said—fittingly enough—in the Sunflower County town of Indianola: "You can pray until you faint, but if you don't get up and try to do something, God is not going to put it in your lap." Gloria Dickerson is not waiting for change to come to the Delta simply by getting on her knees and praying. She is getting out there and creating the change herself.

When Dickerson returned to Drew, she did not like what she saw. "What I found when I got back was that a lot of people were apathetic, and that some of them didn't have any hope. They would say, 'Things have always been this way, they'll probably stay this way.'" Feeling sure that people would be inspired to act if they saw that things can change, she began by doing community education, first with adults and later with young people. Her work with young people evolved into the Emmett Till Academy, which seeks to educate students about the civil rights history of the Delta and to teach history that is not taught at school. What I have observed at the meetings of this group is how the students connect with the history shared by individual members of the community.

One summer evening, I sat in the room in one of the spaces We2Gether occupies on Main Street as students were working to put on *Mrs. Carter and the Sunflower Seven,* a play based on the story of how the Carter family integrated schools in Drew. The production was a collaboration with StoryWorks, a documentary theater company that transforms journalism into theater and audio dramas. The background for the play was *Silver Rights,* a book by activist Constance Curry that chronicles the story of the Carter family and their integration of Drew's public schools. Curry, in her work with the American Friends Service Committee, helped the Carters navigate life after they were thrown out of their home by the plantation owner. Curry often worked covertly and behind the scenes. Yet rather than focusing the book on her own activism, she made Matthew and Mae Bertha Carter and their children the story's central characters. The book's title is a reference to the way elderly Black Southerners pronounced the word "civil," making it sound as if those rights were a precious and valuable metal.

The play was being directed by StoryWorks's Jenna Welch, whose background in journalism influences her belief in the power of transforming facts into art. The idea behind every play Welch directs at StoryWorks is not just to dramatize a story, but to tell the story with accuracy. She also believes the story must be presented in a way that allows the audience to relax and experience it without feeling overwhelmed. Welch stresses to me that the final act of each play is the community discussion that follows. "That is the civic education component of our work," she explains. And like each performance, Welch notes, the conversation takes a different shape each evening.

On the day I watched the initial rehearsal, Welch and Dickerson were still looking for an actor to portray civil rights activist and NAACP leader Amzie Moore, who helped the Carter family navigate their life after their time on Pemble Plantation. After the night riders' drive-by shooting at the

Carter house, it was Moore who called the FBI and convinced them to begin an investigation. When they asked me if I knew of anyone who might be interested in portraying Moore, I decided to volunteer. Though I am not an actor, I was not the only first-time actor in the room. None of the students had ever been involved in a theater production either. And if I wanted to understand how theater worked to change people's minds and attitudes, it seemed being a part of the production was the best way to do that.

For the young people involved, putting on the production of *Mrs. Carter and the Sunflower Seven* was a complete act of faith. For months they had studied the story of the Carter family, explored its history, and learned of the family's most dramatic moment. The challenge of all the actors—including me—was to put on a production that would engage the audience and generate discussion. That meant we all had to make the audience believe we were the people we were portraying.

There was nothing glamorous about the production. There was no curtain in the Drew Middle School theater, and the space was nothing more than a stage on the edge of a school gymnasium floor. There were limited props and the costumes were simple and unassuming, much like the Carters themselves. Key to the production's effectiveness were the images of the Carter family, along with images of the Delta landscape, that were projected onto a screen behind the actors at strategic moments.

During the community discussion about the play each night, the conversations were animated and the audience seemed to connect with the story. Six of the Carter children also joined the cast on stage after each performance, and their insights about seeing themselves portrayed onstage made for an emotionally charged discussion. The Carter children spoke openly about the emotional abuse they suffered, whether it was being shunned by teachers and fellow students or being regularly pelted with spitballs. At the first performance, several of the young actors portraying the Carters became teary-eyed after hearing how the play had affected members of the family.

The community conversation took on a different tone each night. While some members of the audience were seeking to understand how the actors came to understand their roles, others felt as if they were engaging with the Carters' story for the first time. Some of the older members of the audience who remembered the story as it happened seemed to feel liberated to tell their own stories. Sometimes instead of posing questions about the play, as Welch anticipated, they shared testimonials, which I attributed to the play having given members of the audience permission to discuss this history openly, perhaps for the first time.

For the three performances and during the week of rehearsals leading up to them, I heard the actor portraying Marian Wright give a powerfully delivered monologue in which she noted that the freedom of choice system placed a "cruel and intolerable burden" upon Black parents. After the final performance, I began to wonder if that cruel and intolerable burden was still being carried by the Delta's Black citizens. That burden was certainly evident in the school where the performance took place, which was not in the best physical condition. The air conditioning worked, but sometimes it leaked from the ceiling on the stage during our rehearsals. And even though it was just two weeks before the school year began, there were numerous repairs and renovations in process that were unlikely to be completed by the time students arrived. Although a few white people were present at the performance and the community discussion after the play, they were people who I would argue already understood the nature of the Carters' sacrifice. It made me wonder about the people not present, the people who did not understand this story. That question led me one afternoon to look at the campus of North Sunflower Academy, the segregation academy that was founded in 1966 after the Carters integrated Drew High School.

North Sunflower Academy is merely a collection of ungainly, tan-colored corrugated metal buildings surrounded by a tall chain-link fence. The color of the building even blended in with the soil surrounding it on the dry, hot summer day I visited. Had I not known it was a school, I would have thought it was some form of correctional facility, given the way it was clearly designed to keep intruders out. I stood outside with my camera, seeking to gain a visual perspective that would capture the spirit of the place. Eventually I set my camera down and just stared at the utilitarian buildings and the football field, all set off the road and virtually free of any connection with the Black citizens of Drew. It looked like a place constructed in haste—which it was—with more attention paid to function than to form. Then it occurred to me that the students who attend this school exist in a realm separate from the predominantly Black school on the opposite side of the road a half mile back. Like the Black students, they also carry a cruel and intolerable burden, yet their burden is different from that of the Black children I spent a week with portraying historic events onstage for three nights. I'm not even sure they recognize the burden of the legacy of segregation that their school perpetuates.

Although it took some time for the young Black Drew residents in *Mrs. Carter and the Sunflower Seven* to recognize the weight of the history they were acting out on stage, by the final performance I felt they were at least aware of the forces that shaped their present circumstances. As I stood outside North Sunflower Academy, I asked myself the same question Gloria Dickerson did in response to the Kellogg Foundation: "Well, who is doing that work?" It didn't take me long to come up with an answer: nobody.

Yet it is institutions like North Sunflower Academy that have shaped the educational landscape of the Mississippi Delta. As I stared at the tin-sided buildings of North Sunflower Academy, I kept wondering about how much the existence of this school and the separate realm of whiteness it has created affected the public school that sits just down the road from it.

CHAPTER 10

"JUSTICE IS A BLIND GODDESS"

*The real trouble is that you have given us
schools too long in which we could study the earth
through the floor and the stars through the roof.*

—REV. H. H. HUMES

In many Mississippi Delta towns, abandoned houses and buildings dot the landscape, yet one lonely structure stands out in the town of Drew. If you turn right at a collection of boarded-up school buildings on Highway 49 and drive toward the center of town on Green Avenue, you'll find the building that once housed Drew High School. Years of declining enrollment and a state-led takeover of the school system led to the closure of the school in 2012 and the consolidation of high schools across Sunflower County. Little of the Art Deco building is left standing except the archway of green and white columns enwrapped in gold-beaded rope. Inside that archway stand the structure's burned ruins.

Just weeks before the building was to be awarded historic preservation status, a group of seven teenage arsonists set fire to the school. The young people had heard from neighbors about what a nuisance it was to have this large empty building in the middle of the town and thought no one would care if it burned. None of them had an idea of the way the history of the building represented the struggle for equal educational opportunities for Black people in the Delta. While arson is never justified, the question remains why the students would even know of that history, given the way segregation has become a way of life in Drew and other Delta towns. The educational inequities that were fought in that building continue to be a burden for every child in the Delta, including those seven teenagers who set the building on fire. In fact, the boarded-up school buildings on the edge of town were built for Black children during segregation, a harsh reminder of the way inequity in education has long been a part of the Delta and is now evident in a landscape filled with decaying abandoned schools, including those built under a system that was allegedly separate but equal.

Soon the building that housed Drew High School will be leveled. There may never be a historical marker proclaiming this now burned-out building as one that played a role in challenging the freedom-of-choice integration system in the 1969 Supreme Court case of *Alexander v. Holmes County Board of Education*. Instead, there will be a massive empty space left in the town. It's not something Matthew and Mae Bertha Carter could have imagined when they chose to send their seven children to Drew High School. They made the decision to integrate the school because they knew the all-white school board was much more concerned about providing an adequate education for white children. If the school district wasn't going to give equal resources to Black children, the Carters reasoned, why not send their children to the school that fulfilled the educational needs of the white and powerful? Yet just one year after Drew was fully integrated as a result of the *Alexander v. Holmes* decision—the Carter family was a plaintiff in a related NAACP lawsuit that challenged segregated schools in Mississippi—the school was 80 percent Black. By the time the school closed, consolidating with a school in nearby Ruleville, it was virtually all Black.

But the school that played a part in Drew High's declining white enrollment still stands. That school, North Sunflower Academy, was part of a highly organized white exodus from the public schools in the Delta. Across the Delta there were other schools just like it, offering white students and their families a way to maintain a segregated way of life as courts ordered schools to integrate. And this mass departure led to the abandonment of the public school system by white families. At the time, those who left said they were trying to maintain "quality education," a phrase that did not disguise the racism that led them to retreat from public education. And that same justification is used today, despite more than fifty years of shrinking resources for public schools since whites abandoned the system.

North Sunflower Academy's enduring presence is linked to the now-charred ruins of Drew High School. Had the members of the community found a way to live together, the building that was clearly a source of community pride might still be standing and vibrant. You don't place something in the very center of town if it is not an important institution for the community. Gloria Carter Dickerson, who as Matthew and Mae Bertha Carter's daughter stood at the center of her town's integration fight, remembers in vivid detail students talking about leaving Drew High School and moving to the academy so that they would not have to go to school with Black people. Except they used a less polite term than "Black people."

North Sunflower Academy and white academies across the Mississippi Delta stand as a reminder of the ways the Delta served as a model of resistance to social change that accompanied the long Black freedom struggle. Some would argue that the entire state of Mississippi resisted the push toward racial equality in the 1960s, but that resistance was experienced most viscerally in the Delta. The Delta is a place that sits apart from the rest of the state in the minds of most Mississippians; it always has. Yet the region also shows us the attitudes of Mississippi and America in ways that we think are the exception but actually are the norm. We simply refuse to see the ways the Delta perpetuates white supremacy or acknowledge its existence, just as we fail to see the ways this country does the same.

The places that have come to be known as "segregation academies" also stand as symbols of white Delta residents' preservation of a way of life rooted in the segregationist past and at odds with the interracial realities of the modern-day South. Back in the 1930s, sociologist Hortense Powdermaker thought the region's future would not be permitted to work itself out from within. Outside forces would instead bring change. "The process of acculturation in the community is and will increasingly be subject to the effects of forces from without, upon each group separately and on the community as a whole," Powdermaker wrote.[1] But her prediction did not hold up. She underestimated the ability of white Delta residents to cling to the ideas of the past even as forces from without demanded change. The more external forces asserted themselves, the more white Delta residents doubled down, carving out a realm into which they chose to escape, not caring about who might get left behind or the institutions that might be destroyed in the process. Powdermaker believed magazines, books, and radio would bring white residents of the Delta into closer touch with the world at large and away from the closed society of the 1930s. Instead, a new closed society has taken shape in the form of private schools founded to maintain segregation. There is no sign a different world will be opening up.

When Powdermaker's *After Freedom* was published in 1939, no one anticipated how advances in telecommunications and the introduction of something called the internet would connect people, even in a region like the Delta where broadband access is limited. But today, even in this hyper-connected digital age, white Delta residents exist largely in a separate social and cultural space. The most segregated social space in the Mississippi Delta—after the church—is the classroom. After more than five decades of school integration and social change in America, it is time for white Delta residents to recognize that a multiracial society is a fact of life and stop placing their children in a racially segregated realm. Yet that change does not seem to be coming soon. Or ever.

What failed to happen in the Mississippi Delta and all over the United States after integration is a process of reconciliation that addressed inequities of power and access in society. By "reconciliation," I don't mean just restoring broken relationships or engaging in some superficial joining of hands but learning how to live together. Blacks and whites in the Delta lived a profoundly divided past, and the legacy of that past has never been confronted with openness and honesty. Instead, separate spaces—educational, social, and political—were created, which led to broader social and educational inequality. As a result, the divisions of the past persist.

Take the Delta town of Cleveland, the home of Delta State University. When this vibrant college town fully integrated its schools in 2017, the issue of reconciliation was part of the discussion. A federal court order combined all-Black East Side High School with Cleveland High School, which was 40 percent white and 60 percent Black. Leaders anticipated the combined school would be about 70 percent Black and 30 percent white. "You can't have consolidation without reconciliation," noted a member of a panel in Cleveland that sought to make integration and consolidation go smoothly. Even with this attempt at reconciliation, there has still been white flight, with white enrollment in the consolidated school dropping 7 percent. Bayou Academy, a segregation academy founded in 1964, is one of two private schools in Cleveland that have taken in many of the fleeing white students.

What happened in Cleveland, Mississippi, mirrors what happens across the country: when minority enrollment at a school is higher than 60 percent, the families of white students often withdraw them based on the perceived inferiority of a school that is mostly Black.[2] What is different in the Mississippi Delta is that the existence of private academies prevents towns, even ones like Cleveland, from achieving some form of reconciliation. Without this small town's private academies, spaces that were created for white flight, the schools would be more integrated.

In a 1979 interview with Robert Patterson, one of the founders of the segregationist White Citizens' Council, he claimed that white Mississippians did not accept that their society was moving toward integration. He even challenged his interviewer to prove that white Mississippians accepted integration, asking, "Why do they all live in the suburbs, and why do they move out of the neighborhood when Negroes move in? And why do they send their children to private school? And why do they manipulate and move to go out to an area that doesn't have many Negroes in it so they can send their child to a virtually all-white school? . . . They haven't accepted integration. They've run from it."[3]

But the flight from integration is not something that just happened over time; it was planned. A group of powerful men—of course, they were all white men—planned an exit strategy from integrated schools for every white child in the Delta. These men formed the Mississippi Private School Association (MPSA) in 1968. By 1972 the organization had an enrollment of 30,515 students spread across 110 schools in four states. In 1964, Mississippi had fewer than twenty private schools, most of them private Catholic parochial schools. The number of private schools soared to more than two hundred by 1971, one year after court-ordered integration, and many, but not all, of them were accredited by the MPSA. Since the Delta was majority Black, private schools took over quickly and fed into the fear of integration that had been stirring since the *Brown* decision in 1954. It wasn't white flight—in the rural Delta there is no suburb to which a family could flee. Instead, the flight took place within communities where all could see it, creating separate schools that effectively thumbed their noses at the idea of education as a public good and social equalizer.

Segregation academies came to exist across the Delta because the people who founded them believed that Black and white students should be educated separately and because there was nowhere else to go. They wanted nothing to change. As Gray Flora, who studied the rise of private academies for his doctoral dissertation at the University of Mississippi, explained to me, "Private academies in the Delta and across Mississippi created a mirror image of public schools as they existed before integration." Some of the newly established academies adopted the same fight songs, mascots, and other traditions as their public school counterparts. In the Delta, the private school movement dramatically shaped the education landscape.

The founders of private academies also believed they should no longer support the public school system now that they no longer had a need for it. And when an institution is no longer needed by a part of the community, it falls into decline. That is exactly what happened to the education system of the Mississippi Delta. As Flora reminded me one afternoon just steps from where James Meredith entered the University of Mississippi, "If a community is going to pull time and resources out of the public school system, you're going to create inequality." More than half a century later, the impact is visible. And the attitudes of the past persist.

When Drew's school system was placed in the hands of a state conservator, nearly half of the funding of the school came from the state and only 20 percent came from local taxes. At the time, Republican state representative Rob Roberson said school takeovers and consolidations are unavoidable. "Do I believe that some of these people feel disenfranchised?" he said when asked about the takeover trend. "I honestly think that that's their belief. But I also believe they have to take some responsibility in moving the ball."[4]

What politicians like Rob Roberson and others fail to acknowledge is that disinvestment from public schools in Drew and towns like it across the Delta is directly related to the existence of segregation academies. The open secret is that these are also places where white supremacy still thrives. The racism of these schools was once cloaked in the idea that they provided a "quality education" or that they upheld Southern traditions. In my discussions with recent academy graduates from the Delta, today they are taught that the schools were established to uphold Christian traditions and things like prayer in school. It is only when they begin to take history classes in college that they learn they were told a lie.

Roberson's accounting also mirrors the narrative that towns in the Delta generally use to explain the existence and persistence of segregation. According to that narrative, malfeasance and inept leadership contributed to the downfall of the public schools, whose continued failings keep the academy system alive. The opposing narrative, however, is that white leaders and residents starved the public schools of necessary resources after decamping for the academy, an institution perpetuated by racism. The truth is that the public schools were indeed starved of resources, and the narrative of ineptitude in school leadership is both false and serves to keep them starved of resources.

"Like Confederate memorials or a still-standing plantation home on tour, segregation academies remain part of the southern landscape," wrote Delta native Ellen Ann Fentress in an essay for the online journal the *Bitter Southerner*.[5] As someone who was shaped by school integration in Mississippi, I have some familiarity with how segregation academies came to be a part of the landscape. I watched the system take shape in real time and recall white students leaving my integrated school one by one in shamed silence. Now the existence of segregation academies appears to have been normalized. There is no shamed silence—just silence. But the question that has evolved over more than half a century is, can racial justice be achieved in the Delta without integration? James Baldwin once called white America a "burning house." "I do not know many Negroes who are eager to be 'accepted' by white people," he wrote in the *New Yorker*, noting that whites "had robbed black people of their liberty."[6]

I do know that the early years of school integration felt like being thrown into a burning house in which you were forced to survive. But I also know that, like the now-ashen remains of Drew High School, the fire did not have to be set.

When I ask Delta-born novelist Steve Yarbrough for his memories of attending a segregation academy in his hometown of Indianola, he shares two recollections with me. One is short. The other, more complicated, memory sears his consciousness to this day. First, he tells me that the textbooks he used at Indianola Academy were all marked "Property of the State of Mississippi," an indication that while his school was private, its mission and existence was sanctioned by the state.

The next recollection he shares with me is of his Black childhood playmates. This is not a story about a segregation academy graduate bragging about having had Black friends. That is not Yarbrough's style. As longtime friends and writers, our conversations are always brutally honest, almost as if we are behind the grate of a confessional recalling our human failings through the years we have known each other. Except we don't necessarily want to keep what we are talking about sealed and confidential. From his tone, I know what he is about to tell me is about loss and regret. "Until I was six years old, I just played with Black kids. There were no white kids within about two miles. There were Black kids within two hundred yards. So, that's who I played with, and I didn't even think about it."

For the first three years of his education, from 1963 until 1966, Yarbrough attended public schools in Sunflower County. This was before integration became a remote possibility in the Delta and his father felt the need for him to be shielded from even the possibility of sharing a classroom with Black people. But when he started at his then-segregated public elementary school, his father demanded he stop playing with his Black neighbors. "Right before I went to school, my dad said, 'No, you can't play with, you know, those N-word children, anymore. You can't do that. You're going to school now, so things change.' And I guess he knew his admonition would go in one ear and out the other. Then I came home from school, and after about four or five days, he caught me playing with the Black kids again. And he pulled his belt off and he whipped the shit out of me. And I did it again about three or four days later and he whipped me about twice as long then, and I got the lesson, I absorbed it. And I didn't play with the Black kids anymore. I didn't play with Black kids until I went to college and played football."

Suddenly, a pensive expression comes across Yarbrough's face. He shakes his head and pauses. Then he tells me, "In the most basic way, those Black kids were my friends. And you don't do bad things to your friends, you interact with them. And so, this was the way it always was in the Delta. If people can't get to know one another, if they don't grow up playing with one another, and thinking this is a normal thing, well, you get what you get. And then you don't have any stake in the economics of that other group. You don't worry that they're growing up in shacks with no running water, no bathrooms. Or that their schools don't have enough resources. But you remind yourself, 'Well, at least I have that.' And that's how white folks in the Delta continue to view Black people as somehow different in a basic way and don't worry about their welfare."

Steve Yarbrough and I have been friends since he gave up a football scholarship at Delta State University, transferred to the University of Mississippi where we were both undergraduates, and decided to work as hard at becoming a writer as he did at playing football. In four of his novels— *Visible Spirits, Prisoners of War, The End of California,* and *Safe from the Neighbors*—Yarbrough explores what the Delta's past can tell us about the present, whether it is the effect of racism on the life of a Black postmistress in *Visible Spirits* or the long-term impact of the 1962 Ole Miss riot on a history teacher in *Safe from the Neighbors*. The connection between the past and the present is what he and I often talk about. Very early in our conversation about private schools in the Delta, he tells me about the shame he feels for having attended an all-white segregation academy in the early days of school integration, even though he won a state football championship there and got to play two years in college. "I live in a different world than the one I grew up in. I don't think in the same way I was conditioned to think while I was growing up."

What he was conditioned to think was that his whiteness made him superior. Still, Yarbrough doesn't believe that just because he lives north of Boston today that his community is free of racism. "I know lots of white liberal Bostonians who won't set foot in Roxbury," he says with a chuckle, referring to one of Boston's largely Black neighborhoods. Yet what he thinks makes the Delta different is the legacy of the plantation system that historically exploited Black labor. "Some of the white people my age who own plantations and had their superiority drummed into them keep this idea of superiority alive." And he thinks the academies reinforce the dominance of white political and economic interests. "I'm sure it is not as brutal as it was when I attended the academy. The teachers are probably not saying the N-word in the classroom, but that sense of superiority is what keeps these schools alive. How can that message not be conveyed to these kids?"

This feeling of difference from his Delta upbringing keeps him away from reunions of his championship football team. "You must understand, I loved playing on that championship team. But I am ashamed of where I went to school. And I believe I should be ashamed of where I went to school. I also think about how much richer my life might have been if I had been taught from an early age that the differences between me and those who looked different were superficial and the similarities the very thing that makes us human." It's not something his former teammates understand. When he told a classmate about his shame, the response was, "I believe you are telling me the truth, but I don't know how you arrived at that perception."

Yarbrough's friends can't understand his perspective because their children also attended segregation academies. And if those children of his classmates remain in the Delta, their children will do the same. Now that the academies only talk about how they are places for a good Christian education and overlook the history that led to their founding, people can compartmentalize the shame Yarbrough feels. Or feel none at all. Plus, now that these schools admit a small number of Black students—some of them student athletes—they can brand the schools as nondiscriminatory.

Keeping up an image of segregation academies as nondiscriminatory is not a new practice. The original constitution and bylaws of the Mississippi Private School Association (MPSA)—the organization that shaped the private school movement—do not contain an official admissions policy on race. Yet the meeting minutes of the MPSA from 1971 show that members agreed that any member school admitting a Black student or faculty member would be asked to leave the association. The schools were allowed to adopt an admissions policy that was nondiscriminatory in name only so that they could reap nonprofit tax benefits. For years, these private schools maintained a gentleman's agreement to not admit Black students or faculty, while also lying to the Internal Revenue Service about their discriminatory practices.

Although the gentlemen's agreement on not admitting Black students is no longer in effect, it doesn't mean that things are easy for Black students who choose to attend private academies. That was the experience of Mia Word at a segregation academy in the 2010s, where she was the sole Black face in a sea of twenty white students. By the time she left in eighth grade, there were three Black students. Word had started going to the academy after her family moved back to the Delta from suburban Atlanta. Her mother simply wanted to find a school that would provide a consistent level of instruction, which she found was missing from the local public school. While she is not angry about her time attending an academy, Word tells me that she knows that the same people who were teaching her were also sowing the seeds of racial distrust. "My teachers truly tried to be egalitarian, but it was clear that they would rather pay more attention to the white students than to me." Her peers noted how she was treated differently, which she believes sent a message to them that she did not belong.

Now a graduate of Harvard and a published poet—her family eventually moved to the Memphis suburb of Southaven, Mississippi, because of the rigor of the town's public school system—Word believes that it is difficult for any Black student to fit in at a Delta private academy: the history of how such schools were founded has not been confronted and still lingers in the air. "Integration of the academies, I believe, is much like the integration of schools in the 1970s. The teachers were trying to be fair, just like I've heard about those in the 1970s, but worried about the way they might be perceived in the wider community." As someone who integrated schools in the 1970s, I found that Word's experiences rang true. Back in the 1970s, everyone knew the rules had changed, but no one knew what the new rules were. And there was little dialogue about what the new rules should be.

Now, more than seventy years after the *Brown v. Board of Education* ruling that outlawed segregation in the nation's public schools, states across the country are pushing for universal vouchers to fund private school attendance. More than thirty-five states have created voucher programs to send public dollars to private schools. At Steve Yarbrough's Indianola Academy, books were the only thing funded by Mississippi state tax dollars—perhaps through an under-the-table arrangement but still with the state's tacit endorsement. With universal vouchers, most of private school tuition could be covered, pulling even more money from public schools.

Private school vouchers are being touted as a call for "freedom of choice," which is what segregationists called for in the wake of the *Brown* decision. The *Alexander v. Holmes* decision even overturned freedom of choice in public education, noting how the system of token integration placed a "cruel and intolerable burden" on Black families. Today, even though this issue was supposed to be a legally settled matter, the term "freedom of choice" is back, but with a different approach and framing. In January 2018 Empower Mississippi, a school-choice advocacy group that supports publicly funded vouchers for use at private schools, held a rally at the state capitol. Then governor Phil Bryant likened the fight for public-to-private education options to the fight for integration in the 1950s and 1960s: "*Brown vs. Board (of Education)* changed the laws in the land," Bryant declared. "You're fighting today for the same belief. Your civil right, your civil liberty to take your child and enroll them in a school of your choice—not one that the federal or state government is telling you to put them in."[7]

Because segregation academies don't turn a spotlight on their history, we fail to see connections between the past and the present when it comes to issues like private school vouchers and school choice. Yet I think there is a bigger issue: the history of segregation academies is indeed there for us to see; we just choose to overlook it. Segregation in schools has become an accepted norm in the Delta, just as it has across this country. And to find out how much young Delta residents know about the ways segregation academies came to be—as well as to learn how normalized segregation has become—I decided to assemble a group of students to discuss the history and formation of these schools.

From 1880 through the 1960s, public schools for Black children in the Mississippi Delta were so poorly funded that they set up their students for a life of second-class citizenship and servitude. During the Mississippi Summer Project in 1964, otherwise known as "Freedom Summer," the idea of a type of summer school that would provide an alternative curriculum sprang up in the Delta and across Mississippi. Charlie Cobb of the Student Nonviolent Coordinating Committee (SNCC) proposed the idea of establishing Freedom Schools that would enhance the education of young Black Mississippians and encourage them to "articulate their own desires, demands, and questions" and "to find alternative and ultimately new directions for action."[8] At the time, Mississippi's public schools had what historian William Sturkey calls a "policy of deliberate censorship" that withheld information about the Civil Rights Movement and limited discussions of citizenship rights and Black history.[9] The Freedom Schools sought to provide educational enrichment that would empower young Black Mississippians to become full citizens and reach their full intellectual potential.

Although voter registration activities were the most publicized aspect of Freedom Summer, the Freedom Schools were successful in motivating students to understand more about their history and to be engaged citizens. In 1998, more than thirty years after Freedom Summer, three Teach for America/AmeriCorps teachers in Sunflower County realized that there was still a need for an educational program that would challenge and engage young people in the area. To help meet that need, Chris Myers Asch, Shawn Raymond, and Gregg Costa founded the Sunflower County Freedom Project.

Chris Myers Asch had taught fifth grade in the town of Sunflower with Teach for America before leaving to spend a year in South Korea on a Fulbright fellowship. During his year abroad, he had the chance to reflect on his teaching experience and the Delta. He came to realize that young people in the Delta had tremendous potential and deserved a much wider, richer array of educational experiences. "When I was teaching, my students arrived at school at 7:30 a.m. and left at 3:30 p.m., a much longer school day than most American students," Asch recalled when I asked him to look back on the founding of the Freedom Project. "Yet the district did not offer physical education, art, music, foreign language, or any other courses to enrich their academic experience. The reason, I was told, was both economic and pedagogical, since the district felt the students were so far behind that they needed to spend all their time on the 'basics.' They rarely took field trips and faced corporal punishment if they misbehaved. The school resembled a prison, with its barbed-wire fence surrounding the playground and the regimented expectations." Yet his students loved coming to school. But, he realized, that changed by high school, when more than 30 percent of the students dropped out.

Asch concluded he had unfinished business back in the Delta. In the summer of 1998, he set up community meetings for families to talk about the kind of education they thought their children deserved. "People rarely talked about 'the basics,'" Asch recalled. "Instead, they talked about drama, music, history, field trips, health education, foreign languages, and other 'extras' that their kids were denied. It reminded us of the kind of curriculum that SNCC's Freedom Schools had offered back in the 1960s."

The Freedom Project started as a summer program, but today it operates year-round and offers middle and high school students intensive academic enrichment, mentoring, educational travel, physical education, and art classes. In the summer, students tenth through twelfth grade are offered college courses. For those who go to college, the Freedom Project offers mentorship support during the undergraduate years. And it follows the tradition of the 1960s Freedom Schools by seeking to supplement the education students receive in public schools and encouraging intellectual curiosity. The current executive director, LaToysha Brown—who was once a Freedom Project student—allowed me to talk with a group of four students who are intensely interested in history. Back in high school, Brown had begun to wonder why she had so little interaction with her white peers in the town of Indianola. She knew that some of the current Freedom Project students might be wondering the same thing.

The Freedom Project's building sits in the middle of the town of Sunflower, with the town's namesake river flowing nearby. On the day I come to talk to the students, I enter the building to a young voice singing Sam Cooke's "A Change Is Gonna Come." The young singer stops when she

The Mileston store and post office in October 1939. When my father, Warren Eubanks, arrived ten years later, the store looked very much the same. And when my parents married, their first residence was within walking distance just a few houses down the road.

Sharecropper houses like these once dotted the Delta landscape and were a reminder of the reliance of the region on cotton. Today, only a few of these "shotgun" dwellings exist in and on the edges of cotton fields, like ghosts from a forgotten past.

(TOP) Tchula Hardware in the Delta town of Tchula today is owned by Eddie Carthan, the town's first Black mayor. Although he has witnessed much change, Carthan says, "It's going to take a Moses to change the Delta, and this time Moses might actually be a white man or a white woman."

(LEFT) The historic marker for Providence Farm. The green and gold historic marker only tells part of the story of the cooperative farm's history, noting that the farm ceased operations "due to civil rights era tensions." The ambiguity of that description, combined with the now deserted setting, speaks to the ways tension in the Delta often leads to erasure.

Although shotgun houses may not be found in cotton fields, they still exist in Black residential neighborhoods of Delta towns. Many houses, like these in Greenwood's Baptist Town, are owned by absentee landlords, with only about a third owned by their residents.

This boarded-up Piggly Wiggly grocery store in the town of Ruleville serves as a reminder of how many Delta towns are so-called "food deserts." Rural counties in the Mississippi Delta average one supermarket per 190.5 square miles.

Just weeks before Drew High School's art deco building was to be awarded historic preservation status, a group of seven teenage arsonists set fire to the school. This now burned-out building was to be recognized for the role it played in challenging the Delta and Mississippi's freedom of choice integration system in the *Alexander v. Holmes* Supreme Court case.

Outside the observation tower for Parchman's Unit 29 sits a sign that reads "Brethren, I could not myself to have apprehended but this one thing I do, forgetting those things which are behind, and reaching forth unto those things which are before." The verse reappears across the grounds of Parchman, an odd and fatalistic choice since many of Parchman's residents may never exit these grounds once they enter.

Mont Helena was built in 1896 atop a sacred Indian burial mound in the middle of a cotton field. This Colonial Revival mansion is a reminder of the way this entire region was built on spectacle and rooted in unfettered wealth and power.

The freshly plowed fields in Tunica stand in contrast to the lights shining from the adjacent Sam's Town casino, putting the past and the present side by side. Yet those fields still exist because wealthy landowners are benefiting from farming, as well as from leasing their land to the casinos right beside those fields.

John Ware was born in 1938 to a sharecropping family on the Stansel Plantation in Ruleville, pictured here. While its former plantation commissary still stands, its fields of cotton have been replaced by rows of solar panels, transforming it into a solar-electricity farm.

sees me, but I assure her I was enjoying her voice. When I tell her that the river Sam Cooke references in the song is the Sunflower River, she gives me a surprised smile.

Freedom songs are a way to center the students, so Jeremiah Smith, the program director for the Freedom Project, gets the students to sing "Oh Freedom" together. It is an appropriate spiritual since it is one that focuses on freedom in the here and now and includes a fitting refrain that we also sing: "No segregation."

I begin the discussion with a reading of the poem "Justice" by Langston Hughes accompanied by a PowerPoint image of a blindfolded Lady Justice. The poem describes a battered Lady Justice wearing a bandage to cover "two festering sores / That once perhaps were eyes," as well as the ways that Black Americans can see how the justice system keeps them from equal treatment in US society.

I use the poem to begin a discussion of the history of school integration, pointing out that the injustices of the education system in the Delta are hidden by bandages that were put on more than fifty years ago, and those bandages keep us from seeing the inequities. We begin with the *Brown* decision, which they all know ended *Plessy v. Ferguson*'s doctrine of separate but equal. Next, I take them on a timeline of school integration in the Delta; discuss the role that the white establishment's massive resistance played in delaying *Brown*'s implementation, which was supposed to happen "with all deliberate speed"; and end with covering the *Alexander v. Holmes* case that ordered integration and should have ended massive resistance. One young perceptive seventh grader then spoke up. "*Brown* left room for loopholes, and *Alexander v. Holmes* addressed those loopholes," he said.

After discussing this history, I asked the question, "Is it legal to have a school where only students of one race can attend?" There was silence, and I assured them I was not asking a trick question. Then one student replied, "No, it's not legal. But some schools you have to pay for, and those were made just for white people."

When I asked if they knew why those schools you have to pay for were started, it was clear they did not connect the history we had just discussed with the academies. They had never even heard the term "segregation academy." The segregation that was a daily part of their lives was presented to them as if it were normal, as simple a matter as "white people pay to go to school and Black people don't." Just as there were once a number of rules and restrictions that governed the system of Jim Crow—guidelines that sociologist Hortense Powdermaker referred to as "the little things that prick"—this new form of segregation seemed to also have its own set of rules. As one student noted, "When Black students go to all white schools, there are a different set of expectations." Although I could not get her to come up with the difference in expectations, what the group decided was that in integrated schools they would be seen as inferior, which to them meant there would be no room for them to make mistakes.

Judging from the expressions on their faces, they were ashamed that they did not understand the connection between segregated Delta schools and the existence of the academies, something they characterized as an "open secret." They all had learned about the *Brown* decision, but no one knew that the all-white private schools were a way to subvert the *Brown* decision and marked the next phase of massive resistance. But there was one other myth that they wondered about: Were the white academies better schools? I assured them that they were not. Yes, the buildings might be in a better state of repair, but there was little else that differed except that the academies were majority white.

Instead of volleying more questions at them, I asked them to write down why they thought they had not learned any of this history in school. Here are a few of their responses:

> "They did not want us to know what happened. They thought it would upset us too much. They kept us blinded like Lady Justice."

> "It was too uncomfortable to talk about it. They limited our knowledge of this history, kept us from learning what actually happened when schools integrated."

> "They did not tell us because they want to maintain the status quo. The best way to do that is to keep us ignorant and uninformed."

Then there was this longer response: "It's crazy how all this 'bad' stuff has been happening under our noses. To be honest, I feel a bit more informed and plan to start breaking the cycle of ignorance. I will probably start looking at a lot of things more closely. What I have learned today has set me on a new path on the journey of righteousness."

Finally, I read to them the line from the *Alexander v. Holmes* case that the freedom of choice system placed a "cruel and intolerable burden" on Black families. Next, I asked them, "What is the burden we are all carrying? Do we still have an intolerable burden?" This time, their responses came much faster. One student said, "The intolerable burden is that we still have segregation. No one ever made an effort to do anything about it." Another commented that "the cruel and intolerable burden has become a way of life. But we can't do anything about it. The intolerable burden is driven by fear, and we are afraid that things might get worse. But if we acknowledge this burden, it might actually lead to even less funding than we have for schools now. We are afraid of losing the education funding we already have. It is fear of losing what little we have."

Then it occurred to me that what keeps this system intact is fear mixed with shame. The shame drives the fear—the fear of having even less school funding, worse buildings, and fewer resources.

As I headed north from Sunflower on Highway 49 that evening, I drove past North Sunflower Academy, then took a fleeting glance at the boarded-up, formerly all-Black Drew Rosenwald School. Later, I thought about the burned-out ruin of the Drew High School building. The conversation that day, along with seeing and thinking about these symbols of educational inequality, made me realize that racial justice cannot be achieved in the Delta without integration. Without integration, young Black children in the Delta will continue to see themselves as inferior and whites in the academies will see themselves as superior. The cycle will never end, the festering sores on the eyes of the blindfolded goddess of justice will never heal, and we will all continue to carry a cruel and intolerable burden.

Just seven miles up the road from Drew stands the Mississippi State Penitentiary at Parchman. Everything about it—its history, its remote, nearly treeless location, its very name—equates with punishment of a violent, vindictive variety. And it is also a place that carries a different cruel and intolerable burden.

CHAPTER 11

THE WRONG SIDE OF THAT FENCE

Never will forget that day
When they taken my clothes
Taken my citizen's clothes
And throwed them away
Wonder how long
Before I can change my clothes?

—BUKKA WHITE,
"When Can I Change My Clothes?"

I f the blues is a mythological musical genre, then the Mississippi State Penitentiary at Parchman is the creator of many of the mythologies in-herent in the music. The twenty-eight square miles it occupies on the Delta landscape exists in a realm of its own, one that is a notorious container of cruelty as well as one that has inspired music and literature that combine equal measures of truth and myth. Blues singer Bukka White warned those who might find themselves inside the Delta's famous prison, "Oh, listen you men / I don't mean no harm / If you wanna do good / You better stay off old Parchman farm." Folklorist Alan Lomax, who recorded songs and field hollers of workers at Parchman in the 1940s, observed in his book *The Land Where the Blues Began* that every Black man in the Delta knew he could end up on the wrong side of that fence separating the prison from the surrounding fields of the Mississippi Delta and a life of freedom.[1] Sadly, that is still true today.

If the United States' penal system is the modern-day plantation, the architects of the system learned how to create that exploitative structure from Parchman, which was already an established plantation when the state of Mississippi purchased the land in 1901. When it opened in 1905, the prison immediately became a profit-driven farm that grew cotton and other crops and soon became Mississippi's largest source of revenue out-side of income taxes. Back then, convicts worked ten hours each day for six days a week and slept in long brick-and-lumber buildings called "cages" that were produced on-site. Men were largely employed in farming, but some worked in the prison brickyard, sawmill, cotton gin, or prison hospital. When women were housed at the prison, they made clothes and bedsheets for the entire prison. From the very beginning, crime and punishment at Parchman was racialized, since Governor James K. Vardaman saw the plantation as a means of dealing with "criminal Negroes." That is why Black men feared the place: they knew it did not take much to land them inside its confines.

Given its remote location, Parchman originally had boundaries rather than a system of walls and fences built to keep prisoners inside. Parchman's administrators hired convicts they considered trustworthy to work as armed guards. Known as "trusty guards" or "trusty shooters," they were separated from the general prison population and could shoot to kill any inmate they thought was trying to escape. Trusties functioned very much like plantation slave drivers, since they did the bidding of Parchman's superintendent and sergeants, who functioned like plantation masters. And prisoners were treated like slaves.

Today the trusty system is gone at Mississippi's oldest prison, but Parchman remains a place of deadly violence. Nine deaths were reported there in January 2020, the result of stabbings, beatings, and suicides. The cotton fields have been replaced by fruits and vegetables, and the Mississippi Department of Corrections says work in these fields addresses "inmate idleness." As the Mississippi DOC website notes, "Parchman holds a unique place in the prison system for reasons other than its age. [Parchman] is also home to Mississippi Prison Industries Corp. (MPIC)'s work program for its textile and metal fabrication." The website also boasts that those incarcerated at Parchman "provide more than 100,000 hours of free offender labor each year to adjacent municipalities and counties, as well as assisting other state agencies." Black men still fear ending up on the wrong side of the prison fence, since they make up nearly 65 percent of Parchman's population.

The other component of labor at the prison is the guards and infrastructure needed to run the place. In the Mississippi Delta, the prison industry is one of the region's largest employers. Yet because of the violence inside the prisons—and there are both private and public prisons across the Delta—there is a shortage of guards. Eighty percent of the guards are women. The Marshall Project found that violence against guards at Parchman is as much of a problem as inmate violence.[2] That means everyone inside the prison system is at risk for violence.

And then there is the violence that lives outside the prison walls, the violence in the crime in Delta towns such as Greenwood and Clarksdale and in Sunflower County, where Parchman sits. The rate of violent crime in Greenwood and Clarksdale is more than double the rate for the entire state of Mississippi. According to research by the University of Michigan's Poverty Solutions project, Leflore County and Coahoma County—which include Greenwood and Clarksdale, respectively—and Sunflower County are also all communities of deep disadvantage where between 31 and 36 percent of the population lives below the poverty line. In fact, these counties rank in the top twenty-five most disadvantaged counties in the nation because they have so many residents who live in what is defined as "deep poverty." The Poverty Solutions research also found that the rate of violent crime in a community is directly tied to the rate of intergenerational mobility.[3] That is, if a place has been disadvantaged for generations—and that disadvantage has been maintained and works to the advantage of those at the upper end of the income scale, as it has been in the Mississippi Delta— its violence can only be cured by increased economic opportunity.

In his 1937 study of the Delta, *Caste and Class in a Southern Town*, sociologist John Dollard argued that the lack of economic mobility among Black people in the Delta led to violence against those who were similarly oppressed.[4] While that may have been the case, there was also the omnipresent threat of violence in the form of lynching, which led many Black Delta residents in the 1930s to leave as part of the Great Migration. Those who remained found themselves in an emotional climate shaped by violence that persists to this day. If violence is the way the weak assert power, violence in the Delta appears to be a consequence of both a history of violence and years of perceived weakness that have led to learned helplessness. Yet no one in power wants to confront this tangled history of brutality and bring about the type of economic opportunity that would be transformative.

The path to increased economic opportunity is in no way tied to work in prisons or in maintaining prisons. If you are subject to violence both inside and outside prison, an uncontrollable cycle is put in motion. The myth of Parchman is that the people inside its walls are keeping other Delta residents and all Mississippians safe by reducing crime and violence outside the prison's boundaries. But in actuality, this remote prison only perpetuates the very problems incarceration is supposed to confront and solve. In her book *Are Prisons Obsolete?*, Angela Y. Davis observes that "[prison] relieves us of the responsibility of seriously engaging with the problems of our society, especially those produced by racism and, increasingly, global capitalism."[5] Places like Parchman keep Americans from confronting the poverty, educational inequity, and lack of economic opportunity that exist in places like the Mississippi Delta. In the Delta, locking people up prevents real conversations from taking place about the intergenerational violence, rooted in poverty and neglect, that has led many of its residents to sit inside enclaves surrounded by barbed wire on a great expanse of Delta land called Parchman.

Mississippi has an incarceration rate of 1,021 per every 100,000 people, one of the highest rates in the nation.[6] In 1983, just over seven thousand Mississippians were incarcerated. Today that number has grown to twenty-seven thousand Mississippians. The increase in Mississippi's prison population seems to align with the state's ever-decreasing education funding, which was at its peak following the education reform bill of 1982.[7] Since the Mississippi Adequate Education Program began in 1997, it has struggled to fully fund public education, only meeting its funding obligations to education twice in that time. Mississippi ranks forty-sixth in education spending, and the poorer school districts many of the prisoners come from have less to spend per pupil than those with healthier tax bases. Combine an underfunded education system with poor access to health care and a social safety net with huge holes in it, and you have set a trap for a segment of your population to fall into the criminal justice system, along with suffering, shame, pain, and death.

Although no prison occupies as much space as Parchman, there are numerous facilities throughout the Mississippi Delta. In fact, the counties of Bolivar, Issaquena, Leflore, Yazoo, Holmes, and Washington all have prison facilities. More than forty miles to the south of Parchman in the Delta town of Greenwood, the state has taken over the site of a former private prison and is now using it to house three hundred women. Eight miles to the north in the town of Tutwiler is a private prison, one that residents of the town thought might become its economic savior when it opened in 1999. More than twenty years later, the economic circumstances of the town are the same, and some would even argue that the economy is even worse, particularly after the COVID-19 pandemic.

To confront the way Parchman looms over the myth and reality of life in the Delta—and mirrors many of the problems of the American penal system—I decided to go inside the prison. I have taught at Parchman in the past, but my students were largely inmates who were scheduled to be released. This time, I chose to conduct a memoir writing workshop with a group called the Prison Writes Initiative in the part of Parchman known as "Unit 29," which houses men who are imprisoned for life. "I have instructed the Mississippi Department of Corrections to begin the necessary work to start closing Parchman's most notorious unit—Unit 29," Governor Tate Reeves announced on January 27, 2020. Yet it has not been closed. The areas that were in the worst physical condition, with water and sewage flooding through them, are allegedly shuttered. While some units may have been closed, Unit 29 is still filled with men who, as Bukka White would say, have all had their citizen clothes taken away and will never get them back. One inmate even wrote an essay about longing to find out what happened to the "cheap blue Men's Warehouse suit" he wore to the trial where he was sentenced to life in prison. In his words, I heard the echo of Bukka White wail across a modern-day Parchman.

Since my first visit to Parchman to teach writing and literature in 2019, I have come to see prison writing as a unique body of literature that offers a commentary on the conditions that exist broadly in American society, specifically in the Mississippi Delta. The themes of the prison writing I have encountered flow seamlessly between poverty, abuse, education, and mental health, all issues that affect the lives of people in the Delta. As one prisoner wrote, "Poverty comes with an entourage" that includes "tragedy, crime, shame, pain and death. All of which I have gotten to know on a first-name basis." The men I have encountered over the years write about their past lives of poverty and deprivation in a way that is clear-eyed and lacking in sentimentality. Along with the bleak violence they are familiar with as part of their daily lives inside prison, they also intimately know the violence that exists outside the prison walls. Getting a group of eight men to write about their memories, both the good and the bad, helped me understand the problems of the Delta and forced me to confront the depth of the issues that live inside and outside prison walls.

———

Writers sometimes bloom in the darkest of circumstances, even inside the walls of a prison. Although the sun is shining brightly on the day I arrived for the first of my memoir writing classes, it seems the sky has darkened as soon as the prison gates close audibly behind our car. In the driver's seat is Louis Bourgeois, who runs the Prison Writes Initiative. He tells me that he is no longer aware of the clanging of the gates, since he enters the prison at least twice every week. I remind him that I can never stop hearing the sound that makes me feel as if I am being locked away, even though I know that I will be leaving in two hours.

Parchman's Unit 29 is a gray concrete building surrounded by a tall fence topped with razor wire that rests securely on miles of never-ending flatness and endless sky. Observation towers are placed strategically around the corners of the facility. While the prison grounds have no high fences, the prison units exist as separate fortresses, successors to the long wooden barracks that were once here. The journey from the gates of Parchman to Unit 29 takes the traveler past a mixture of modest brick and white clap-board houses, all of which once housed prison officials and employees. The most decrepit and weather-worn houses appear to be empty, although a few show outward signs that they are occupied. Each time I arrive it feels as if I am traveling on a town's main street rather than a road through a prison. That might have been intentional since at one time families of the employees in those houses lived on the grounds of the prison, often with prisoners working as house servants to the families. Generations of children grew up on these grounds. There was even once a grand residence for the prison superintendent that resembled a plantation house, but it is long gone. Off in the distance, away from the units surrounded by gates and observation towers, a graveyard with a white arched gate sits in the midst of clear blue sky. From a distance it looks like it could be the gates of heaven. As you get closer you can see words just under the arch that say "Parchman Cemetery," with a cross on each side. Beyond the gate are hundreds of white crosses, marking the graves of Parchman's long-dead prisoners.

Although I could not find anyone who grew up on Parchman's main street, I did meet someone who regularly played on the grounds of Parchman as a child. Stacey Sanford grew up in Tupelo but regularly visited her grandparents in Grenada, a town on the edge of the Delta. Her grandfather ran the machine shop at Parchman—one of her uncles worked there as well—and she spent a great deal of time at a place she just knew as "the shop." "I didn't even realize I was on the grounds of prison until I was in high school," Sanford tells me one afternoon at a coffee shop in Oxford, where she now lives. She even still wears a ring an inmate who worked in the shop gave her made from stray bullet casings, as well as an assortment of other gifts. To Sanford, nothing about her regular trips to the grounds of Parchman seemed out of the ordinary.

Sanford's time playing on the grounds of Parchman fell between the mid-1980s and the early 1990s, when she was between the ages of five and twelve, in the years after Parchman had been subject to a round of court-ordered reforms and before the years of mass incarceration. The men who worked with her grandfather were in vocational training—more than twenty inmates worked in the shop—which had become part of Parchman. Also, the prison had just become all male—before that change, there were roughly two hundred women imprisoned at Parchman—bringing the prison's population at the time to just under four thousand. Her grandfather and uncle were the last of the almost exclusively white workforce that ran Parchman. She has no memories of her grandfather's truck undergoing a vehicle search before entering the prison grounds, as the car I ride in is routinely searched, or of seeing any of the prison facilities off in the distance. That surprises me, as I can see that prison buildings are visible from the machine shop, which I often drive past. Her memories of Parchman as a bucolic place rather than as a prison remind me that the children who grew up on the grounds of Parchman probably saw the place the same way.

After a drive down what I think of as Parchman's main street, you zigzag down weathered blacktop roads speckled with filled potholes—the prison roads are a grid that from the air appear as large rectangles—you arrive at Unit 29. Occasionally, men on horseback in prison stripes wander past, a reminder of the old trusty system that once existed here. "Parchman is a praying prison" the sign announces as soon as you get past the security gates. Every room includes a Bible verse prominently placed at eye level. Religion—particularly Christianity—plays an outsized role at Parchman.

Outside the observation tower for Unit 29 is a sign that reads, "Brethren, I could not myself to have apprehended, but this one thing I do, forgetting those things which are behind and reaching forth unto those things which are before." The verse reappears across the grounds of Parchman. These are words from the apostle Paul, who is looking forward to the day when he will see the face of Christ rather than looking back at his failures. Paul is forgetting everything that was behind him, including the stoning of Saint Stephen the Martyr, who cried out as he was being stoned, "Lord do not hold this sin against them." It seems an odd and fatalistic choice to place outside a facility that houses men who are in prison for life. Paul gets to do a victory lap; these men never will. Until they die inside this perpetual conflagration built from concrete and barbed wire, their sins will always be held against them.

The biblical references displayed on the grounds of the prison remind me that historian David Oshinsky once remarked that there were two reasons why Parchman exists: one was the desire for profit and the other was racial control. Now that Parchman is no longer a major source of state revenue and the staff is largely Black, religion has become the means of controlling the inmates. Today Parchman is all about sin, since once you enter its gates there is no chance for true redemption.

While there are various courses offered to inmates in Mississippi's prisons, the only higher education degree available at Parchman is an associate's or bachelor's in theology from the New Orleans Baptist Seminary. The program was established to train inmates to be what are known as "inmate religious assistants," so, unless a prisoner chooses to be a member of the clergy after release, the program is only useful inside prison walls, not outside them. It is also an educational option only for inmates with ten years remaining on their sentence, plus they must have no rule violations and a high school diploma. Half of incarcerated people in Mississippi lack a high school diploma or its equivalent, and many only read at a sixth-grade level.

The eight men who are part of my class all have high school diplomas. In preparation for the class, they have all read an essay by Henry Louis Gates Jr. called "Lifting the Veil," in which Gates explores the ways he chose to explore the subtext of African American life fully in his memoir *Colored People* rather than keeping aspects of Black life "behind the veil." I chose this essay to let them know that when they are writing about their past, they need only lift up the veil covering their past as much as they would like. Initially, the class is made up entirely of Black men, who quickly tell me that the idea of a veil placed over the lives of Black folks is one with which they are familiar. A week later, two young white men join the class, and they also understand the idea of the veil. For the Black men, the veil is rooted in the racism that marginalized them from a broader society before they came to prison. For the white men, the experience of prison was the veil that now concealed them, rendering them strangers and exiles from the world outside.

Half of the men are from the Delta, and those who are from other parts of the state committed crimes in the Delta that landed them in Parchman. One was born near my father's hometown in Choctaw County, Alabama, and ended up in the Delta, just as my father briefly did. Lacking the type of education my father had, his life took a different path. Even today, class and education serve as shields from the Delta's violent culture. But none of these men had enough wealth or social standing to keep them out of prison. Their stories remind me of how violence is baked into the history and culture of the Delta and manifests itself in the prison population.

I think of Heraclitus's axiom that "geography is destiny," but I don't proclaim those words in front this group. What I begin to understand is that geography does not have to be destiny. From each of them I learn that the men, regardless of race, had once lived a life of poverty. And crime was seen by each of them as a means of relieving the pain of poverty.

It doesn't take long to recognize that they already see the connection between the places they are from and the circumstances that led to life imprisonment. Instead, I begin the class with a writing exercise that I often use: I ask them to find one small detail from their past, then write from the flood of memory for ten minutes and just see where the writing takes them. "Sometimes memories—often the best and the worst—burn inside us for a lifetime," I tell them, quoting memoirist Mary Karr. "These memories 'burn inside us for lifetimes, florid, unforgettable, demanding to be set down.'" It sets their writing in motion, their pencils audibly scratching their yellow pads.

After the ten minutes are up, I ask each of them to share what they have written. Most of them go deep into the memory vault of childhood, recalling fishing trips and family gatherings. One man opens his with, "Everything changed when we moved to Foley," recalling how a childhood move disrupted his life in a way that he feels led to his imprisonment. Another writes, "I remember when I had a fan club," thinking of his days as a high school football star and trying to understand how he moved from being idolized by his peers to being distanced from them in prison. Yet another remembers that the town where he is from is one of "bright lights and dark corners." Then he writes that he fell into one of those dark corners, which in turn led him to Parchman.

At the end of our first two classes—by the second class, we have shrunk from eight to four men though later expand back to eight—I ask them to begin to craft a short memoir essay, one that we will workshop in a future class. Their ideas for their essays are sound and by the second class they lift the veil off their past even more, since they feel they can trust me. As I leave, I realize Dostoyevsky had it right: "Pain and suffering are always inevitable for a large intelligence and a deep heart." There is a great deal of intelligence among these men, along with much pain and suffering.

To keep them focused, each week I introduce a piece of writing, ask them to analyze it, and write a passage inspired by it. Reading Kiese Laymon's essay "World's Finest Chocolate" helped the men contemplate how they could capture their lives in a voice that felt as authentic as Laymon's. Another week we read an essay by David Owen called "Scars," in which the author contemplates the physical scars held on his body and the memories associated with those scars. This prompts one of the men—I'll call him M.—to contemplate the psychological and physical scars he bears and how he intends to live with them. He writes:

> My trials and tribulations have certainly been painful and have left deep psychological scars that have shaped who I am today. As have the years I've spent in prison, which have indeed left me with more physical scars than I came in with.
>
> The best thing I can think to do with all these scars—psychological and physical—is to learn to live with them; embrace them; accept them for what they are: Proof that I am human.

What I learned from these discussions about writing and the craft of writing is that each man in the class had a desire to frame the life he led inside Parchman carefully on the page for all the world to see. Still, I kept pushing them to look beyond the vast, flat landscape they inhabited, one they could only view through a high steel fence capped by razor wire. It proved difficult. Their world inside Parchman was defined by regulation of contraband items, the work they were told to do, conflicts with other inmates, and the corruption and neglect of the prison administrators. I wanted to get them to blend the past before prison and the present conflicts inside the prison walls, and begin to recognize how the confluence of those parts of their existence affected their interior life, as well as the ways their life inside prison in some ways mirrored what existed in the world outside Parchman.

In seeking a piece of writing that would get them to begin to think about those ideas, I chose James Baldwin's "Notes of a Native Son," an essay that shifts between place and time. Baldwin takes the reader into the evolution of his feelings about his father, from hatred to mourning—the essay revolves around his father's death—as well as the evolution of his views on racism in America, which move from innocence to a clear-eyed acknowledgment that racism must be confronted. "Notes of a Native Son" is an intimate essay that captures Baldwin's emotional evolution toward an understanding of his complicated feelings.

What I did not know when I assigned this reading was that Baldwin had visited Unit 29 at Parchman in 1983. Baldwin had come to Mississippi to attend the annual Medgar Evers Homecoming celebration. He had been friends with Medgar Evers, who had served as the first field secretary for the NAACP in Mississippi until he was assassinated outside his home in 1963. Baldwin had visited the Evers' family home to sign books for them, just months before Medgar Evers was killed. On this trip to Mississippi twenty years later, according to Mississippi state senator John Horhn—who accompanied Baldwin as a twenty-five-year-old employee of the Mississippi Arts Commission—Baldwin sought to honor Evers's memory by connecting with prisoners at Parchman, first at death row and then at Unit 29.

The men all connected with "Notes of a Native Son," and not just because Baldwin had visited Parchman. They all felt he understood their lives, which had been shaped by abuse, discrimination, poverty, and oppression just like Baldwin's. One of the men, like Baldwin, had been a boy preacher. As a young Jehovah's Witness in a suit and tie, he could sell more copies of *The Watchtower* than anyone—a boast he made repeatedly to me. By the age of six, this man I will refer to as R. was giving five-minute speeches before his entire congregation. He identified with Baldwin's conversation with his father when he told him that he would rather write than preach. The two white men who joined the class the day Baldwin was assigned were also moved by the essay; the emotional events Baldwin recounts in his essay—his father's death, his sister's birth, and his own birthday, all falling on the same day—mirrored their own emotional lives and made racial discrimination feel real rather than theoretical.

But something happened the day I taught Baldwin that stuck with me as much as the men's enraptured response to Baldwin's essay. One of the students, whom I will call E., had just received a letter about a legal appeal that had been pending. He held the sealed envelope in his hand and turned to the class with a huge smile on his face. As E. was telling all of us about the letter that he hoped held good news, a guard stomped into the room and took the envelope from the man, opened it, scanned the letter and the envelope, and then abruptly handed it back to E. Then she informed him that he was never to open any mail himself. "That is my job. You don't have the right to do that," the guard informed E., and then quickly turned on her heels and left the room just as abruptly as she had entered.

E. asked to be excused from class to read the letter and later returned and contributed to the discussion. When he came back, I was visibly distracted. E. recovered from this encounter faster than I did. This was my first time seeing a guard treat an inmate with disdain—almost as if he were not human—and I couldn't stop thinking about it. It made me wonder about what the guards were taught and what guided their interactions with inmates. I realized then that I knew more about the inmates than I did about those who watched over them.

That motivated me to seek out someone who had some insights into how a place like Unit 29 at Parchman worked. I decided to seek out a former chaplain, Maurice Clifton. In light of the intense focus on religion, particularly Christianity, at Parchman, I wanted to understand why the response to such a small infraction like the one I witnessed was lacking in Christian charity. Parchman says it is a "praying prison," but what exactly were people there praying for? That's not something I could ask the guards or the warden. I had to go beyond the platitudes and proclamations of religiosity I encountered on the prison's doors and bulletin boards.

Before Maurice Clifton became a chaplain at Parchman, he served twenty-two years in federal prison for aiding and abetting the sale of 6.5 grams of crack cocaine, as well as a simultaneous twenty-year sentence for the theft of $2,500 through wire fraud. At the time of his arrest, someone arrested for a powder cocaine offense would have needed 1.5 pounds of the substance to receive the same sentence, revealing the inequities in sentencing between the two forms of cocaine. He maintains that he is innocent of the charges, although he admits that he was once involved with hustling drugs. "They wanted me for what I did before and that they could not catch me doing," Clifton tells me one morning in a coffee shop in Jackson, Mississippi, where he now lives.

While in prison, Clifton worked for Federal Prison Industries, Inc. and mastered the company's SAP manufacturing system. He enrolled in dozens of classes on a wide range of subjects, including advanced microcomputers. But most importantly, he kept his eye on the politics of US criminal justice reform. Clifton was released from prison in 2020 under the First Step Act, a law aimed at reforming federal prisons and sentencing laws. He knows what life is like inside a prison as an inmate and as a prison employee.

Clifton also knows what life is like growing up poor in the Mississippi Delta. He is the twentieth of twenty-three children—"same mom, same dad" he adds as a point of clarity. His parents worked as sharecroppers in Bolivar County, though he says he never saw himself as poor because he never went hungry. Yet neither of his parents had any formal education. "My mother never went to any school," he tells me. When his father retired in 1977, when Clifton was twelve years old, the family moved to Mound Bayou. "We had to move out of the sharecroppers' house, since they no longer had any use for us." Still, Clifton realizes that his family remained part of the sharecropping system longer than most families like his. He also realizes that because of that accident of history, he grew up in a different Mississippi Delta than the one that exists today. He doesn't see his own dalliance with crime as related to the region's current landscape. "Instead of going down a road less traveled," Clifton says, referring to getting an education, "I saw a path that was a shortcut," referring to his years of selling drugs. Several of his twenty-two siblings went to college, and Clifton briefly went himself, going so far as making the dean's list as a nursing student before deciding to drop out. When he didn't register the next semester, his adviser came to his house to encourage him to re-enroll. "I asked my adviser, 'What you make?' He said, 'Oh, about $88,000.' I said, 'Well, I'll make that in a month, Doc.'" His adviser responded, "Yeah, Maurice. But I sleep at night." That exchange didn't hit Clifton until seven years later. He was twenty-four when he had that conversation; at age thirty-one he went to federal prison.

When I ask Clifton about how poverty and violence intersect, he interrupts me and tells me that he believes that it is lack of opportunity that intersects with violence, revealing his hopeful outlook on the world. He doesn't like to use the word "poverty" because he sees it as a label. "I see my role as a chaplain as healing," he says gently, since he sees himself as a man of God. Yet when I tell him the story of the inmate having the letter snatched from his hands, his tone changes. The guards, Clifton believes, are trained to be oppressors. "When guards are hired, they take them through a class. The training takes them through a dehumanization process, one that directs them to not see any inmate as a human being. That means that every day they do their job, they see part of their job as stripping inmates of their humanity. And that is what you saw inside Parchman when that letter was snatched away."

Then Clifton begins to sketch out on a piece of paper the power structure of the prison as he sees it: the gangs and their pecking order, as well as the ways the juvenile justice system feeds young people into the prison system. But what strikes me, as he finishes this visual outline, is that the same forces that exist inside prison as Clifton sees it—gangs, drugs, money, violence—exist outside the prison on the streets. The guards are the controlling authority in the prison, whereas gangs, local police, and a group he calls the "Alphabet Boys"—the Drug Enforcement Agency (DEA), the Federal Bureau of Investigation (FBI), and the Bureau of Alcohol, Tobacco and Firearms (ATF)—hold a primary role outside prison.

"There's just so much that goes on inside Parchman that you can't see. It's a veil, it's a veil," Clifton says to me while shaking his head in frustration. Even after careful study of the outline that Clifton constructs for me, I realize that there is much about Parchman that is unknowable, no matter how hard I try to understand. The mysteries are intentional: the purpose is for no one to figure out the system and for all to remain mired in it. The drawing also reveals how much Parchman and the Delta exist as worlds unto themselves that have little connection with prevailing cultural norms. Yet Parchman and the Delta also exist as threads intertwined with the story of America, because they both represent problems that we refuse to acknowledge and resolve. As long as we ignore the way poverty and violence intersect in places like the Delta, more Parchmans and places like the Delta will come to exist across this country.

Clifton's description of a veil over Parchman reminds me that we should all care about the actual human effects of incarceration. And we should also care about the intersection of poverty and violence outside the prison walls that sets a path for so many to end up in the prison system. Yet the question remains: How can we care about the effects of incarceration if most Americans never see it?

Toward the end of my time teaching at Parchman, a boxing ring is set up in the gymnasium where class takes place. In my previous visits, it wasn't there. When I comment on its presence, one of my students says it's there just so the men can fight as a spectacle for each other. "They treat us like we're not human," the man I call R. says to me. The idea that prisoners need to box, he thought, reinforces stereotypes about incarcerated men and their character. Refuting those stereotypes, he leans into his identity as a writer. "I write because it frees me," R. tells me. "Nothing that happens in that boxing ring has anything to do with freedom."

What I realize is that the writing class gives these men a sense of dignity. For two hours each week they are writers. When they leave class, the prison system tries to take that dignity away, but by clinging to the identity of writer, they can maintain some level of self-respect. As one student wrote in a poem in class, writing makes him feel that he's "not just another notch on the devil's belt." Although I have a sense of what his statement means, I am certain I have no idea how it must feel to be a notch on Satan's belt. Yet that idea is viscerally real to him.

Both inside and outside Parchman there is violence, both physical and emotional, as well as substandard living conditions. A Department of Justice report in 2022 noted that Parchman inmates have been subjected to "an unreasonable risk of violence due to inadequate staffing, cursory investigative practices and deficient contraband controls," adding that "these systemic failures result in an environment rife with weapons, drugs, gang activity, extortion and violence, including 10 homicides in 2019."[8] It is the constant specter of violence that inspired a prisoner I will call L. to write these words:

> Is life a repeat, or is it just prison life? Yesterday is gone, and never to be
> any more. And we really can't even think of tomorrow, because it only
> exists in our mind.

In the beginning of my time at Parchman, I asked students to write about life before prison, thinking those memories would somehow take them out of a place that, if I am being truly honest, scares me like nothing

I have encountered on a deserted city street. The truth, I realized, was that I wanted them to write about life before prison because the life they have inside prison is unimaginable to me, just as it is to millions of Americans. Now I know why Parchman haunts my very soul, having learned that there is a thin line between those on the wrong side of the fence and those on the right side. Each time the gate closes behind me, I hear it because I know there is little that separates me from these men. Having listened to their stories from childhood, I see the pieces of their experiences mirroring my own.

My students all took to heart the adage from Mary Karr that I introduced to them on the very first day. They wrote about the memories that burned "inside them for lifetimes, florid, unforgettable, demanding to be set down." And those memories were of their time in prison. It is a life they know better than the one they once knew outside Parchman. As the prisoner named R. wrote:

> I've witnessed so much corruption, violence, and death throughout my 20 years of incarceration. . . . I've witnessed inmates, including myself, denied medical treatment. Any time an inmate gets sick, it is the duty of the correctional officer to go through the proper procedures to ensure that the safety and wellbeing of the inmate is protected. I haven't met a correctional officer in the Mississippi prison system that has read the Mississippi Department of Corrections policies to know what is expected of them.

One prisoner wrote of his experiences of lockdown at Parchman, noting that "Unit 29 lockdown is a hell house" of suicidal prisoners and horrible living conditions. Once lockdown is over, it is "just like getting out of prison and going free." In his essay he refers to a character he calls "Slick Joe," a prisoner who preys on the women guards.

> I tell them [the women guards] to not let Slick Joe talk them into doing anything wrong. Because if she gets caught with drugs, a contraband cell phone, cash money, or having sex with Slick Joe, she will end up in the Sunflower County Jail, and Slick Joe will go on lock down for a very long time. But positive advice doesn't reach them all. Slick Joe is destroying many of these young ladies' lives, since when they get caught, they lose everything.

Reading this prisoner's essay confirms that prison is a place that puts into motion an uncontrollable and unending cycle of violence and deception. Maurice Clifton reminded me that there is so much that goes on inside Parchman that we will never see because it is hidden behind a veil. Yet there is also so much there that we refuse to see or choose to ignore.

In March 2024, a bill was introduced into the Mississippi State Legislature that would have closed Parchman and sent inmates to other prisons in the state. One argument for the bill was that the state had no reason to spend so much to improve the conditions in the prison when there were existing facilities in better repair. Juan Barnett, the state senator who introduced the bill, noted that Parchman is the way it is because of a lack of investment to ensure it is a secure and safe facility. What prompted the push for the bill was the release of videos, captured via an illegal cell phone, of violence and poor living conditions at Parchman, as well as several deaths by suicide. Yet none of the legislators visited the prison to see the conditions for themselves.

Although the bill failed, the debate over the bill's merits focused on improving the prison facilities rather than examining the reasons we incarcerate so many people in Mississippi. All of this should remind us that if we view correctional reform as simply closing problematic units and monitoring the presence of technology—technology that made those of us outside the prison walls aware of the violence and deprivation inside—the slow living death that exists at Parchman, at Mississippi's other prisons, and in prisons across America will continue. And the slow death by poverty and violence that exists outside Parchman in towns across the Delta will also continue until we begin to understand that the number of Mississippi Delta residents we incarcerate is correlated with poverty rates, a poor education system, and few job opportunities that pay a living wage.

It took death to bring attention to the crisis of neglect and abuse at Parchman. Unless citizens and policymakers begin to focus on the systemic issues that led to the neglect and abuse, both inside and outside the prison, the death in Parchman and in prisons across the country like it will continue.

CHAPTER 12

YOUR BLUES AIN'T LIKE MINE

I'm getting up so early in the morning,
I believe I'll dust my broom

—ROBERT JOHNSON, "Dust My Broom"

Clarksdale stands apart among towns in the Delta because of the way it blends the more urbane side of the region with the rougher country edges that reside in the cotton fields surrounding its borders. Rather than being shaped by the industry and influence of the Mississippi River like the towns of Greenville and Rosedale, Clarksdale bears the imprint of the railroads that spread across this flat expanse of land after the Civil War. The Victorian and Greek Revival houses clustered toward the end of Clark Street serve as reminders of the way the town's wealth was shaped by the timber and cotton transported on the railroad lines that converged here. The Italianate mansion once owned by the Cutrer family stands out from every other house surrounding it and seems to anchor the street. Playwright Tennessee Williams spent a great deal of time there in his youth and gained literary inspiration from the characters that once attended grand parties there. Like other houses at the end of Clark Street, its grandeur feels more Gilded Age than Old South plantation.

The town's founder, John Clark, cleared the land for timber in the late 1840s, which led the way for the cotton fields that followed when the town was founded in 1871. Of course, he placed his name on the town, which was first called "Clarksville"—the revision to "Clarksdale" perhaps used to differentiate it from a dying river town located further south in the state, near the Louisiana border. In the early part of the twentieth century, some even proclaimed Clarksdale "the golden buckle" of the cotton belt, given its role in the business of the Delta's main crop.

The railroad viaduct that has long divided Black and white Clarksdale still exists, though the train that once rolled through to Memphis and points north and south has long since ceased operation. Back in the early 1900s, a

Black man by the name of Nelson Jones built the first house south of those tracks. The lower floor was used as a saloon and the upper floors were a rooming house, of course for Black people only, on the basis of where it stood in relation to the town's racial dividing line. The house bore a large sign outside proclaiming the building as "Nelson Jones's New World." And since then, the side of Clarksdale across the railroad tracks has been known as "the New World," the name enduring among local people even though Jones's house is long gone.

Yet this place called the New World was not just inhabited by Black people. Along Issaquena Avenue, which runs between what might be called the old and the new world of Clarksdale, there were merchants who came to the Delta from Italy, China, and Lebanon. The Italians and Chinese were the descendants of people who arrived in the 1870s to supplement the agricultural labor force after the end of slavery. The Lebanese arrived in the 1880s to escape religious and political persecution in their homeland. The presence of these immigrant groups, including Jewish families from Eastern Europe, reveals the collision of cultures in Clarksdale, all of the groups seeking just to survive as small business owners. But what differentiated this part of Clarksdale, what marked the end of Issaquena Avenue as the "New World" district, was not the fact that it was the Black section of town with merchants whose origins were from around the globe. What separated it from the rest of Clarksdale was the music that flowed across the once narrow street, a style that came to be known as the blues.[1]

The blues had its origins among those who worked the levees, roads, cotton fields, and prisons. Back in 1901, Harvard archaeologist Charles Peabody found he was mesmerized by the music he heard from the Black workers who assisted him on a dig outside Clarksdale. Though he never called it the blues in his article "Notes on Negro Music," Peabody mentioned all the elements of the form in his description: the bending of notes, the use of three chords, and the themes of hard luck, love, and violence. He described the music as being "subdivided into melodic and rhythmic; the melodic into the sacred and profane, the rhythmic into general and apposite."[2] Later in 1903, bandleader W. C. Handy arrived in Clarksdale to be the director of the Knights of Pythias Band and lived on Issaquena Avenue. As Handy traveled through the Delta, playing dances for both white and Black audiences, he began to incorporate a sound he heard while waiting for a train in the town of Tutwiler a few miles to the south. What Handy heard was a man playing slide guitar with a knife and singing, "Goin' where the Southern cross' the Dog"—referring to the crossing of the Southern and Yazoo & Mississippi Valley railroads in Moorhead, forty-two miles to the south—which Handy adapted into "Yellow Dog Blues."

Issaquena Avenue marked where the blues was transplanted from the fields and levees into towns, first in Clarksdale and, later, the railroads as the people who created the music moved north, first to Memphis and, for some, later to Chicago. On Saturday nights, when people from surrounding farms and communities gathered to shop, eat, socialize, and listen to music, the part of town known as the New World would be so filled with jubilant revelers that people in this part of the Delta said you "couldn't stir the place with a stick." Of course, gambling and prostitution were part of the mix, so the presence of vice contributed to the crowds, composed of both Black and white people. Clarksdale may have been segregated, but there was lots of integration on a Saturday night.

Today there are rarely enough people along Issaquena Avenue to stir with a stick. On most Saturdays, there are remnants of the nightlife that once made this street bounce, with echoes of music in the background, but during much of the year it feels empty. The exception is the annual Juke Joint Festival, which brings throngs of tourists to events at the old New Roxy Theater—with music on every street corner, a carnival-like atmosphere, and the famed spectacle of monkeys riding dogs herding sheep—but the crowd is urban, international, and largely white. Some of them might be staying in a renovated sharecroppers' shotgun house at a place called the Shack Up Inn for $100 a night. "Guests can immerse themselves in the living history found within these restored sharecropper shacks," the promotional material proclaims. But that living history is hidden because these shacks now come equipped with heating, air conditioning, and a hot shower. There are no gaping holes in the floor where snakes and other critters might come visit at night, like they did in real sharecropper shacks. And there is no information that tells visitors what living in a Delta shotgun shack was truly like.

The Shack Up Inn is located on the site of the Hopson Plantation, one of the oldest plantations in Mississippi. The commissary for the plantation still stands and its presence casts a dark shadow. This was the place where sharecroppers were forced to buy food, clothing, and other items on credit and end up in debt to the plantation owner. Founded in 1852 by Howell H. Hopson, the plantation also introduced the world's first cotton picker, in partnership with the International Harvester Company, and the first mechanically picked cotton crop. Hopson also pioneered the aerial application of pesticides. Both innovations effectively ended the system of sharecropping. Yet no one tells visitors that the houses where they sleep emptied out because the laborers who once lived in them were forced to leave after technology and chemicals had made their jobs obsolete.

In its marketing material, the Shack Up Inn tells visitors that its shacks "are for people who appreciate history, the way it was. . . . Shacks are loved by artists, musicians, writers, and just plain cool folks. (Some people seem to think our shacks were slave shacks, not so.) They were sharecropper houses and or tenant houses." All of this seems to say, "Don't ask us any questions related to the real lives of people who once lived in dwellings like these free of modern amenities. Sharecropping may have replaced slavery as a labor system, but let's not discuss how the sharecropping system kept people oppressed in ways that mirrored slavery. To ask any questions about any of this is uncool."

In the world of blues tourism, the line between the past and the present is sometimes blurred or obscured. The Shack Up Inn is the most egregious example of this blurred line, but other evidence of this can be found on the streets of Clarksdale. What was once the white side of town, the other side of the viaduct on Issaquena across from the New World, now feels subsumed into that district. Today the blues is no longer relegated to a certain section of Clarksdale because, in a town that has lost a third of its population in the past twenty years, the tourist dollars that come from the blues must be drawn from everywhere, from every street running through town. Tourists are coming and going in Clarksdale, but longtime residents are leaving. "I'm getting up so early in the morning, I believe I'll dust my broom," Robert Johnson once sang. "Dusting my broom" meant "I'm getting out of town in a hurry, to leave for good." If you were talking about a relationship, it meant, "I'm putting you down. I won't be back no more."

In this town that helped bring the blues to the world, it's clear that lots of people have left and won't be back. "I believe, I believe my time ain't long," goes the refrain at the end of "Dust My Broom." It's almost as if the town of Clarksdale heard that refrain resounding through its streets soon after they emptied out as cotton became an industry of shrinking importance and people moved out, compounding the economic loss. The only thing they had left was the blues, so they decided to transform its sounds, rhythms, and refrains into an economic development plan. But for many residents of Clarksdale, particularly Black residents, the question remains: Is the exploitation that characterized sharecropping and the cotton industry being repeated as the town focuses on drawing tourists from around the world? It's a hard question to confront when the visual representation of that exploitative past is used to attract tourists in the present.

If the blues sung by the people W. C. Handy and Charles Peabody encountered was a means of doing, seeing, and being in the world—and shaped by pain and resistance to oppressive forces—the question remains of what happens to that music when it is seen as central to the town's economy rather than part of a larger history of struggle and resistance. Does it lose its sense of structure and style? "The very existence of the blues tradition is irrefutable evidence that those who evolved it respond to the vicissitudes of the human condition not with hysterics and desperation, but through the wisdom of poetry informed by pragmatic insight," wrote cultural critic Albert Murray in his essay "The Storyteller as Blues Singer."[3] Which leads me to wonder, does the blues respond only to the vagaries of commerce rather than the human condition when it is commercialized? Slavery, sharecropping, mechanization, and migratory labor are just a few of the ways the power structure of the Delta has sought to exploit its people and what they produced. Is blues tourism just another form of exploitation to add to this list?

The blues as an art form emerged immediately after the overthrow of Reconstruction. The music became an alternate form of communication in a period during which Black voices were silenced. As Shelby "Poppa Jazz" Brown told noted folklorist William Ferris:

> They got the blues because of how they made the folks here plow and hoe and chop cotton at daylight in the morning. They would get out there and work so hard they would sing "Hurry, hurry Sundown. Let tomorrow shine." They wanted the sun to go down so they could stop work. They worked too hard and they learned the blues from that.[4]

As someone who never had to work a cotton field and who always knew where his next meal was coming from, I have a different relationship with the music that is native to this land that shaped me. When asked about my connection with the blues, I always describe the art form as poetry wrapped in a struggle for survival. What I have found is that when I read Delta blues songs together, all the expressions of personal trials and pain form a Homeric, rhythmic epic poem that tell the numerous stories this flat expanse of land holds, as well as a few that have been hidden or masked. As someone who has studied literature my entire life, I think of the blues as a literary form more than a musical one. And I frame the blues as literature because I can never claim a connection to the personal pain that shaped the music. Though I am well acquainted with grief and pain, the blues from whence I came is not the same that sprang from the deep Delta soil.

But if I am being honest, I have not always viewed the blues in this way. To give you some perspective on where my thinking began, I must flash back to my nineteen-year-old self and the bicentennial summer of 1976. It was in that year of celebrations of patriotic pride that the north Mississippi town of Houston hosted a blues concert by Bukka White. White was born just south of Houston, so this was a homecoming concert. My family was then living in this town in the north Mississippi hills, a long way from where I grew up in the Piney Woods. I knew who Bukka White was, but I must confess that he was not at the top of the list of acts that a 1970s college student who loved rock and roll wanted to see. The summer before, I had seen the Rolling Stones in Memphis, who had local bluesman Furry Lewis warm up the crowd. My youthful insouciance did not allow me to connect the music of the Stones and Furry Lewis or, for that matter, Bukka White.

I saw Bukka White less as the legend that he was and more as a symbol of a past I felt disconnected from or even ashamed of. Now I know that in 1937 White recorded a minor hit, "Shake 'Em On Down," in Chicago, but that year he was also convicted for his role in a shooting incident and sentenced to Parchman Penitentiary, where John Lomax of the Library of Congress recorded him in 1939. He famously penned the song "Parchman Farm Blues." That song concludes with these words, the last of which echoes the words of a civil rights anthem:

I'm down on Parchman farm
But I sho' wanna go back home
But I hope some day
I will overcome

After his release from Parchman, White recorded twelve of his best-known songs at a Chicago session in 1940. During the war he settled in Memphis and worked at a defense plant. In Memphis he also performed with blues legend Frank Stokes, among others, and helped his younger cousin B. B. King become established on the local music scene.

White was brought back into the spotlight by John Fahey and Eugene Denson during the blues and folk revival in 1963. Ed Pearl, a West Coast club owner who presented White in 1963, called the bluesman "the bearer of the torch" of Delta blues. Both Fahey and Denson remembered White as a "very proud man whose spirit had not been broken."[5] The way I remember him was a man in a dark suit and tie, with a well-pressed white shirt. To my youthful eyes, he just looked like a slightly hipper version of a Baptist preacher.

When my mother told me that not only were we going to Bukka White's concert, but we were also having dinner with him, I was not entirely thrilled. In fact, I could barely disguise my disdain. "The blues is the music of oppression," I remember bellowing at my mother, echoing the way my friends thought of the music that I had grown up listening to on the clear-channel radio station WLAC from Nashville during the numerous trips I made across the Delta with my father. (WLAC and stations like it broadcast across the rural South free of frequency interference from other stations.) Both my mother and I were grieving the death of my father just three months before. She was trying to give me something to look forward to, while I was just trying to remain closed off in my grief.

But that wasn't all I was thinking about. The way I saw it then, the blues was a form of music shaped by the soul-crushing Delta plantation system. It was also too close to the world of Jim Crow, a system that is part of my living memory. I saw my generation as playing a role in putting all signs and symbols of oppression in their final resting place. From my trips to the Delta as a child, I had connected the oppression of Jim Crow with the blues. As I grew older, I learned that I was not alone.

My response makes sense now that I understand that like most university-trained Black intellectuals, I was distancing myself from a non-print, nonverbal Black culture that those of us who thought ourselves educated bluntly labeled as "ignorant." On a pop-culture level, I was part of a generation raised on Memphis and Motown soul, the music of the Black middle class. The blues was part of a Black working-class tradition, one that my generation of Black Southerners was seeking to place at a distance. What I failed to recognize at the age of nineteen was that to understand the very place I was from, I had to turn to the blues for many of my answers. That did not come until many years later.

What I wish my nineteen-year-old self knew was that the blues was the music of the resistance to the oppression of the plantation, not the music that could only be associated with the plantation. In an oral history interview conducted just a few weeks after I met him during that bicentennial summer in Mississippi, White told an interviewer he felt the blues music he played had its origins in what he described as "slavery times," since a few of the people who taught him music had once been enslaved.[6] Had I been a bit more enlightened, I would have learned about that connection directly from Bukka White and engaged with a man with a living link to Mississippi's history of enslavement. That interview was conducted in a hospital in Beverly, Massachusetts, in July 1976—just about a month after I met him—where White was recuperating after suffering a stroke on a flight from Memphis to Boston. I saw one of his final performances. By February 1977, he was dead.

Now I know that the blues are a means of articulating what life was like in the Delta and demonstrate a toughness of spirit, not subservience. There is that daily anguish of the blues that Poppa Jazz talked about, the conflicts between farm laborers and overseers that Bukka White refers to in his music, but there is also a subversiveness to the music. The Devil is mentioned quite often in the blues, but the Devil here is not necessarily Beelzebub himself; rather, he is the white man keeping the Black man down. By conflating the Devil and whiteness, the blues singer is expressing frustration in a way that is coded.

Though I am now fully engaged with the blues and its cultural meaning, this awareness has taken me years. Moving into an apartment off Issaquena Avenue in Clarksdale, with the viaduct to the New World just a block away, was a full-circle moment for me. I understand why people come to Clarksdale to connect with the blues, since the signs of its presence are everywhere, whether on Mississippi Blues Trail markers or in the music that plays somewhere in this town every night. Yet most tourists I meet in blues clubs, from Ground Zero to the grittier Red's, come to Clarksdale just to have a good time. As music writer Preston Lauterbach reminded me one day as we discussed the disconnect between the blues and its history,

"For every one of us who tries to understand the truth that exists inside what created the blues, there are hundreds more people who are just here to party." These people don't want to be reminded of the pain associated with the blues. I don't want to lash out at these fun-loving tourists, making the inverse argument of what my nineteen-year-old self would have made yet filled with a more aged haughtiness. When I think about it, I am reminded of what Bukka White's cousin B. B. King would have probably said to me: "Crying won't help you now, since you've been so mean to me." But I do realize my generation of Black Southerners' disconnection from and avoidance of this music is part of what for more than half a century has separated the blues from race, pain, resistance, and the land of its origin with only the backbeat left throbbing in the background. Yet I believe it is not too late to reconnect the blues with its origins—and I wonder if the cultural tourism in modern-day Clarksdale has a role to play.

In Clarksdale, the past has a way of popping out and hitting you like a sharp lightning strike. There is always something in your field of vision that reminds you of the richness of the past as well as the pain. The old Greyhound bus station where civil rights protests took place is just down the street from where musician W. C. Handy arrived and soon connected with the blues. Across the street stands what looks like a fire escape, but it was once the colored entrance to the Paramount Theater. The "Colored Entrance" sign is long gone, yet because this and other segregated entries were such a key part of the architecture of Jim Crow, for those of us who remember them they are difficult to overlook. Each morning when I walk past, I look up and stare at its zigzagging stairs. I want to plead to the souls who once traipsed up to that balcony to speak to me through the ages. Its rusting awning, weathered by more than a hundred years of sun and rain, reminds me that at one time I would not have been allowed to occupy the apartment I have just a few doors down.

Next to the stairs of the theater is an entrance boarded up with white plywood and these words etched on it in red letters: "Let me be strong enough to overcome the fear of shedding another layer." I'm not sure what this means, but each time I read these words I turn my gaze toward a small opening through which feral cats enter and exit. I also see empty pizza boxes, a sign that a person or group of people are also using the space as shelter. This type of poverty and abandonment is something the Delta needs to shed, yet it is part of the fabric of life in Clarksdale. It's hard to avoid it.

The presence of poverty is not driving tourists away from Clarksdale. In 2019, visitors to Coahoma County, home of Clarksdale, spent more than $68 million, according to a 2019 report by the Mississippi Development Authority. Yet only 13 percent of the jobs in the county are tourism related. Clarksdale may have gone all in on blues tourism, but the question that people both discuss openly and whisper around town is, who benefits from visitors who come to experience the land where the blues began, whether they are just passing through or staying for a major blues festival? Is blues tourism a sign of real change for the future of the people of the Delta, or just something to deceive those who visit to feel as if progress is in motion?

I began to examine that question in Cat Head, a shop that bills itself as "Mississippi's Blues Store." The store features blues records, books, and merchandise, but is also a clearinghouse for Clarksdale's seven-days-a-week music scene. The person in the center of it all is Roger Stolle, a man in his mid-fifties whose unlined face makes him look at least twenty years younger. Perhaps the secret of his youthfulness is that he left corporate marketing with the May Department Stores Company to explore the blues and music in Clarksdale more than twenty years ago. "I came to Clarksdale for the blues, but I stayed for the people," he tells me from behind the counter of his shop, where he keeps a framed copy of the first 25-cent piece he made in his business, which he sees as a monument to his thriftiness. His first sale was paid for with a ten dollar bill, a two dollar bill, and some change, but he decided to frame only the quarter from that transaction. Stolle's ability to, as old Delta folks would say, "squeeze a dollar 'till it hollers" is part of the secret to running a business that is rooted in passion but also must pay the bills.

Stolle's interest in music began with the death of Elvis Presley in 1977, when he became obsessed with Presley's relationship to the blues. Elvis's life, death, and music made front-page headlines even in Stolle's hometown of Dayton, Ohio. Soon he began to pay attention to the Elvis recordings that moved him, such as versions of Mississippi-born classics like "That's All Right" and "Mystery Train," as well as Deep South–penned blues and R&B songs like "Good Rockin' Tonight," "Milkcow Blues Boogie," and "When It Rains, It Really Pours." Then he began to examine songwriting credits and liner notes, and a blues fan was born.

After working in corporate marketing for more than a decade, Stolle made his first visit to the Delta in the 1990s to take what he called his "Dead Man's Blues Tour," because he thought everyone who wrote and played the music he loved was gone. He quickly discovered that a few folks he thought were gone were among the living in and around Clarksdale. "On my first visit, the welcome signs to Mississippi said, 'Mississippi, Feels Like Coming Home.' And then when I kept coming back and people told me stories about music, race, and history, I was drawn to the people. And then I decided to move here."

Stolle didn't just move to Clarksdale on a whim. It took him six years to decide to move South from his corporate job in St. Louis, and he had a purpose. "My idea was to help other like-minded individuals and entities organize and promote the blues from within—and by all means necessary." Clarksdale had what he referred to as a great "blues infrastructure," with musicians, history, and venues, but he felt it just needed to be promoted and organized into something people could rely on. "I figured if we were the only town with blues and music between Memphis and New Orleans, when people were traveling between those two places maybe they would stop here, if they knew it had an active music scene."

More than twenty years later, Clarksdale has music on stage 365 days of the year. But it is clear Stolle is not getting rich on Clarksdale's music. Although he is passionate about blues in a way free of academic theories and jargon, he does worry that the music is becoming more the province of people who only understand the structure of the music and not the experience from which it originated. His work, as he sees it, is to keep the legacy of the blues alive, and he is quick to remind those who visit his shop to think beyond the beat of the music. He wants them to connect with the history.

"In Mississippi we have a blues trail, a country music trail, a freedom trail for civil rights history, and now a writers trail. I fear when we are attracting tourists here, whether to the Delta or elsewhere, we are pushing them into one thing. What they need to understand is how all this creativity that springs from the Delta and Mississippi is connected. Right now, I don't think many people see the connections."

Kinchen O'Keefe directs tourism for Clarksdale and agrees with Stolle, who serves as a volunteer with the tourism bureau O'Keefe directs. While Stolle wants to keep the history behind the music alive, O'Keefe wants the tourism associated with the music to be part of what sustains Clarksdale.

O'Keefe, who is known as "Bubba," is a Clarksdale native who remembers when the streets of downtown were more vibrant. His father was the mayor of the town in the early post–World War II years, when Clarksdale was more prosperous but functioned under a system of segregation that kept the blues relegated to the Black side of town. He's not ignoring the racial history of exploitation in the Delta. That would be hard to do, given that his grandfather was the superintendent of the state penitentiary at Parchman and helped develop its feudal system of using convicts to farm the land, with the substantial profits from its cotton crop going directly to the coffers of the state of Mississippi. His ancestors didn't sing the blues, but rather created the system that led to the music. "I'm painfully aware of how my history is tied in with the old Clarksdale," he tells me in his office, which is located in the town's old train depot. But he is passionate about building a new Clarksdale.

When I ask O'Keefe who benefits from blues tourism, he agrees after some probing that no one is getting rich off this niche industry. He's done some real estate speculation and redevelopment, including renovating old buildings and converting them to loft apartments for tourists. Soon I discover that although he no longer owns it, he developed the building where I am living. But O'Keefe says in a self-deprecating tone that he is not a good enough developer to be called an entrepreneur. He sees his work as building a creative class in Clarksdale. "Money kills creativity," O'Keefe tells me one hot afternoon, and not with a hint of irony in his voice as he gazes out at the summer heat rising from the street.

As O'Keefe tells me his philosophy of tourism as a means of building community, I can't help but think of those in Clarksdale who have visible wealth, most of whom are connected to cotton and agricultural businesses in some way. I often drive past their columned and gated homes out near the Clarksdale Country Club. Many of these residents have lives that exist outside of the Clarksdale created by newcomers like Roger Stolle and the musicians and artists from around the country and the world whom I encounter at music venues and other gatherings. The creative class O'Keefe is seeking to create is in no way part of the private Clarksdale Country Club golf tournaments with cash prizes in the mid-five figures that I witness from afar and hear about in passing. The sheltered world of the planter class is still in place in Clarksdale, and blues tourism isn't drawing them out into the creative world O'Keefe speaks of so passionately.

Although O'Keefe feels tourism needs the support of the more monied people in Clarksdale, he doesn't see them as the people he is targeting. He's interested in visitors from abroad or those whose families left during the Great Migration but are now returning. A group of French tourists stood in the lobby the day I visited. And just the day before a woman had come from California to do family genealogy research. "What I want to build through blues tourism is a sense of hope in this town," O'Keefe says. "And I want everyone to feel welcome. There are people in this town who don't know hope exists. Despair comes next. I'm just trying to keep despair from taking over this town."

Yet O'Keefe knows that tourism is not the cure-all and that despair exists in this town. When I went just a few blocks across town and visited the office of Clarksdale mayor Chuck Espy to continue the discussion about the role of tourism in shaping Clarksdale, the only response I could elicit was, "Tourism has its place." I couldn't even engage him to talk about the tourism at all. Crime and public safety were more of a concern, given that Clarksdale has one of the highest crime rates in the state of Mississippi. Since 2019, Espy has even been paying people convicted of crimes to leave the city out of personal funds. When I asked about his public safety goals for Clarksdale, he was passionate about this initiative. "If you're just simply a gang member, a criminal, or a drug dealer, move out of this city now. We'll help you start a new life somewhere else." He didn't even flinch when I expressed surprise at this approach. "You'll never solve the Delta's issues if you simply maintain the status quo," Espy explained. But he also feels solving the problem of crime will lead to more jobs and told me that 25 percent of the new jobs in the Delta in 2022 were created in Clarksdale.

Roger Stolle, Bubba O'Keefe, and Chuck Espy represent three different perspectives on Clarksdale, the blues, and tourism. Stolle is the newcomer to the Delta but is aware of the history and has a strong interest in preserving the connection between Clarksdale's history and the music it nurtured. O'Keefe is the consummate insider and native who truly loves his hometown and doesn't want it to fall into despair. Both men are white. Espy is a Black mayor of a majority-Black city in which economic power is held by powerful, monied white people. He is passionate about solving the problem of crime but also about getting more people employed, since he believes there is a link between unemployment and crime. By not discussing tourism, he is echoing what many Black Clarksdale residents believe:

the town's emphasis on blues tourism comes at the expense of the needs of its poor and Black residents.

These conversations about tourism, crime, and economics led me to think about how the variation in the lived experience among the people in Clarksdale leads to similar gaps in what different residents think of the Delta's past, present, and future. Chuck Espy's message seems to be that poverty and oppression may have created the blues, but that he needs to keep those forces at bay today, even if it means shipping people out of town. The Black residents I spoke with weren't skeptical about blues tourism. It's just that they wanted a broader emphasis on not only the blues but the arts in general, as well as local civil rights history.

Roger Stolle and Bubba O'Keefe are both aware of the skepticism surrounding blues tourism and expressed the need for a civil rights museum, given Clarksdale's role in the Civil Rights Movement not just in the Delta but in Mississippi as a whole. NAACP leader Aaron Henry's drugstore on Fourth Street in the New World neighborhood was once the center of civil rights activities. Henry was also involved in the Southern Christian Leadership Conference and brought Martin Luther King Jr. to speak in Clarksdale in 1958. The lot where the drugstore once stood is now empty, since the building burned in 1993. An iron silhouette of Henry with outstretched arms rests on a barren spot, along with a sign that says, "Aaron Henry stood tall here." A marker notes the amount that has been raised for a civil rights museum. The needle has been stuck at $20,000 for the past few years, although the project received a $50,000 contribution in 2023. Yet the impression the sign gives is that progress is frozen.

When you move beyond the blues in Clarksdale, the dynamic between historic preservation and community development seems to be askew. Mississippi Blues Trail markers dot the streets of downtown. The Mississippi Writers Trail marker for Richard Ford stands outside the stately Carnegie Public Library, where he wrote his novel *The Sportswriter*, and Tennessee Williams's marker greets visitors to the Cutrer Mansion, one of the sources of his literary inspiration. The Mississippi Civil Rights Trail marker for Aaron Henry, however, stands in front of an empty lot.

One spot in Clarksdale seems to have all the elements of blues, literary history, civil rights, and the birth of rock and roll all wrapped together. The Riverside Hotel was a hospital when Bessie Smith died there in 1937 after an automobile accident. It closed soon after Smith's death and became a hotel in 1944. After a mention in *The Negro Motorist Green Book*—the guide for safe places to stay during the Jim Crow era—the hotel did brisk business with Black travelers between Memphis and New Orleans, particularly musicians. Ike Turner wrote "Rocket 88" there, which is said to be the first rock and roll song. Duke Ellington, Sam Cooke, Muddy Waters, John Lee Hooker, Howlin' Wolf, and Robert Nighthawk all stayed there. Sam Cooke's iconic "A Change Is Gonna Come" pays tribute to the nearby Sunflower River and may have found its inspiration from a stay at the Riverside Hotel.

Once again, the Riverside Hotel is closed. Since it is considered one of the most endangered historic sites in the country, it has received a significant grant for its restoration. When it reopens, it holds the potential to create a competing vision for how to preserve and promote the Delta's rich musical and civil rights history. But for that competing vision to become a shared one, the various parts of Clarksdale must reach a consensus.

On the wall of a building across from the old Greyhound bus station stands a large image of Aaron Henry along with Vera Pigee, who helped charter the NAACP in Clarksdale and was also a local hairdresser who used her salon as a base for activism. Back in the fall of 1961, Pigee and fellow NAACP member Idessa Johnson challenged the state's segregation laws at that same bus station where her portrait stands today.

Pigee's image serves as a reminder of the profound and meaningful role Black women played in the Civil Rights Movement, not just in Clarksdale but across the South. Her image and Henry's are also a reminder that this is the future site of the North Mississippi Civil Rights Museum, which Black Clarksdale sees as completing its vision of the town and making this place not just about the blues but connecting it with the pride and resistance that underlie the music. Right now, the building stands empty. Yet the vision for completing the space is evident in architectural renderings that decorate the windows. They show that this once and future museum will not just be a memorial to the past. Along with being a museum, the building will be a community gathering place, a theater, and a place to help develop the next generation of entrepreneurs in Clarksdale. It is all part of the work of the social justice nonprofit Higher Purpose, run by Tim Lampkin.

Lampkin tells me his mantra is, "Do good work and make a difference in the community." He's very serious about his work, and each time we speak, he places a time limit on our conversation to make sure he remains focused on his work. When he tells me that he works, sleeps, and eats just to develop and support Black-owned businesses in the Delta, I know from the tone of his voice he's not kidding.

Like other Black Clarksdale residents and Mayor Espy, Lampkin sees a role for tourism. He just thinks there needs to be more focused discussions about the actual benefits of tourism, and that perhaps the singular focus on tourism is keeping Clarksdale and the Delta in general from examining ways to create systemic and intentional change. Right now, that change is not coming about through tourism. Lampkin feels those in power in Clarksdale should be asking, "How can we have an economic strategy that embraces tourism and also helps to create opportunity in the community and lead to economic justice?"

After working in a sales job, Lampkin eventually found himself employed by a large bank. His time in banking put him face-to-face with the inequities inherent to small business lending practices. There was an obvious disparity between who was at the table funding community-based businesses and who was not at the table but had better knowledge about community needs and opportunities. "When it came down to who was making the decisions about who got funding, I realized the people making those decisions didn't have any connection to the lived experience of the people who could have benefited the most. I decided that I never wanted to be in a position where I was doing things to the community versus doing things *for* the community." So, Lampkin left banking and decided to start Higher Purpose in 2016.

What Lampkin likes about his work now is that he is helping people to create businesses to have a better life rather than just fostering a type of entrepreneurship that is about getting rich. "One is about survival and the other is just about the pursuit of success," Lampkin tells me as a way to distinguish between his brand of entrepreneurship and the kind large banks finance. He also reminds me that some potential funders are leery of the work he does. "When I say my work encourages entrepreneurship, that seems fine. But when I say I am trying to build a network of Black businesses in the Delta, some people get worried." In other words, the old plantation ethos is still at play in the Delta.

Higher Purpose owns the building that will house the civil rights museum and the group's other pursuits. A large foundation grant made the purchase possible. The challenge now is raising the money to fulfill the vision Lampkin has for this space. He says he is committed to creating some form of radical change in Clarksdale and the Delta, much like Vera Pigee did with her activism along with the group of women now known as the "Beautiful Agitators." But he recognizes that none of this can happen without a real reckoning in Clarksdale and across the Delta. "We need some type of community healing and discussions about the legacy of the Civil Rights Movement. There also needs to be a shift in power with respect to our political leadership. We're not building a pipeline of new leaders who can create change."

Reconciliation is the missing piece of the Delta's reckoning with its civil rights past, from school integration to politics and voting rights. In fact, the entire nation is missing this piece, and this lack of active engagement with the past is keeping the country and the Delta frozen in a version of the past that never existed. What makes the Delta different from other parts of the country is that the inequities of the past can be felt in the very air that surrounds you, and the need for that reconciliation is deeper than the deep layers of rich alluvium that cover this land. In Clarksdale you can see those past inequities covered up or masked by the veil of hipness: for many tourists and people living in the town, it is simply a beautiful ruin rather than a place with a deeply layered and painful past.

America developed through a dual-caste system; this inequity exists in every city and hamlet across this country. Clarksdale and the rest of the Delta particularly suffered through this dual-caste development, through additional inequities tied to cotton and the plantation system that took hold after the end of slavery. Yet Clarksdale has a rich and unique history, one that may be getting watered down as it seeks to market an invented idea of itself built on the bones of its history.

Living in Clarksdale changed my relationship with the blues. Now I understand how the blues expresses the life of the people of the Delta and what they have confronted. Still, the version of the blues that this town sells is not the blues I have come to know and love. When I listen to the blues now, I hear a struggle for equality that echoes across time. Clarksdale's blues seem to be forged out of equal parts ambition and willful blindness.

Writer Albert Murray believed that no one has ever been able to get rid of the blues. "You can only drive them away and keep them at bay for the time being. Because they are always there, as if waiting and watching."[7] The blues are waiting and watching on the streets of Clarksdale, yet I sometimes wonder whose blues are echoing across its streets. The words and music sound authentic, yet something about the spirit in the music doesn't feel true.

CHAPTER 13

CASINO LIGHTS

You know it's a cryin' old shame
Workin' man works every day
Meet up one of them good old Georgia Skin men
Let him make a fool outta him

—BUKKA WHITE, "Georgia Skin Game"

If you drive north from Clarksdale on famed Highway 61, you'll run into the Delta town of Tunica. Tunica sits just thirty miles south of Memphis, Tennessee, yet it stands a world apart from the world of the Bluff City. Delta writer David Cohn famously said that the Mississippi Delta began in the lobby of the Peabody Hotel in Memphis: "If you stand near [the hotel's] fountain in the middle of the lobby, where ducks waddle and turtles drowse, you will see everybody who is anybody in the Delta."[1] During my childhood travels around the Delta, Tunica and its environs always felt like the end of the Delta; in comparison, the streets of Memphis felt foreign and otherworldly. Perhaps that is because as a child, I found the fields in and around Tunica to be so vast, almost limitless. Arriving in Memphis and confronting its urbanity meant leaving behind the Delta's limitless flatness and expansiveness. Memphis too was a Southern space, but for me it stood apart from the Delta rather than being a part of it.

In Cohn's statement, one can see how perspective works in the Delta. If you are a planter, Memphis is a place of beginnings associated with prosperity, a place to be seen a certain way by one's peers. Those who work the fields may never leave Tunica for Memphis, except on a passage further north to Chicago. For one group, Memphis feels like a paradise to display one's wealth and standing by being seen in a lush hotel lobby with a twice-daily procession of ducks. For another, Memphis is a path that leads to a possible escape from poverty and penury.

Like much of the Delta, Tunica is home to vast fields planted in cotton, rice, and soybeans, with a few commercial catfish ponds dotting the landscape. Tunica's boundless agricultural expanses, like all of those in the Delta, were created by clearing the land of a jungle-thick covering of trees. Tunica also stands at a bend in the Mississippi River that has changed its course so often that what was once Mississippi shore a century ago is now Arkansas territory.[2] Now a new created environment has been placed on top of the one created at the turn of the nineteenth century. Across the vast fields that stretch to the Mississippi River levee stand tall hotel casinos that look like they belong on the strip in Las Vegas. The Hollywood Casino and Sam's Town are separated by both a boulevard and a field planted in cotton, corn, or soybeans, depending on the year of crop rotation. It is an odd juxtaposition, as if somehow the lobby of the Peabody has been displaced to the Delta, yet without the status and grandeur. These huge placeless spaces have been plopped onto an environment created by humanity, as well as time and the Mississippi River. And there are no ducks in the lobby, only the smell of stale cigarette smoke wafting its way from the floor of the casino.

The tall buildings and bright lights are new to this part of the Delta, something bluesman Robert Johnson could not have imagined when he was growing up on the Abbay and Leatherman Plantation down the road from where the casinos now stand. For more than thirty years, Tunica has embraced the gambling Johnson captured in his song "Last Fair Deal Gone Down," a work song that tells the story of gambling and romance on the Gulf and Ship Island Railroad. "If you cry about a nickel, you'll die 'bout a dime," Johnson once sang in a high and expressive voice. Unlike the Delta, the Mississippi Gulf Coast long had a culture of gambling, albeit illegal gambling for much of the twentieth century. Now the gambling games of Georgia Skin that were played on the railroad cars Johnson sang about—whether bound for the Gulf or in transit to the coast—have come to the plantation land where he spent his youth, if in a more comfortable and sophisticated setting.

When civil rights activist Jesse Jackson visited the Delta town of Tunica in 1985, gambling was the last thing on his mind. Instead, he rallied its residents by acknowledging that their town was a place that had "dropped out of the bottom of [President Ronald] Reagan's safety net."[3] Jackson said he was "disappointed about the collapse of government at all levels on the problems of these people." In front of a packed audience at Rosa Fort High School, Jackson led the crowd in chants of "War on poverty!" and "I am somebody!"—the latter one identified as Jackson's signature.

Five US congressmen accompanied Jackson and pledged to help the community move forward with legal help and college tuition assistance. Few remember that promise. But what everyone remembers is that Jackson proclaimed the town of Tunica to be "America's Ethiopia" because its poverty and lack of electricity and indoor plumbing were more akin to the living standards found in a country overtaken by war, famine, and natural disaster. The Black community of Kestevan Alley—otherwise known as "Sugar Ditch"—became a focus of national attention because of reports of hunger and parasitic and bacteriological infections. What had earned the neighborhood its nickname was not sugar but raw sewage, since many residents had no sewer connections. People lived in collapsing shacks filled with vermin. The poverty rate of the county was then 56 percent. When CBS's *60 Minutes* visited Sugar Ditch in 1985, reporter Morley Safer compared it with South African townships, noting that the only difference was that in Tunica "apartheid is there for all Americans to see."

Nearly a decade later, casinos and gambling were introduced as a commercial force that would save the Delta economy. Legal gambling came to Tunica County in the early 1990s bringing the promise of prosperity to an area known for its extreme poverty and racial segregation. Gambling came to the Mississippi Gulf Coast as well. But over twenty years after the casinos opened, the gambling landscapes of the Gulf and the Delta are completely different. Gulf Coast casinos merely made legal what was once illegal and were compatible with a place that already had a culture of resort vacationers. Constructing casinos in Tunica was a way to create a new resort and resort culture, built on the romance of the Delta and the Mississippi River, with its connection to riverboat gambling in the early twentieth century.

Gambling traditionally took place on Mississippi riverboats to avoid anti-gambling laws in Mississippi and other states along the river. Now, the gambling could take place on land, free of restrictions and with the generated tax revenue going to Tunica County. The advent of casinos in Tunica was also pitched as a way out of poverty for the region's residents, as if the money that bettors gambled would magically materialize into jobs. But the advent of casino gambling has not completely lived up to its promise. The county's unemployment rate in July 2024 was 4 percent, fairly average for Mississippi. Even with revenues of roughly $759 million from casino gambling, a county that ranked among the nation's poorest in the 1980s still has roughly a third of its residents living in poverty. The people who lived in the infamous Sugar Ditch may now have indoor plumbing, but they are not much better off economically than they were when Jesse Jackson visited in 1985.

Mississippi writer Kiese Laymon famously remarked that "no meaningful promises are made or kept in casinos."[4] If you look at Tunica today, you understand exactly what he means. The promise that gambling could create an economic miracle and transform Tunica was based not on sound planning, nor was it a promise that could ever be realized. Today, Harrah's Casino is shuttered and empty, a victim of the Great Recession of 2008. Thick blades of grass poke through holes in its now-empty asphalt parking lot. The building that once housed the headquarters of Mississippi's Casino Gambling Commission is scheduled to be demolished. Sam's Town has demolished some of its hotel space since it was not being used. Wind farms are being constructed to compensate for the tax revenues that casinos are no longer bringing in. The shining buildings that remain represent only the prospect of an economic miracle, not evidence of one.

Tunica's approach to its decisions about casino gambling was akin to a cotton farmer speculating on his next crop, albeit with a little less precision. Cotton farmers calculate their profits based on the expected price, expected yield, and the number of acres planted, but in the end what they do is play the odds that in one year cotton might be more profitable than another crop, such as corn or soybeans. It seems as if in Tunica, the back-of-the-envelope calculation on long-term profitability of casinos was based more on irrational exuberance than a well-thought-out calculus. This poor county in the Delta believed that casino gambling would put it on an upward trajectory that would change its tragic moniker from Little Ethiopia to Little Las Vegas on the Mississippi Delta. The land itself is still being farmed for cotton, soybeans, and corn, which I see as a sign that those who leased land to the casinos were not willing to give up all their land on a risky bet. They knew that one day someone would have to pay up when that marker came due, though seemingly no one else took the odds into account.

Alongside Highway 61 stands a Tunica welcome center that is steeped in the culture and artifacts of the blues. The rustic-looking wood building and its neon signage are intended to evoke the feel of a Delta roadhouse juke joint. It is a sign that this part of the Delta thought it was going to turn a corner that combined blues tourism with gambling. Instead, what it found was that you can't compartmentalize poverty into an economic or cultural box, add a new entity into the mix, and instantly expect things to change. It is impossible to determine the manner in which a region's path out of poverty might unfold in particular contexts and conditions over time. Or how that supposed train to prosperity might come to a screeching halt.

Randall Towns doesn't remember Tunica without casinos. He was born in Clarksdale in 1990, the year the state legislature legalized casino gambling in Tunica, and was two years old when the first casino opened. At the age of seven, when his family moved to Tunica, the casinos were fully operational and were still expected to be the driver for a new economy in the Delta.

I met Towns outside the Tunica History Museum, where he is a maintenance worker. On the day we met, I had come to visit the exhibitions at the museum, which I remembered from a previous visit. When I found the exhibition space locked, he kindly informed me that the facility was under renovation. Unable to gather the history of Tunica from the museum walls, I improvised and he agreed to tell me about how he sees the impact the casinos have had on the town he calls home.

"I grew up gambling, that's why I still gamble at the casinos," Towns tells me with some pride in his voice. He grew up in a single-parent household where, he said, "I essentially raised myself." After getting kicked out of school in the eleventh grade, he was sent to the Oakley Training School, a juvenile justice facility run by the Mississippi Department of Corrections. After getting his GED, he tells me he "got baptized and found God."

Like many Black Tunica residents, Towns doesn't think the casinos have changed the town for the better. "Casinos have run this town dry. You can't even find a quarter on the ground," he tells me. When I ask him what he means by that, he says, "This is a town where a lot of people need help. The casinos were supposed to change this town, but they didn't."

Much like David Cohn's idea of where the Delta begins, the feeling about whether Tunica's experiment in casino gambling is a success is a matter of perspective. For Black residents, the amenities that came to the community from the casino's tax revenue—such as the museum where Towns works, an Olympic-sized swimming pool, and a professionally designed golf course—don't really benefit them. When I ask Towns if he uses any of these facilities, he says he doesn't but points out they are open to all.

Yet he does agree with me that the spending from the tax revenue has not benefited working-class people like him.

Even with the presence of casinos, Tunica County has a poverty rate of 31 percent, a little over half of what it was during its days of being labeled "America's Ethiopia." As the *Washington Post* reported in 2015, of the hundreds of millions of dollars that Tunica earned from gambling between 1993 and 2015, just a tiny bit—about 2.5 percent, according to county records—was used on social programs to help county residents who live in poverty.[5] While county leaders thought casino gambling would allow this very poor region to catch up, they underestimated the depth of the poverty that exists here. Tunica may no longer be America's Ethiopia, but it is still much like the rest of the downtrodden Delta in its concentration of Black poverty.

To begin the casino gambling experiment in Tunica, the political class had to convince the landowners that they would benefit from this new revenue source. Since the vast majority of local landowners are also descendants of the county's plantation class, they owned much of the land in the county and many lived in the separately incorporated town of Tunica, which has a vibrant and well-maintained downtown, unlike many in the Delta. The town of Tunica and the county exist in separate municipal realms, yet poverty infringes on both places. For example, what was once known as the "Sugar Ditch" is inside the city limits of Tunica. Yet quite a few of the landowners who lived in the town of Tunica were already wealthy, having inherited their wealth from parents, grandparents, and great grandparents, but, given the decline in the cotton industry, the members of this landowning class were not building new wealth. In the Delta's past, this would have been the group resistant to bringing in a new form of industry. But they did not resist this time, perhaps because they stood to make millions of dollars selling and leasing their land in the county to the casino industry.

In the first decade of the casino's existence, Tunica had an abundance of jobs and unemployment dropped to 4 percent. Yet its residents only moved from being the unemployed poor to being the working poor. At 31 percent, Tunica County may have a lower poverty rate than other counties in the Delta, but it is still more than double the national poverty rate.

During the boom times, Tunica County moved to slash property taxes to the lowest level of any county in the state, an overture to businesses and investors. Once again, the beneficiary was the wealthy landowner. But now the casino boom is over. Harrah's Casino has been demolished, and the county has been looking to repurpose the long-vacant hotel portion of the property. In the spring of 2024, county officials considered a proposal for repurposing Harrah's Hotel, as well as another hotel called The Veranda, as a facility to house unaccompanied migrant children. The proposal was met with some opposition, but the fact that the proposal was even considered indicates that Tunica's days as a tourist destination are over.[6]

Randall Towns may still gamble at the casinos, along with other local people, yet the reason he gave for his regular visits was that there was simply nothing else to do in Tunica. Judging from the empty parking lots on Saturdays and the buildings set for demolition, people outside Tunica don't see the town as the destination many had hoped it would be. With other casinos in neighboring Arkansas, there is little reason to cross the Mississippi River to come gamble in Tunica. But the casinos cannot survive simply on local business, which makes the town's economic future uncertain. As Towns put it, "With other casinos around now, why would you want to come to Tunica?"

For years, people touted that the "Tunica Miracle" had arrived, since it appeared that America's Ethiopia had been transformed into the "Diamond of the Delta." Promotional pamphlets about the county proclaimed Tunica to be "One of America's Success Stories." At the height of the Tunica Miracle, Tunica was the country's third-largest gambling destination, behind Atlantic City and Las Vegas. The opening of casinos in nearby states was the first disruption, as it led to a decline in casino business. Then came the COVID-19 global pandemic, which shuttered the casinos. While other destinations have slowly recovered, Tunica has not been able to get the casino business back to pre-pandemic levels. At its peak, Tunica had nine casinos; now it only has six.

The casino gambling experiment in Tunica promised more than it could ever deliver. The Tunica Miracle was only temporary, not permanent. The tax windfall that Tunica County felt with the advent of casino gambling blinded its leaders to a cruel fact about the industry they placed their hopes on: the riches the gambling industry brings are fleeting. When the county cut property taxes, it only benefited the wealthy. As the *Washington Post* reported in 2015, 76 percent of the county's property tax revenue comes from just a hundred property-owning entities and a small number of in-dividuals among the 3,200 who own land in the county.

Tunica's leaders failed to see that casino gambling is a cultural ame-nity, not a panacea for the economic woes of a county that was once the poorest in the nation. Maybe Tunica's economy would have had a stron-ger post-pandemic recovery had there been more diversified economic development along with the casinos. Instead, the county saw gambling as a way to forge a new future rather than one piece of an overall economic development strategy.

Even with a more diverse economy, the historical economic structure of the Delta would have held Tunica back. As former Mississippi gover-nor William Winter observed in 1985, "There remains the other South [the Delta], largely rural, undereducated, and under-productive and underpaid, that threatens to become a permanent shadow of distress and deprivation in a region that less than a decade ago had promised it better days." The promise of better days came from the Civil Rights Movement, which forced the end of public discrimination, but did nothing to change the economic and social structures of the Delta, including who held economic power. And the economic structure of Tunica changed little from the civil rights era to the time casinos landed on the landscape. Just like in the agricul-tural economy of the pre–civil rights era, it was the landowning planter class that benefited the most from the advent of casino gambling rather than the underclass that Mississippi leaders thought the casino industry would lift out of poverty.

The policy challenge Tunica faced was to simultaneously achieve eco-nomic development and poverty reduction. But the link between the two was weak, since there was never a reckoning with the historical systems that cre-ated the deep intergenerational poverty that had long existed among Tunica's Black citizens. The economic development that was on offer did not begin to touch the ideas and attitudes that created the poverty of the Sugar Ditch neighborhood and elsewhere in Tunica and allowed it to linger for decades.

Then there is the question that begs to be asked: Is casino gambling actually a policy prescription? Tunica's leaders saw themselves as creating a new market for jobs, which they did. But what Tunica reveals is that mar-kets are not enough. The jobs that were created were mostly low-paying and did not allow for much economic mobility.

Social scientists who study the impact of casino gambling find that it is in education where communities see the biggest gap between promise and reality when it comes to the benefits from gambling revenue.[7] Schools and school populations typically experience few positive gains, and Tunica is no exception. Twelve percent of gambling revenue was devoted to the public school system, and it led to virtually no improvement. But property taxes are the main source of funding for school districts, and Tunica County cut those taxes during the casino boom, effectively cutting the flow of tax revenue to schools. A 1997 state report chided the district for "wasteful" and "imprudent" spending, citing its renovations to buildings and "large" raises for school staff. What the report did not consider was the substandard state of the school buildings that warranted those renovations.

The support that property taxes provide schools was not much of a concern for those wielding economic power, since in Tunica as in the rest of the Delta, the vast majority of white students in Tunica attend private academies instead of the public schools. Consequently, Tunica had long neglected the state of its school buildings. Yet once again, it is the ingrained structures of the Delta and the failure to confront them that have the real impact on Tunica's education system. Ronald Love, who once served as an administrator in Tunica's schools, summed up Tunica's issue best in response to a reporter from *Fortune* magazine in 2007. "It is like Tunica suffers from a hangover from 100 years of poverty," said Love, who was hired to supervise the schools when the state took control of the district in 1997 for failing to meet basic performance measurements. "There are vestiges of it everywhere: in education, in local politics, in the housing. And when you have been the poorest of the poor, well, an infusion of resources might lighten your load, but you still have the hangover."[8]

Even though Tunica's high school graduation rate has moved up to nearly 89 percent, just two points above the national average, nearly all students receive free and reduced lunch. So, despite signs of educational progress, poverty is still a factor in the daily life of students here. The school remained under receivership by the state of Mississippi for nearly a decade before it was released in July 2024. The school district now has one of the highest per pupil expenditure rates in the state, at $17,737 per student, compared with a state average of $11,738.[9] But Tunica still has a hangover, and casino gambling revenues are not helping them get over it.

Most visitors to Tunica will never look beyond the shiny casinos that remain on the landscape even after the gambling bust, or the new roads that take them to and from those glitzy gambling halls. Television ads still run to attract visitors to Tunica, and, of course, these commercials make a visit to the casinos seem more glamorous than it really is. The visitors who still come to Tunica will drive past the well-preserved offices of the Abbay and Leatherman Plantation and maybe stop and read the Mississippi Blues Trail marker that proclaims the plantation the oldest and largest in the Delta, as well as the boyhood home of legendary bluesman Robert Johnson. And maybe they will think real progress has been made, through economic forces that transformed this land from sharecropper shacks to towering hotels. What they won't see or begin to understand is that these amenities built for tourists have had little impact on the lived experience of most residents of Tunica. The tourists never have to confront the fact that the structures that built the largest plantation in the Delta are still intact. The plantation was simply replaced by the casino.

The failure of casino gambling to bring change to Tunica shows that the long-term structures that create inequality must be confronted for real change to begin in places of deep disadvantage like Tunica. The town's policymakers never thought beyond the boom years and were concerned with giving benefits like tax cuts to those who needed them the least. Tunica's experience with casino gambling also shows that if our society remains unfocused on policies that work, and only preoccupied with the social class and racial identity of those whom effective policies help, our cycle of recklessness will continue to constrain our capacity to envision policy alternatives.

In the Mississippi Delta—and in communities like it across America—geography and culture are destiny. Until we see the linkage between geography and culture and begin to understand how the culture of the Mississippi Delta binds all people together, both Black and white, we will remain stuck in a version of our past that only feels like the future.

When Bukka White sings the "Georgia Skin Game," the tone of his voice sends a message to the listener that he knows he is about to be swindled out of his money and made out a fool. Like most blues songs, "Georgia Skin Game" reflects on the catastrophe confronting the singer. And like Bukka White and his Georgia Skin Man, Tunica must now confront the bad luck and trouble it created, both in the deep and recent past.

CHAPTER 14

RESILIENCE AND SALVATION IN THE DELTA

You may be high, you may be low
You may be rich, child, you may be poor
But when the Lord gets ready
You've got to move

—MISSISSIPPI FRED MCDOWELL,
"You Gotta Move"

During my time exploring this great alluvial plain, I have come to think of the Mississippi Delta as my own Sargasso Sea, a liminal space of madness where my thoughts are sometimes lost between the darkness and the intermittent light that can be found in this land's glowing sunsets. The Sargasso Sea, surrounded by the Atlantic Ocean, is also the only sea that exists without shores. It is an extended region surrounded by ocean. When I look at the Delta that is what I see: people unmoored and adrift at sea, though they live on a great expanse of land with the richest soil in North America, from the farm cooperatives of Mileston to the plantations and casinos of Tunica. It is a place adrift between what some see as the glories of its past and the tragic poverty and abandonment of the present.

I've come to realize that to understand the Delta, you must experience it not just through the history and rhythm of the blues, but through the struggles and stories that created the music. The blues isn't just about pain: inside those songs are hidden cries for freedom and liberation. And the only way to connect with the spirit of those ideas is to connect with the land and the people.

To connect with the land, I often stop and walk the fields of the Delta, imagining what it would be like to walk them and have to pick cotton rather than stroll down the rows while my boots get caked with mud. Sometimes, just to get closer to the land, I will ride my bike on the Delta's relatively empty roads that go east and west to get closer to the scenery and experience the silence. When I begin to look at all the facets of the Delta—the topography, the people, the culture, and all its natural and human-made beauty—I see a story not just about this place, but about America itself.

To see the Delta through stories and struggles, I talked with two men who have worked the Delta's soil. John Ware was born in 1938 to a share-cropping family on the Stansel Plantation in Ruleville. His parents and their ten children, seven boys and three girls, lived in a three-room house. "Every day my mother would go into the kitchen and say, 'Lord have mercy, what am I going to cook today?'" thinking of how many of them there were and how little they had. "But she would always come up with a meal," Ware said with an air of pride. "And she said if you didn't leave something, you didn't have enough."

Ollie Morganfield grew up in Mayersville on a farm, but says he never really worked on a farm. Born in 1943, his father and his famous uncle, McKinley Morganfield—known as Muddy Waters—grew up on the Stovall Plantation outside Clarksdale and knew the sharecropper's life. Although his father did not become a famous blues performer, he made sure his children never had to work the fields the way he did.

Morganfield left the Delta and served in the Air Force for ten years. He then returned to the town of Glen Allan to work at the Yazoo National Wildlife Preserve, at first working on reforestation of the area and later as an equipment operator. Morganfield is proud of the years he spent with the Mississippi Fish and Wildlife Service helping to maintain a piece of the natural Delta. "I've always been a naturalist," he told me one warm spring afternoon. "I like a natural habitat."

Ware and Morganfield are deeply rooted in the Delta. Both feel that the experience of growing up here taught them how to survive but also to recognize the ways their families were able to shelter themselves from the rampant exploitation ingrained in the culture of the Delta. In their lives I began to see how the Black working class of the Delta had a social vision for their lives that manifested itself in the way they worked to build lives of dignity in a place that sought to rob them of that dignity. These are two men who have navigated the Delta's seas without shores and survived.

When Ware's family worked the fields, all the plowing was done with mules. Looking back, it seemed ordinary to Ware. "But it is still hard for me to understand how a mule could pull a plow all day and look like he was just walking. And the boss man would come by and tell Daddy, say, 'Willie, don't work that mule too hard.'" The message was that the mule's welfare was more valuable to the plantation owner than the welfare of Ware's father. Laboring daily in the Delta's unrelenting heat was risky for both man and beast.

Like every other sharecropping family in the Delta, they planted cotton in the spring of the year. After the planting was done, Ware was allowed to go to school. In the fall, he could not go to school until the crop was harvested. "We got maybe $30 out of fifty-five bales of cotton," Ware recalled as we sat in his house in the town of Indianola. "Now, my daddy didn't know what a bale of cotton cost, he didn't know how much it cost to plant it, or to cultivate it. He had no way of knowing." Which meant he may not have received his fair share each year when accounts were settled.

I am unsure of whether it was accident or luck, but I happened to meet a member of the Stansel family who was in possession of the plantation's records for the years when the Ware family worked there. When I looked at the now-yellowing ledger from 1938—the very year John Ware was born—I saw exactly what Ware recalled to me that afternoon in his house in Indianola. The only difference was that it was $33.05 rather than $30, but he was close enough. There were numerous charges against the family's accounts, and the nature of those charges was not clear from the ledgers. After I saw the plantation records, I could see why his father decided to move to another plantation. But that was difficult because he was indebted to the Stansels. "If you moved to another plantation, you still had to pay the man at the other plantation. But my father always found some way to settle up so we could move on. But your hands were still tied. You couldn't go anywhere."

Somehow his father found a way to keep his hands from being tied. They lived on three different plantations while Ware was growing up, and each time they moved, their motivation was to find better living conditions. This didn't mean a bigger house, since sharecropper houses were all the same. What the Wares wanted was to be allowed to grow their own vegetables, which many plantations did not allow. The last place they lived they were even allowed to keep a cow on the property, which gave the family a source for milk. Ware made extra money for the family by selling copies of the *Pittsburgh Courier*, a Black newspaper that advocated for civil rights. "I sold more papers during the Emmett Till trial, mostly to white people who were trying to figure out what was going on and what Black people were thinking," Ware recalled.

When I walk cotton fields in the Delta, I imagine myself as a farm laborer back then, and it simply does not seem humanly possible to do that labor in such long rows, even with many hands picking. I figured the invention of the cotton picker led to these rows being as long as they were, but Ware let me know that assumption was wrong. "Every ten acres, there was a house in these fields. There might be two houses per 50-acre plot." These were only three-room houses, so they did not occupy a great deal of space. Ware says he could pick three hundred pounds of cotton a day. "If you didn't pick that much, you might get a whupping."

Ware believes that education is what allowed his family to progress. He and his siblings worked to put each other through college. Ware attended Rust College for two years, but then left so he could work to support a sibling's education. His intention was to go back to college, but he never returned because he married and started a family. Instead, Ware apprenticed to a Black dentist to become a dental technician and learned to make dentures. He worked at his job for fifty-two years and was able to not only ensure the education of his sibling, but all of his children, two of whom are now dentists. When I asked him what was his motivation for the work he did, he told me a story:

> At the age of seventeen, a dentist made my mama some teeth, and they didn't fit. And she would cry. And I couldn't stand to see her cry. I told her, "Take them out. I'm going to make you a pair." She backed up and looked me straight in the face, "Boy, you can't make no teeth." I said, "Mama, I'm going to make you a pair of teeth." Again, she said, "Boy, you can't make no teeth." I said, "Mama, I'm going to make you a pair of teeth." And sure enough, the next year, a dentist needed somebody to do his janitorial work. And I took the job to do his cleaning for him around the office. And when I took the job, I took the job for one purpose. And that was to learn what those teeth were made out of, so I could make her a pair of teeth.

Through his apprenticeship he learned to make dentures. And by 1959, five years after he declared to his mother that he would make her some teeth, Ware did.

Ware has lived in the same house with his wife for more than sixty years. As we step outside as I leave, he reminds me that the cotton fields that once surrounded his house have now been filled with houses. "We raised five kids here. All the kids have gone. And all the houses that I had prayed and asked God to give them, the kids got. But I didn't get my dream of an education. The dream that I had, I don't have. They have it. That's why, because I bent my back."

Ollie Morganfield is a slim and quiet man. He doesn't like to talk much. When I ask him probing and direct questions about his work in the Yazoo National Wildlife Preserve, he is resistant to speak about his work in superlatives. After we have a conversation at his tidy white house right near Lake Washington in the town of Glen Allan, I suggest we head over to the nature preserve to take a look at the place where he worked for twenty-five years. He smiles at my suggestion and seems eager to get in the car and go to a place that he has described with great affection.

His grandson, Keith Johnson, drives us to the nature preserve and Morganfield provides directions. Johnson is a musician, carrying on the musical legend of the man he calls his "Uncle Muddy." When I ask Morganfield if he plays an instrument, he tells me quietly, "I run a little bass," meaning he plays bass guitar. Johnson nods and tells me that he does more than just run a little bass. He can really play.

When we stop the car and look out over Steele Bayou, Morganfield moves from being quiet and reserved to being quite animated. He points toward the trees he planted twenty years ago and tells us there are more trees along this stretch of land than anywhere else in the Delta. "This nature preserve is more like the way the Delta was before it was cleared for farming," Morganfield tells us, pointing toward the field that lies across the bayou and contrasting it with the lush green nature preserve.

For twenty-five years, Morganfield built bridges, planted trees, and helped maintain the wildness of the nature preserve. As we walked around, I was surprised when he said quietly, "You know, I feel like this is my land." It's not so much that he feels ownership of the land as that his deep love for it fosters that kind of connection. He sees this nature preserve as part of his earthly legacy. As we walk, Morganfield talks at a good clip about migratory waterfowl, alligators, and the wading birds that come through the nature preserve. He pulls out his binoculars to observe the birds and points out alligators moving through the bayou. Part of Morganfield is embedded in the soil.

There is a section of the nature preserve named for Holt Collier, the Black man who took Theodore Roosevelt on his famous bear hunting expedition in the Delta. Morganfield tells me that quite often, white people tell him he looks like Holt Collier, who is revered by white outdoorsmen and hunters in the Delta. A formerly enslaved man, Collier allegedly fought with the Confederate Army in the Civil War. Morganfield's body language tells me that he doesn't like the comparison with Holt Collier very much. With a smile he tells me, "Well, Holt Collier was a hunter. I am a naturalist. I'm different."

Although the Mississippi Delta is a Southern space, we often forget that it is also an ancient one. The region was formed long before national political and racial divisions were projected onto our borders and into our consciousness. As Ollie Morganfield reminded me, the fields of the modern-day Delta serve as a direct contrast to the primordial environment that existed before the land was cleared. Morganfield and John Ware feel connected to this land, yet in different ways. Morganfield feels he has helped preserve the Delta's natural environment. Ware saw the land as a something he needed to work just to survive. Oddly enough, the cotton field that Ware's father plowed with a mule is now a solar farm rather than a cotton farm, which can be read as a sign of positive change or the beginning of a new extractive economy that is only available to those with land.

What the two men share is that their families helped make the Delta what it is today. And both men, as John Ware would say, bent their backs so their children would not have to do the same thing. Although well into his eighties, Ware had an idea of what might help the Delta build a new future. "These towns need high-speed internet and all of this that other people have, you know, then maybe these towns would grow." In an economy that is increasingly rooted in the digital world, even a man in his eighties realizes that it is difficult to build a new economic future for the Delta unless it has an infrastructure rooted in the twenty-first century.

The Delta's entire economic base is rickety. It's something I heard from people attending the annual Glen Allan picnic, which is a way for former residents of the town to stay connected now that they have moved on to other parts of the Delta, Mississippi, and other points north and south. Each year, over two hundred people attend, according to Darren Hughes, who organizes the event. Hughes reminded me that "the community didn't offer much, so all of these people you see here had to leave." Now each year they come back and reconnect with the place that shaped them. Hughes lives in Greenville, but misses being in the town that he feels nurtured him into adulthood. And everyone else I spoke with at the picnic had a similar story.

The Delta didn't develop much industrially in the early twentieth century, as white elites were determined to fence out any competition for Black sharecropping labor. Of the few factories that did set up shop, most have closed down over the past few decades with the decline of US manufacturing. Small-scale farming never became a path to prosperity, owing to mechanization and consolidation in agriculture.

In the twentieth century, people like Ollie Morganfield and John Ware found a way to make hope exist for their families. That is harder to do in the twenty-first century in a place that in many ways is stuck in the previous century. Across the Delta there are people and families living in poverty who don't know hope exists. I have encountered them in Greenwood's Baptist Town, in Clarksdale, and numerous other towns across the Delta. These people are in schools with few resources to provide an education and a vision for life. Years later, some of the people from those same schools may be found inside the prison walls of Parchman.

In the Delta, the question remains: How do we create an environment of opportunity for all people in all towns and places? As Americans, we forget that it is the welfare of the poor that tells us how this country is faring and what our service to the country should be. Finding ways to decrease the number of poor Americans has long been part of this country's story, from the Great Depression to the Great Society. The Delta, like our national struggle to end poverty, is our national story because it is one we cannot seem to resolve. And like our national story, the story of the Delta is one of ongoing struggle. Like John Ware, we should all be bending our backs as part of that struggle.

CHAPTER 15

A VEILED MIRROR

Some these days, you gonna be sorry
Some these days, I'm going away

—CHARLEY PATTON,
"Some of These Days I'll Be Gone"

The Mississippi Delta is often portrayed as a unique part of the American South, a place more Southern than it is distinctively American. But the forces and policies that shaped the culture of the Delta were American at their core. While we often think of poverty as the circumstance that sets the Delta apart, culture and mythology have played a role in creating the notion of separateness regarding the Delta, in the way Americans see the region as well as the way residents of the Delta see themselves.

Myths have allowed the romantic idea of the Delta to overshadow the region's social and economic realities, rendering them less clearly visible to the outside world, particularly to those who have never been exposed to the bare realities of the place. The Delta's myths have been shaped by Tin Pan Alley songwriters, its own blues music, the eternal mystique of the Mississippi River, and by ordinary people, like those who see spending a night in a sharecropper's shack as a way to connect with the place and its legacy. Politicians and policymakers have also contributed to those myths by painting the Delta as a region shaped by welfare dependency, when in fact it is a place populated by the working poor who are merely struggling to survive in a place lacking in opportunity. Roughly 4 percent of all Delta residents receive cash welfare benefits, hardly enough to create a massive culture of dependency. Yet stereotypes about poverty in the Delta persist because there is a disconnect between our policies and the realities of the lives of people in the poorest region of the poorest state in the nation. Instead of addressing the systemic and institutional causes of poverty—and listening to the people of the Delta to determine what they need to overcome those forces—poverty is seen as rooted in individual behavior. Myths like these make it easier to see the circumstances of the Mississippi Delta as linked to a sense of geographical determinism and personal failings than to more powerful and sinister circumstances. And that is why the myths persist.

The Delta is also a place of bleak beauty, its magnificent richness and flatness shaped by the wild rivers that run through it and by the land itself. Beauty and suffering are equally salient traits of the Mississippi Delta, yet emphasizing the land's grandeur can obscure the suffering that shaped the land. Or perhaps sometimes we choose to focus on the beauty of the place because if we acknowledge the splendor of the land, the suffering that exists for the people across its great expanses seems less urgent since its people live in the presence of beauty. As Joan Didion once wrote, we tell ourselves stories in order to live. But sometimes the stories we tell ourselves allow us to live in ways that shield us from life's harsh realities.

Of course, there is the issue of race. Although many native Mississippians will deny it, race and racism have also shaped the Delta's mythology. Whether one is looking at education or the economy, slavery or sharecropping, the forces of white supremacy define the Delta's past and present. As Americans, we must confront the fact that the circumstances of people living in the Mississippi Delta continue to be ignored because the population is poor and majority Black. Americans have been conditioned to think that Blackness and poverty are wrapped together in a covenant that somehow determines the destiny of the Delta's people. It is time for that kind of thinking to end. Also, the Delta is a majority-Black rural place, but today much of the attention on rural America centers on white rural America. Like white rural America, the Delta is plagued by poor health care access, failing infrastructure, and farming job losses. We must begin to study what these two sides of rural America have in common.

Despite the optimism of the people of the Delta, many feel that no amount of struggle against the original sins that defined the region can save it. As one former Delta resident said to me, "Just depopulate the place. Nothing else can change it." What that solution fails to confront is that the very people who shaped the Delta, who cleared its land, built the levees that controlled the river, and upon whose backs was built the wealth extracted from this land are being asked to flee the home they built for themselves and others. This proposed remedy for the Delta's ills seems to be saying, "Now that the work has been done, simply dispose of the people whose ancestors made this land what it is today."

The most important thing that exploring the history and culture of the Delta has taught me is that if Americans continue to think of the Delta as an outlier with regard to the way inequality and race have shaped the lives of people in this country, we will fail to recognize that there are other regions and places that have also been shaped by racism, extraction, and dispossession. The region some refer to as the midwestern Rustbelt is urban—unlike the rural Delta—and shaped by manufacturing, but forces of globalization and automation have transformed it from a place of prosperity to one of hopelessness, much like the Delta. When I look at photographs of a decaying post-industrial Braddock, Pennsylvania, taken by LaToya Ruby Frazier, I see not only the place she is from and has documented so profoundly, but I also see the Delta. As Frazier herself has said, "I go to a new place, and I see Braddock everywhere."[1] When I go to a new place, I see the Delta. And this nation has many Deltas.

The Mississippi Delta is a mirror to America, yet we continue to place a veil over the mirror to keep from seeing the imperfections that exist in the Delta and places like it in the rest of the country. Failing to look closely in the mirror prevents us from seeing how the systems of power that shaped the Delta also have manifested themselves in other regions and places, particularly those that are radically different in topography and demographics. When we fail to confront the interrelatedness of the history of different regions of the country, we allow the situations that shaped the inequities to persist. Far too often, we fail to acknowledge that the Mississippi Delta is not the only place in America where the richness of the land was worked by the poorest people who profited the least from that abundance. Cotton was not the only extractive industry in America.

In *The Most Southern Place on Earth*, James Cobb's deep and detailed history of the Mississippi Delta published in 1992, the historian concludes the book by asking his readers: As economic disparity and indifference to human suffering in this country grows, have the forces that made the Delta the South writ small now seeped into the rest of the country, rendering parts of the entire nation the Delta writ large? From Cobb's perspective of more than three decades ago, he thinks the answer is yes, as he argues that the economic and social polarization we associate with the Mississippi Delta "may be observed wherever and whenever the pursuit of wealth, pleasure, and power overwhelms the ideals of equality, justice, and compassion and reduces the American Dream to a self-indulgent fantasy."[2] There are numerous places around this country that have been shaped by the level of profit generated by the land and level of devastation to the landscape. The contemporary Delta remains tethered to its past because what we see in the present-day inequality in the Delta is the result of forces that have intentionally undermined the forces of change. Those who have reduced the American Dream to a self-indulgent fantasy held political and economic power in the Delta that allowed them to trespass on the lives of the less powerful. And now they have convinced many Americans that poverty in the Delta and places like it is just something we have to live with.

Across America, there are numerous places shaped by inequality, but we choose not to see them, or we think of them as exceptions or fail to see them as connected to places like the Mississippi Delta. That is why, in order to see the Delta's history and culture more clearly, I chose to go beyond its borders and see the ways the circumstances of the Delta exist in other forms. When viewed from the outside, the Delta is more than just the most Southern place on earth.

The cotton fields of the Mississippi Delta and the hills of eastern Kentucky may be distinguished by their radically different landscapes, yet focusing on the differences in region, culture, and topography risks overlooking the similarities between these places. Both places were shaped by a single commodity—the Delta by cotton and eastern Kentucky by coal. There were much fewer plantations in Kentucky, but the corporate bosses that shaped the coal industry there were just as powerful as the Delta's plantation class. The Delta is majority Black and eastern Kentucky is majority white, but both places have been shaped by the poverty of the people who live there. Poverty rates in coal country mirror those of the Delta. Visiting Appalachia with the Mississippi Delta on my mind and talking with the people who live in its hills and hollows shortened the distance I had perceived between these two points on the map.

Mississippi lacks mountains, yet twenty-four counties in its northeastern region fell within the service area of the Appalachian Regional Commission, a Great Society program that sought to bring economic development to the Appalachian region. By using a map doctored by a group of politicians, Mississippi was reimagined as Appalachia, giving Senators James O. Eastland and John C. Stennis a way to bring Great Society funds to the whitest part of Mississippi. These are the same senators who sought to obstruct the economic empowerment of Lyndon Johnson's War on Poverty in the Delta because of its linkage with the Black freedom struggle through programs such as cooperative agriculture, community improvement in segregated neighborhoods, and Project Head Start. Instead of helping the state's poorest region, these leaders remade part of the state into Appalachia to establish watersport recreation areas, highways, and historical landmarks celebrating the white settlers who took the land from the native Chickasaws and enslaved people of African descent.[3] Mississippi's segregationists found a way to circumvent the War on Poverty's required participation of Black and low-income residents by creating an alternate way to bring federal largesse to the South in the years after the Civil Rights and Voting Rights Acts.

Yet the rationale for the work of the Appalachian Regional Commission was different in the part of the region that had real mountains. New and improved four-lane roads and other infrastructure projects came to the more mountainous region of eastern Kentucky, but those improvements were not made just to transport people. They also made it easier for coal mining trucks to make their way through the mountains. Eastern Kentucky is a region shaped by coal mines, many of which were once owned by large corporations such as U.S. Steel and International Harvester. Towns were often named after mine owners, just as some Delta towns were named after plantation owners. Paternalism was key to maintaining a stable labor force and keeping out the unions. With commissaries, company stores, and housing owned by the mining company, coal mining towns effectively functioned like plantations. Although there is little mining going on today, the coal industry has had a lasting impact on the region. Instead of rusting cotton gins, Appalachia has abandoned coal mines.

While the continued use of pesticides has a lasting impact on the environment of the Mississippi Delta, the legacy of the coal industry has brought environmental disaster to eastern Kentucky. In 2000, toxic waste left over from coal mining broke through an abandoned mine shaft and dumped 300 million gallons of toxic sludge into area rivers, thus contaminating the water system of Martin County. The spill was thirty times larger than the Exxon Valdez oil spill in 1989.[4] But I had never heard about this catastrophic event until I came to Martin County.

In eastern Kentucky, there are few pristine places where coal has not had an impact on the land. The byproducts of the coal industry, particularly those that have made it into the water table, have dramatically affected the life and health of eastern Kentucky residents. Nina and Mickey McCoy are retired teachers who have become activists for clean water in Martin County. I talked with them on the porch of their restaurant, Metrobilly's, in the town of Inez one afternoon as customers came for lunch. Why, I asked, weren't more people concerned about the water quality? "Some people simply write off the water problems with a shrug and say, 'You live in a coal mining community and coal mining is a dirty business,'" Mickey tells me. In the minds of many in Martin County, the lack of clean water from their taps is a political rather than an environmental and health issue, and the politics that drives that sensibility is the politics of coal. Coal is still a powerful interest in this region, even though there are no working mines in the county. "Because we are environmentalists, we have targets on our backs," Nina, a former biology teacher, told me, referring to herself and her husband. She understands how toxins affect the body, yet some residents refuse to listen to her concerns about the water. What might explain their bias is the influence of the current and former owners of the mining operations, who still hold a great deal of political and cultural power. They deny the dangers posed by the byproducts of coal mining and see the issue of clean water as working against their interests and convince others to see things the same way. Coal's interests have long been tied with those of the commonwealth of Kentucky.

Nina and Mickey's children have both left Kentucky, one for California and the other for upstate New York. To get me to understand the pull of the place, they read to me a sermon their daughter Annalyse gave at a church in Beacon, New York, about her love for her home and her frustration that more people don't share her parents' concern about water quality in the region. "This situation my town finds itself in is only a microcosm of the dysfunction and lack of sustainability mindset that plagues our nation and our world," she states.

Later in the sermon, Annalyse touches on a question that many in the Delta confront: Why don't people just leave if things are so bad? She believes questions like this weaken the power and ability of places like Appalachia to achieve justice, since it allows Americans to separate themselves from the devastating situation confronted by their fellow citizens. "Are we weakening ourselves by giving the few who profit a win, even in our minds?" she asks. "That type of territory is dangerous. What happens to one of us, happens to all of us." It is this lack of communitarian spirit that allows places like Inez to be seen as separate places that can just be discarded.

Inez is not the vibrant community it was during coal mining's boom years, and like most towns in eastern Kentucky, it is a shadow of its former self. The poverty rate may be lower than in the 1960s, but there are fewer jobs now that the era of coal mining is over. Over in Harlan County, another mining community, Mike O'Bradovich remembers when his hometown of Lynch, Kentucky, was at its peak. He grew up in a house owned by U.S. Steel that is no longer there since being torn down when layoffs began in the 1960s. Pointing to the top of a hill, he says, "There were once ten or fifteen houses on that hill. When the layoffs began, they relocated people and tore that whole area off, except for one house." His father had been recruited to work in the mines when he arrived at Ellis Island from Beringia, Yugoslavia. The apostrophe in his name was not an Ellis Island addition but was placed there at the insistence of the Irish Catholic nuns who were his teachers.

Lynch and the neighboring town of Benham weren't all-white coal mining towns. Both towns had a sizable Black population, the result of U.S. Steel in Lynch and International Harvester in Benham recruiting Black miners from the South, primarily from Alabama. Schools were segregated until 1963, when the out-migration of Black families to the industrial North shrank the number of students, making integration an economic necessity given the cost of running a dual school system. Jim Crow remains a part of the landscape of eastern Kentucky, from the now-empty Lynch Colored School to the once-segregated showers for the miners.

O'Bradovich drives me through town and shows me the vacant spot where there was once a two-hundred-room hotel constructed of stone made from local quarries. "It had multiple restaurants, reading rooms, a bowling alley, and social areas. It was the center of town life. It was like our own shopping mall." And this centerpiece of civic life was completely controlled by U.S. Steel, who owned every building in town except for the churches, which were deeded land by the company. But as the town dwindled in population and the mine began to generate less coal in the mid-1960s, there were not enough people coming through Lynch occupying the hotel's rooms. One day, instead of keeping the building in line with local fire codes, U.S. Steel sent wrecking balls and demolished the hotel.

When he left Lynch to attend the University of Kentucky, O'Bradovich did not think he would be coming back to Harlan County. He majored in business and immediately went to work for a mining company in West Virginia after graduation. Then U.S. Steel recruited him to return to his hometown and told him he had a future with them. "They showed me maps of the coal mines and told me, 'We've got fifty years of reserve right here. You can retire from here and so can your son if he so desires.'" O'Bradovich's son didn't want to work in the mines, but even if he did, by the time he was old enough to work there was no coal. "New technology came in that could produce three times the amount of coal as miners. Bigger, faster machines. Remote coal mining. Instead of fifty years, we mined out this place in twenty years." O'Bradovich was able to retire with a full pension, but that option wasn't available to his son, despite what U.S. Steel had promised.

As with cotton in the Mississippi Delta, technology transformed coal mining. And now that the nation is moving away from coal, there is little reason for towns like Lynch to exist. One local mountaintop mining site now is even dotted with solar panels, a sign of how much things have changed.

In Kentucky, the abandoned infrastructure of coal mining dots the landscape of little towns like Lynch and its neighbors Bentham in Harlan County and Inez in Martin County, whether it is the old company store or the mines themselves. "Coal has always cursed the land in which it lies," wrote Kentucky writer and activist Harry Monroe Caudill in his 1963 book *Night Comes to the Cumberlands*. "It mars but never beautifies. It corrupts but never purifies."[5] As I drive the roads through coal country more than sixty years after he wrote those words, Caudill's observations resonate profoundly in the scene before me, in the visible impact of strip mining and mountain-top coal removal, as well as the abandoned mines that small former company towns are seeking to turn into tourist attractions.

Harry Caudill's eloquent descriptions of Appalachia life brought national attention to the impoverished circumstances that were a part of the daily existence of so much of eastern Kentucky's population. Some say that what Lyndon Johnson observed in Martin County, Kentucky, just outside the town of Inez, is what spurred him to launch his War on Poverty. After visiting the home of a laborer by the name of Tom Fletcher, Johnson immediately announced, "I have called for a national war on poverty. Our objective: total victory." Johnson's visit and announcement transformed Tom Fletcher and Martin County into the unwitting faces of the nation's battle, often to the chagrin of residents who resent that each decade writers and photographers make a pilgrimage here to assess how much the War on Poverty changed the place. Martin County became the national poster child for the War on Poverty, effectively putting a white face on a campaign that was aligned with the goals of the Civil Rights Movement. "We will forever be known as the whitest and poorest county in America," a woman by the name of Charlotte Anderson tells me, as I seek out directions to the Fletcher house.

Anderson works at the Martin County Historical Society and is helping me locate Tom Fletcher's house, since I am now one of those writers and photographers local people dread seeing every ten years. Before giving me directions, Anderson and her colleague Loretta Meade caution me about stereotyping the people of this region. Meade said she and her neighbors didn't want to be thought of as "a bunch of isolated hillbillies" in the eyes of the rest of the world. Both women remember Johnson's visit and the excitement it generated in the town. But they feel that even with all that the War on Poverty changed in eastern Kentucky, it created a culture of shame. "We've never been able to rise above it," Meade tells me. But she is unable to pin down the exact source of the shame, except that they feel the images from Johnson's visit froze the place in time. Poverty came to be connected with the place itself.

The directions they give me take me straight to the Fletcher house, which I recognize immediately. It's just that iconic. The house, now painted a distinct orange, stands out from the others on the road, which could be found in any middle-class neighborhood in America. As I look up at the Fletcher house, I think of what Charlotte Anderson and Loretta Meade said about the shame they feel Martin County has never been able to rise above. The shame, I believe, is that the Fletcher house represents the persistence of poverty in eastern Kentucky. There are no longer numerous tar-paper and pine shacks dotting the landscape as they did when Johnson came here. And the road is nicely paved. But there is still a conspicuous poverty here. Poor people and their substandard housing are not just isolated in the mountain hollers that I have also driven through. The Fletcher house puts it all out there to see, and that continues to be a source of shame.

As I step out of the car and walk up the hill to the house, a gentleman in fading blue overalls with a bushy white beard is sitting in a chair on the porch. I introduce myself, tell him I am looking at connections between the Mississippi Delta and eastern Kentucky, and would like to take a photograph of his house and the famous porch where Lyndon Johnson once stood. He tells me that he is a Fletcher and that I am welcome to take a photograph from the side of the house, not the straight-on shot that I had hoped to take. Most of the photographs of the house take in its entire expanse, making me wonder if Fletcher is trying to make his house less recognizable. As yet another stranger with a camera on the porch of this old house, I agree to his terms, and he goes inside as I look for lighting and perspective. After I have taken my photographs, I wait for him to come back, thank him, and politely leave, since in a subtle, nonverbal way, he has told me that he doesn't want to talk.

As I drive away, I begin to think about the Fletcher house and what it means. To me, it is a historic site. But to the descendant of Tom Fletcher that I just spoke with, there must be shame in the fact that he is still living there sixty years later and people are taking photographs of his ramshackle house, which looks much as it did in 1964 except for the orange paint that has been slathered over its fake-brick siding. His silence was a way of expressing his shame.

But it was not just with the Fletchers that I encountered this silence. None of the people I interviewed thought I should use a photograph of the Fletcher house for this book. They felt Appalachia was more than that one house, which indeed it is. Yet I realized none of these people were poor themselves. Social status influences how people see their community and what they want others to see. When those concerns dictate how a community is depicted, we block people who live below the poverty line from our field of vision. In some cases, like the Fletchers, they have been poor for generations. By not showing poverty, we render it invisible.

In eastern Kentucky, as in the Mississippi Delta, I experienced the wealth of the culture, the pride people feel for the land where they are from, and their love for the music that sprang from the soil. Both places have a long legacy of social action that continues today. Traveling to Appalachia taught me that there is a complex interaction between social action and social embarrassment. It's a common experience of humanity. If we are only concerned with avoiding social embarrassment, we diminish the lives of people who live below the poverty line if we don't allow them to be seen. A photograph is not the whole story, but we can't even talk about the story of poverty in places like eastern Kentucky and the Mississippi Delta unless we can see evidence of it.

As Americans, we don't like to see images of poverty because it challenges our idea of exceptionalism rooted in that thing we refer to as the American Dream. That sense of exceptionalism is what prevents Americans from developing moral clarity about the reasons for the persistence of poverty in places like the Mississippi Delta. It persists not because of personal failings or dependence on welfare, but because of systems that have been in place for more than a century that keep people poor and prevent them from moving out of poverty. In the Mississippi Delta and places like it, we must begin to think about how we can build a new framework of justice that will overcome generations of injustice. We must begin to invest in education so that people can find a way out of poverty. Of course, the Delta can't simply educate itself out of poverty, but education is a tool that can help its people move forward. Education can help ease the volatile interaction between poverty and violence that persists in the Delta and provides a path to eventual incarceration.

To transform the Delta, as a nation we must renew our commitment to racial justice and overcome and understand past injustices, even in a country that says all our racial grievances are in the past. The idea of color-blindness only covers up the ways race has been lived in this country and the way it continues to be a part of American life. Patterns of enslavement in 1860 in the Delta correlate with patterns of poverty today, which means slavery casts a long shadow. According to Duke University economist William Darity, closing the racial wealth gap in all of Mississippi, including the Delta, would by conservative estimate require a reparations outlay of $300,000 per person, about $330 billion in total. Our failure to recognize that this wealth gap has its roots in the history of slavery will only perpetuate the wealth gap.

Also, we must begin to invest in Delta communities and ask what people in those communities need to survive and thrive, not make decisions based on what others deem that they should have. Philanthropy can play a role in this by identifying those needs and working with government entities, but foundations can't do it alone. In terms of acting on a more local level, organizations like the Delta Regional Authority and the Appalachian Regional Commission invest in infrastructure and industry, not in people and communities—that should change. Investments in the Delta and places like it should not benefit those who have always benefited from federal largesse.

When I hear individuals make calls for people to flee the Delta, I often ask if they have ever been there. Many of them have not. I then urge them to explore the Delta on foot by walking its fields and levees. The response is often that it is too hot to do that. My response: Come in the spring. Connecting with the land and its people will show that this is a place worth saving.

One of the great things about exploring the Delta in spring is that much of its natural beauty can be taken in on foot. On the edge of the Sky Lake nature reserve, north of the town of Belzoni, you can still experience the land's unique qualities. With trees that date back to before the clearing of the Delta—including a massive 2,000-year-old cypress—you get a sense of what the scenery was like before it was subsumed by the engine of industrial agriculture.

Yes, this is an overwhelmingly flat land, but during spring one need not worry about the relentless heat, often unrelieved by shade, that's part of everyday life here come summer. Once you explore the natural beauty of the Delta, it becomes difficult to shake it from your consciousness. I'm often reminded of Wim Wenders's 1987 film, *Wings of Desire*. In it, a lonely angel wanders the streets of Berlin and encounters a dying man lying on a sidewalk. As the angel sits to comfort him, he urges the man to think of the memories he will take with him from this corporeal realm into the next life. As the man reflects on his time on earth, he suddenly recalls that one of his most beautiful and lasting memories was seeing the Mississippi Delta.

My most lasting memories are of seeing the Delta. As I drive up, down, and around the Delta, I feel my father's presence with me urging me to tell this place's story. As I write these words, it is seventy-five years after my father—the man whose name I carry—first set foot in the Delta. This place was one of his lasting memories and I want it to be that way for others. But at the same time, I want it to live up to the promise my father saw in it when he arrived in the middle of the twentieth century.

The land of the Mississippi Delta generates wealth for a great number of people who benefit from its rich soil. In light of the abundance that springs from the Delta's expansive fields, we must ask ourselves if we can allow poverty to persist in a place that for generations has benefited from the exploitation of the poor to generate that wealth. The Delta and places like it are poor because we allow them to be poor. And that poverty persists because of decades of neglect and policies engineered to keep people poor.

In the Delta town of Friars Point, the evening sun descends with an air of Southern charm that masks the sorrow underlying the land's blood memory. While sunsets in the American West are more dramatic, with their skies streaked lipstick red above mountains and mesas, here the dimming of the day feels haunted. As I walk along the top of a levee, I sometimes imagine the song many of the levee workers sang to the setting sun, which they called "Ol' Hannah."

> *Go down, ol' Hannah, doncha rise no more*
> *If you rise in the morning, bring Judgment Day*
> *Go down, ol' Hannah, doncha rise no more*
> *If you rise in the morning, set the world on fire, set the world on fire*

I often think of the disconnect between the peace I feel and the pain of those who built what lies beneath my feet. An intimate connection with the Delta's landscape doesn't erase its past or its problems, nor does it hide them away. Encountering a place that many claim to know but few choose to understand leads not only to lasting memories but also to a deeper understanding of this country. To change what we see on the Delta's landscape, we must seek to understand it and confront difficult truths about how and why inequality is so much a part of its existence. And one of the ways to do that is to walk its fields, levees, wetlands, and sacred spaces to connect with the land itself. Along the way, you will meet people who will change the way you see the Delta and places like it. As you walk and think about the Delta's past and listen to the voices of its people, begin to imagine its future and remove the veil over the mirror that keeps the region a separate and forsaken place. Look deeply into the Delta's mirror and you will see America staring back at you.

ACKNOWLEDGMENTS

The idea for this book began when I wrote a story for *Wired* magazine on broadband access in the Mississippi Delta in 2015 and then returned to Mississippi to teach at Millsaps College. Upon my return, I started driving Delta roads on weekends without a map. It was during those drives that I wrote observations of what I saw that eventually became this book. At the time, I simply wandered from the main roads and rambled through small Delta towns unsure of what I was searching for. James C. Cobb's masterful *The Most Southern Place on Earth: The Mississippi Delta and the Roots of Regional Identity* helped me find my way and led me to see the Delta as a part of the world rather than a world apart. Along with Cobb's insights, there were many other people who kept me from wandering aimlessly and bolstered my sense of purpose in studying the Mississippi Delta.

I am grateful to my colleagues in the Department of English at Millsaps College who generously gave me their ears during this time of discovery: Laura E. Franey, Eric J. Griffin, Anne MacMaster, Michael Pickard, and Henry Adam Svec, along with then Millsaps president Rob Pearigen and dean and provost Keith Dunn. While at Millsaps, I presented an early version of an essay on Mileston, which evolved into "The Dimming Mystique of Mileston," an essay for the *Oxford American* published in August 2020. Hannah Saulters and Eliza Borné, both then at the *Oxford American*, provided strong editorial guidance on that essay as I began to think of the shape of this book. And I am also grateful to John Gravois, features editor at *Wired*, for assigning my first story on the Delta, and to Alex Heard for asking me to write about the Delta while he was editor of *Outside*.

After Millsaps, the Center for the Study of Southern Culture at the University of Mississippi gave me a home, first under director Ted Ownby and later under director Kathryn McKee. Dr. McKee, along with the center's founding director, William Ferris, and former honors college dean Douglas Sullivan-González, encouraged me to apply for fellowships to support my work, which provided the time and space to write.

The Radcliffe Institute for Advanced Study at Harvard University provided a yearlong fellowship in 2021–2022, supported by the Carl and Lily Pforzheimer Foundation, that was instrumental in helping this book move from an idea toward a reality. The Radcliffe Institute's director, Claudia Rizzini, and the Radcliffe dean, Tomiko Brown-Nagin, gave me the opportunity to present my work as part of the Julia S. Phelps Annual Lecture in the Arts and Humanities. Randall Kennedy of Harvard Law School generously agreed to be a part of my Phelps lecture. Thank you all for your grace and kindness.

At the Radcliffe Institute, Garrett O'Brien and Mia Word served as my Radcliffe research partners during my time there, and I could not have asked for more supportive, curious, determined, and disciplined researchers. I will never forget our reporting trip to the Delta together. I am grateful to the reference librarians at the Schlesinger Library who pointed me toward the collections of June Jordan and Minnie Fisher. And, of course, the members of my fellowship class provided much sound input and critique. I am especially grateful to members of the Mixology Interest Group (MIG) for the thirst-slaking libations and engaging conversations about writing and other important questions, such as whether Vesper martinis are shaken or stirred. You are all too numerous to name here, but I am confident you all know who you are. MIG forever!

Archivists and librarians in Mississippi directed me toward materials that provided historical context for the Delta. At Mississippi State University Libraries, thanks to Jennifer McGillan and Jessica Perkins Smith; at the University of Mississippi, thanks to Sally McWhite and Jennifer Ford. In my exploration of the papers of John Hersey at the Beinecke Library at Yale University, Hersey's grandson Cannon Hersey served as my guide, and I am grateful for his insights into his grandfather's work in the Mississippi Delta.

So many people in the Delta and in Mississippi encouraged this project. Ann Abadie, that quiet force in the arts and humanities in Mississippi, made sure I found lodging during my residency in the Delta town of Clarksdale. My only regret is that she did not live to see this book in print. In the Delta, thanks go to Sydney Bush, Eddie Carthan, Gloria Dickerson, Chuck Espy,

John Fairman, John Dillon Harris, Calvin Head, Rolando Herts, Hermon Johnson Jr., Hermon Johnson Sr., Keith "Prince of the Delta Blues" Johnson, Tim Lampkin, Brenda Luckett, Marquitrice Mangham, Griffin McLaurin, Ollie Morganfield, Bubba O'Keefe, Greenville mayor Errick D. Simmons, Roger Stolle, Watson Turnipseed, John Ware, and Lolvone Williams. Without University of Mississippi student Yasmine Ware, I never would have had the opportunity to meet her grandfather John Ware. A special thanks to Jenna Welch, Charles Coleman, Layla Young (who played a convincing Marian Wright), Amana Wallace, and the entire cast of the StoryWorks production of *Mrs. Carter and the Sunflower Seven*. My dear friend Steve Yarbrough shared his insights into the academy system in the Delta, which shaped my time interviewing students at the Sunflower Freedom Project. At the Sunflower County Freedom Project, special thanks to LaToysha Brown, Sarah Riback, Valerie Simpson, and Jeremiah Smith for gathering a group of students to discuss the Delta's academy system. And thanks to those students: Tamoris Carter, Evionna Petty, Ke'Niya Lewis, and Skilynn Gordon.

My time teaching at Parchman would not have happened without the efforts of Louis Bourgeois and his Prison Writing Project. A special thanks to my students in Parchman's Unit 29 who shared their lives with me: Derrick Harris, Leon Johnson, Trevonte Johnson, Rufus McFadden, Nathan Sumrall, and Matt Willbanks. Former Parchman chaplain Maurice Clifton generously spent time explaining Parchman's inner workings in an intricate diagram.

Outside the Delta, the late Mel Blake shared memories of the last days of the Mileston Plantation in June 2016, in an interview arranged by former Library of Congress colleague Athena Angelos. Curtis Wilkie shared intimate stories of his memories of accompanying Robert Kennedy through the Delta in 1967, and Linda Williams Jackson spoke candidly about what Kennedy's trip meant to her family. Tom and Dorothy Howorth have given me a place to call home in Oxford after my weekend treks to the Delta. Betsy Bradley and Lydia Jasper provided access to the Sara Virginia Jones collection at the Mississippi Museum of Art, and Melvin Johnson and the late L. C. Tucker shared stories of working with Ms. Jones and handling her collection. Jeffrey K. Walters shared his research on Providence Farm with me, which helped lead me to archival material that filled in the missing pieces of the story. Carrie Mae Weems shared her insights into her family's origins in the Delta and their connection to the Delta Cooperative Farm and Providence Farm. David Beito told me stories of Mound Bayou and the Delta Health Center, and Tom Ward generously reviewed my chapters on Mound Bayou. Lawrence Katz of Harvard University and Trevon Logan of Ohio State University shared their perspectives on social change philanthropy. Tom Pittman and Keith Fulcher spent a great deal of time discussing the role of philanthropy in the Delta. Brian Foster shared his perspectives on the role of casino gambling in the Delta. A chance encounter on the streets of Oxford led me to Bill Boyd, who generously shared the plantation records of the Stansel Plantation that were in his possession.

My University of Mississippi colleague Matt O'Neal was instrumental in helping me make connections in eastern Kentucky. Mary Varson Cromer at the Appalachian Citizens' Law Center Inc. connected me with Nina and Mickey McCoy. As I traveled eastern Kentucky, I made other helpful connections I would like to thank: Charlotte Anderson and Loretta Meade at the Martin County Historical Society and Mike O'Bradovich in Lynch, Kentucky.

Music has always been a big part of my life, but this is a book that has been shaped by the songs that sprang from the soil I was writing about and walked upon for four months. Cassandra Wilson's interpretation of "Darkness on the Delta" served as the inspiration for the book's title, perhaps because her rendition sounds more like Mississippi than Tin Pan Alley. JoAnne Prichard Morris took the time to explain to me the significance of the song to the Delta of her youth. Charley Patton, Bukka White, B. B. King, and Bessie Smith accompanied me on Delta roads and helped the landscape come alive. Rufus Wainwright's "Going to a Town" played in heavy rotation, since it is a song that includes a refrain that without fail reminded me that this was a book about America.

Martha Kaplan has always believed in my work, and I am grateful for the time she took finding this book an editorial home, as well as her guidance as the book evolved from an idea to a reality. My editor, Amy Caldwell, has helped shaped this book in ways that improved and refined it, and I am grateful for her graceful approach to editing. Thea Michele Smith helped fact-check the accuracy of the book's statistics and census data. Brian Baughan's copyediting helped polish the book's rough edges, for which I am grateful.

Family has always played a role in my writing, and I am grateful for the time my children, Patrick, Aidan, and Delaney, spent with me in the

Mississippi Delta. Whether they know it or not, their insights always find a way onto the pages I write. And nothing in my life would happen without my wife, Colleen Delaney Eubanks, who has come to understand Mississippi in ways she could never have imagined since that moment all those years ago when I insisted she drive down Highway 61. Yes, maybe all these years later, it's time for both of us to put some bleachers out in the sun way down on Highway 61.

NOTES

As I have noted throughout this book, the South is America's mirror, since it is a region that reflects ideas about this country that many would rather not see reflected in their own visage. And the Mississippi Delta is a place that allows us to look deeply into America's mirror. Although much of the scholarship on the Mississippi Delta cited in *When It's Darkness on the Delta* focuses on the region through a lens of the South, contemporary statistics on the Delta were originally taken from Raj Chetty's Opportunity Atlas website, which traces the roots of affluence and poverty across the nation. Later, I updated those statistics to include the most current census data. Still, the Opportunity Atlas proved essential in comparing the Delta with other parts of the country and in understanding distinctions between rural and urban poverty. It was in seeing how the Delta's issues were connected to issues in other parts of the country that I began to recognize how much this teardrop-shaped piece of land in a distinctive region of the American South reflects the rest of the country.

Four books on the Yazoo-Mississippi Delta were essential background reading and informed my approach to writing about the region: James C. Cobb's *The Most Southern Place on Earth: The Mississippi Delta and the Roots of Regional Identity* (New York: Oxford University Press, 1992); John C. Willis's *Forgotten Time: The Yazoo-Mississippi Delta After the Civil War* (Charlottesville: University of Virginia Press, 2000); John Dollard's *Caste and Class in a Southern Town* (New Haven, CT: Yale University Press, 1937); and Hortense Powdermaker's *After Freedom: A Cultural Study in the Deep South* (New York: Viking Press, 1939). In thinking about the contemporary Delta and the way it relates to other disadvantaged places in the country, the work of sociologists Kathryn J. Edin, H. Luke Shaefer, and Timothy J. Nelson and their book, *The Injustice of Place: Uncovering the Legacy of Poverty in America* (New York: Mariner Books, 2023), helped me place the Delta in its proper national context. Most important of all, *The Injustice of Place* updated what John Dollard and Hortense Powdermaker observed in the 1930s.

Clyde Woods's *Development Arrested: The Blues and Plantation Power in the Mississippi Delta* (New York: Verso, 1998) and William Ferris's *Blues from the Delta* (New York: Da Capo Press, 1984) served as the basis for much of the blues music cited throughout. Woods's idea of a "blues epistemology" shaped the way I wrote about the music mentioned throughout the text. Woods wrote, "Blues epistemology is place-based knowledge of local natural resources, economies, histories and structures of feeling, yet transcends place to connect people based on experiences of oppression." Woods believes one way to understand the Delta and its people is to understand the culture that sprang from that soil as well as the historical and economic forces that created it. B. Brian Foster's *I Don't Like the Blues: Race, Place, and the Backbeat of Black Life* (Chapel Hill: University of North Carolina Press, 2020) provided essential background on blues tourism in Clarksdale, Mississippi.

On the history of the Mississippi State Penitentiary at Parchman and the landscape of the American penal system, David Oshinsky's *"Worse Than Slavery": Parchman Farm and the Ordeal of Jim Crow Justice* (New York: Free Press, 1996) and Angela Y. Davis's *Are Prisons Obsolete?* (New York: Seven Stories Press, 2003) helped interpret circumstances and structures encountered inside the gates of Parchman.

The work of the poet June Jordan and her notes written before her trip to the Mississippi Delta in 1970, found in the Schlesinger Library at Harvard University, inspired me to seek to understand the power of the Delta's mythology. Insights from Jordan's writings allowed me to see the Delta more as an American entity than a Southern one. As Jordan wrote, "Given its mythological reality, comparable to that of Plymouth, The Great Frontier, and Harlem, my purpose is partly to demythologize that place by going there and learning what I can. I submit that this purpose is valuable since only when myth shrinks from reality can we usefully assess the status and experience of that reality."

PROLOGUE

1. Roy Stryker to Marion Post Wolcott, October 17, 1939, Farm Security Administration / Office of War Information Collection, Library of Congress, LOT 12024 (M) (F) (H), LC Catalog record: https://lccn.loc.gov/2004667188.

2. JoAnne Prichard Morris, "The Story Behind 'Darkness on the Delta,'" Hotty Toddy.com, January 16, 2014.

3. Mississippi Association of Educators, "MAEP: Mississippi's Public School Funding Formula," https://www.maetoday.org/maep-mississippis-public-school -funding-formula, accessed May 19, 2025.

4. Bob Moses, "Speech at Stanford University," April 24, 1964, Voices of Democracy, US Oratory Project, https://voicesofdemocracy.umd.edu/moses-stanford -university-speech-text/.

CHAPTER 1: THE DIMMING MYSTIQUE OF MILESTON

All historical correspondence and letters cited in this chapter regarding the founding of the resettlement community at Mileston, Mississippi, are from the records of the Farmers Home Administration, National Archives and Records Administration, Records Group 96, Region 6 (which includes Mississippi).

1. "Robert Moton and the Colored Advisory Commission," *American Experience*, https://www.pbs.org/wgbh/americanexperience/features/flood-moton-cac/, accessed March 4, 2025.

2. David L. Cohn, *Where I Was Born and Raised* (Boston: Houghton Mifflin, 1948).

CHAPTER 2: "IT'S GOING TO TAKE A MOSES"

The Sara Virginia Jones collection at the Mississippi Museum of Art provided background information on Ms. Jones's life and art collecting history. John Hersey's story for the *Saturday Evening Post*, "A Life for a Vote," published September 26, 1964 (pages 34–43) provided background for this chapter, as did notebooks and correspondence in the John Hersey papers at the Beinecke Library, Yale University.

1. Tracy Sugarman, *We Had Sneakers, They Had Guns: The Kids Who Fought for Civil Rights in Mississippi* (Syracuse, NY: Syracuse University Press, 2009).

CHAPTER 3: "WE THOUGHT MISSISSIPPI WAS SAFER THAN ARKANSAS"

Robert Hunt Ferguson's *Remaking the Rural South: Interracialism, Christian Socialism, and Cooperative Farming in Jim Crow Mississippi* (Athens: University of Georgia Press, 2018) served as background for this chapter and led to exploring primary sources in the archive of Eugene Cox at Mississippi State University. Jeffrey K. Walter's "'Hail, Hail Cooperation': The Providence Cooperative Farm and Economic Democracy in Holmes County, Mississippi" (*Rhodes Historical Review* 21 [Spring 2019]) helped me to see not only Providence Farm as a radical space but also how the entire Mississippi Delta functions as a radical space. Will D. Campbell's *Providence* (Atlanta:

Longstreet Press, 1992) provided background on the dissolution of Providence Farm and is the source of the quote used in this chapter's title, "We Thought Mississippi Was Safer Than Arkansas."

1. William Lee Miller, "People in Mississippi," *The Reporter*, December 15, 1955, Papers of Eugene Cox, Mississippi State University Archives.

2. Records of the Resettlement Administration, Records of the Rural Rehabilitation Division, National Archives and Records Administration.

3. Michael K. Honey, *Sharecropper's Troubadour: John L. Handcox, the Southern Tenant Farmers' Union, and the African American Song Tradition* (New York: Palgrave Macmillan, 2013), 76.

4. Jonathan Mitchell, "Cabins in the Cotton," *New Republic* 92 (September 22, 1937): 175.

5. Mitchell, "Cabins in the Cotton," 175.

6. Jerry W. Dallas, "The Delta and Providence Farms: A Mississippi Experiment in Cooperative Farming and Racial Cooperation," *Mississippi Quarterly* 40, no. 3 (1987): 298.

7. Dallas, "The Delta and Providence Farms," 299.

8. Sam H. Franklin Jr., *Early Years of the Delta Cooperative Farm and the Providence Cooperative Farm* (unpublished), 71.

9. Robert Hunt Ferguson, *Remaking the Rural South: Interracialism, Christian Socialism, and Cooperative Farming in Jim Crow Mississippi* (Athens: University of Georgia Press, 2018), 109.

10. Interview with Howard Kester, July 22, 1974, Interview B-0007-1, Southern Oral History Program Collection (#4007), University of North Carolina at Chapel Hill, https://docsouth.unc.edu/sohp/html_use/B-0007-1.html.

11. Murray Kempton, "Intruder," *New York Post*, November 17, 1955, in A. E. [Eugene] Cox Collection, House Box 2, Folder: "Notes on Special Meeting Held in the Tchula Consolidated Community School."

12. H. L. Mitchell, "Report from Mississippi," October 4, 1955, A. E. [Eugene] Cox Collection, Box 17, Folder 8.

13. A. E. Cox to Mitch (surname unknown), September 30, 1955, A. E. [Eugene] Cox Collection, Box 17, Folder 8.

14. Will D. Campbell, *Providence* (Atlanta: Longstreet Press, 1992), 7.

15. *The Decline of Black Farming in America: A Report of the United States Commission on Civil Rights*, February 1982, p. 77.

16. Pamela Browning et al., *The Decline of Black Farming in America* (Washington, DC: US Commission on Civil Rights, 1982), https://files.eric.ed.gov/fulltext/ED222604.pdf; Bureau of the Census, *Fifteenth Census of the United States: 1930: Census of Agriculture: The Negro Farmer in the United States* (Washington, DC: US Department of Commerce, 1933), available at https://babel.hathitrust.org/cgi/pt?id=uiuo.ark:/13960/t9668cs41.

17. Will D. Campbell, *Providence* (Waco, TX: Baylor University Press, 2002), 2.

CHAPTER 4: THE PAST IS A FOREIGN COUNTRY

Ellen Meacham's *Delta Epiphany: Robert F. Kennedy in Mississippi* (Jackson: University Press of Mississippi, 2018) served as the essential resource for this chapter. Meacham's text provided clear historical context for Kennedy's trip to the Delta as well as how the trip was viewed in Mississippi. For additional background, Meacham generously shared her research files for *Delta Epiphany*, taken from the collections of the John F. Kennedy Library in Boston, including a copy of the map Kennedy used during his trip to the Delta. It was that map that served as a guide to the precise route Kennedy took in 1967.

1. *Clarion-Ledger* (Jackson, MS), April 10, 1967.

2. Ellen B. Meacham, *Delta Epiphany: Robert F. Kennedy in Mississippi* (Jackson: University Press of Mississippi, 2018), 88.

3. Peter B. Edelman, recorded interview by Larry J. Hackman, March 13, 1974, p. 10, Robert F. Kennedy Oral History Program, John F. Kennedy Library.

4. Bobby Harrison, "Reeves Makes Clear That Cost Is Not His Reason for Opposing Medicaid Expansion for Working Poor," *Mississippi Today*, October 1, 2023, https://mississippitoday.org/2023/10/01/tate-reeves-medicaid-expansion-costs/.

5. Edward R. Schmitt, *President of the Other America: Robert Kennedy and the Politics of Poverty* (Amherst: University of Massachusetts Press, 2010).

6. Schmitt, *President of the Other America*, 1.

CHAPTER 5: "THE JEWEL OF THE DELTA"

Exploring the collection of poet and journalist June Jordan at the Schlesinger Library at Harvard University provided a fresh perspective on the story of Mound Bayou. Jordan's insights from 1970 seemed contemporary rather than historical. Much of the material drawn from Jordan's collection that served as inspiration can be found in June Jordan Papers, 1936–2002, Box 8, Folder 6, and Box 62, Folder 12, Arthur and Elizabeth Schlesinger Library on the History of Women in America, Radcliffe Institute, Harvard University, Cambridge, Massachusetts.

1. Oral history, conducted December 29, 1979, by Radcliffe College, held by the Schlesinger Library, Harvard University.

2. Quoted in Leon F. Litwack, *Trouble in Mind: Black Southerners in the Age of Jim Crow* (New York: Knopf, 1998), 240.

3. Interview with Minnie Fisher, December 29, 1979, Black Women Oral History Project, Interviews of the Black Women Oral History Project, Schlesinger Library on the History of Women in America, Harvard University.

4. *New York Times*, December 4, 1864, cited in Janet Sharp Hermann, *The Pursuit of a Dream* (Jackson: University Press of Mississippi, 1999).

5. Jefferson Davis's farewell speech to the US Senate, January 21, 1861.

6. David Levering Lewis and Deborah Willis, Daniel Murray Collection (Library of Congress), *A Small Nation of People: W. E. B. Du Bois and African American Portraits of Progress* (New York: Amistad, 2003).

7. Neil R. McMillen, *Dark Journey: Black Mississippians in the Age of Jim Crow* (Champaign: University of Illinois Press, 1989), 48.

8. Cited in Litwack, *Trouble in Mind*, 353.

9. W. E. B. Du Bois, *The Souls of Black Folk* (New York: Modern Library, 2003), 60.

10. Cited in Litwack, *Trouble in Mind*, 353.

11. Du Bois, *The Souls of Black Folk*, 45.

12. David T. Beito, Linda Royster Beito, and Jerry W. Mitchell, *T. R. M. Howard: Doctor, Entrepreneur, Civil Rights Pioneer* (Oakland, CA: Independent Institute, 2018), 75.

13. James C. Cobb, *The Most Southern Place on Earth: The Mississippi Delta and the Roots of Regional Identity* (1992; New York: Oxford University Press, 1994), 113.

CHAPTER 6: RACE, HEALTH, AND POVERTY IN A SANCTUARY FROM SEGREGATION

June Jordan's article "Mississippi 'Black Home,'" published in October 1970 in the *New York Times Magazine*, inspired this chapter. Thomas J. Ward Jr.'s *Out in the Rural: A Mississippi Health Center and Its War on Poverty* (New York: Oxford University Press, 2017), John Dittmer's *The Good Doctors: The Medical Committee for Human Rights and the Struggle for Social Justice in Health Care* (New York: Bloomsbury Press, 2009), and M. Therese Lysaught's moving profile of the life and work of Sister Mary Stella Simpson in the book *Can I Get a Witness? Thirteen Peacemakers, Community-Builders, and Agitators for Faith and Justice*, ed. Charles Marsh, Shea Tuttle, and Daniel P. Rhodes (Grand Rapids, MI: Wm. B. Eerdmans Publishing, 2019) helped bring into focus the issue of health care and poverty in the Delta.

1. Fannie Lou Hamer, testimony before the Credentials Committee, Democratic National Convention, August 22, 1964, https://americanradioworks.public radio.org/features/sayitplain/flhamer.html.

2. June Jordan, "Mississippi 'Black Home,'" *New York Times Magazine*, October 11, 1970.

3. Jordan, "Mississippi 'Black Home.'"

4. Michael Thomas Murphy, "The Politics of Reproductive Rights Legislation in the 'Modern' South," *Nursing Clio*, July 24, 2019, https://nursingclio.org/2019/07 /24/the-politics-of-reproductive-rights-legislation-in-the-modern-south/.

5. "Sit and Die for Lack of $3," *Boston Globe*, July 17, 1967.

6. "His Spirit Still Lives," *Clarion-Ledger*, January 6, 1956.

7. Thomas J. Ward Jr., *Out in the Rural: A Mississippi Health Center and Its War on Poverty* (New York: Oxford University Press, 2017), 139.

8. "The Valley of Poverty," *Life*, January 31, 1964.

9. M. Therese Lysaught, "Sister Mary Stella Simpson," in *Can I Get a Witness? Thirteen Peacemakers, Community-Builders, and Agitators for Faith and Justice*, ed. Charles Marsh, Shea Tuttle, and Daniel P. Rhodes (Grand Rapids, MI: Wm. B. Eerdmans Publishing, 2019).

10. Ward, *Out in the Rural*, 158.

11. Ward, *Out in the Rural*, 170.

12. John Dittmer, *The Good Doctors: The Medical Committee for Human Rights and the Struggle for Social Justice in Health Care* (New York: Bloomsbury Press, 2009), 280.

CHAPTER 7: "HUNGER HAS NO COLOR LINE"

Both Greta de Jong's *You Can't Eat Freedom: Southerners and Social Justice After the Civil Rights Movement* (Chapel Hill: University of North Carolina Press, 2016) and Bobby J. Smith's *Food Power Politics: The Food Story of the Mississippi Civil Rights Movement* (Chapel Hill: University of North Carolina Press, 2023) provided background research for this chapter.

1. Thomas J. Ward Jr., *Out in the Rural: A Mississippi Health Center and Its War on Poverty* (New York: Oxford University Press, 2017), 72.

2. Ward, *Out in the Rural*, 74.

3. Greta de Jong, *You Can't Eat Freedom: Southerners and Social Justice After the Civil Rights Movement* (Chapel Hill: University of North Carolina Press, 2016), 2.

4. Paule Marshall, "Fannie Lou Hamer: 'Hunger Has No Colour Line,'" *Vogue*, June 1, 1970, 126–27.

5. Leigh Ann Ross et al., "The Mississippi Delta Health Collaborative Medication Therapy Management Model: Public Health and Pharmacy Working Together to Improve Population Health in the Mississippi Delta," *Original Research* 17 (September 17, 2020), https://www.cdc.gov/pcd/issues/2020/20_0063.htm.

6. Lyndon B. Johnson, State of the Union Address, January 8, 1964, Bernard L. Boutin Personal Papers, General Services Administration Files, 1961–1964, Brochures, 1961–1964, John F. Kennedy Presidential Library and Museum.

7. Martha J. Bailey and Nicolas J. Duquette, "How Johnson Fought the War on Poverty: The Economics and Politics of Funding at the Office of Economic Opportunity," *Journal of Economic History* 74, no. 2 (2014): 351–88.

8. Ronald Reagan, "Reagan: In the War on Poverty, Poverty Won," address to Joint Session of Congress, January 25, 1988, available at C-SPAN, https://www.c-span .org/clip/joint-session-of-congress/user-clip-reagan-in-the-war-on-poverty -poverty-won/4642456.

9. Bobby J. Smith II, "Mississippi's War Against the War on Poverty: Food Power, Hunger, and White Supremacy," *Study the South* (2019): 11, https://egrove.olemiss.edu/studythesouth/11.

10. James C. Cobb, *The Most Southern Place on Earth: The Mississippi Delta and the Roots of Regional Identity* (1992; New York: Oxford University Press, 1994), 261.

11. "Evaluating the Success of the Great Society," *Washington Post*, 2014, https://www.washingtonpost.com/wp-srv/special/national/great-society-at-50/.

12. Jamie L. Whitten, *That We May Live* (Princeton, NJ: Van Nostrand, 1966), 216.

13. Whitten, *That We May Live*, 141.

CHAPTER 8: SAVING AN OPPORTUNITY DESERT

Discussions with economists Lawrence Katz and Trevon Logan pointed to the work of Hoyt Bleakley as well as the work of Martha J. Bailey and Nicolas J. Duquette to help understand the impact of social change philanthropy and the historical context of Johnson's War on Poverty.

1. Clyde Woods, *Development Arrested: The Blues and Plantation Power in the Mississippi Delta* (New York: Verso, 1998), 2.

2. US Commission on Civil Rights, "Equality of Economic Opportunity," in *Racial and Ethnic Tensions in American Communities: Poverty, Inequality, and Discrimination*, vol. 7, *The Mississippi Delta Report*, https://www.usccr.gov/files/pubs /msdelta/ch1.htm, accessed March 4, 2025.

3. Ted Ownby, "Delta Council," *Mississippi Encyclopedia*, Center for the Study of Southern Culture, July 10, 2017, last updated April 13, 2018, https://mississippi encyclopedia.org/entries/delta-council/.

4. Judith Porter, "What Works and What Doesn't? Perceptions of Economic Development Among Delta Leaders," in *A Social and Economic Portrait of the Mississippi Delta*, ed. Arthur G. Cosby et al. (Mississippi State, Mississippi Agricultural and Forestry Experiment Station, Social Science Research Center, 1992).

5. Associated Press, "Education = Health, Elders Instructs Delta: Final Edition," *Commercial Appeal*, June 26, 1999.

6. "Please Support Efforts to Keep the Kellogg Foundation Delta Initiative Operating," Delta Grassroots Caucus, December 8, 2008, http://www.mdgc.us /articles/2008/12/8/support_effort_to_keep_the/.

7. Anthony F. Pipa, "Building on a Legacy of Community Resilience in Sunflower County, Mississippi," Brookings, January 18, 2023, https://www.brookings .edu/articles/building-on-a-legacy-of-community-resilience-in-sunflower-county -mississippi/.

8. Hoyt Bleakley, "Disease and Development: Evidence from Hookworm Eradication in the American South," *Quarterly Journal of Economics* 122, no. 1 (2007): 73–117.

9. James C. Cobb, *"Somebody Done Nailed Us on the Cross": Federal Farm and Welfare Policy and the Civil Rights Movement in the Mississippi Delta*, vol. 77 (Bloomington, IN: Organization of American Historians, 1990), 936.

10. Methodist Hospital v. Slack, 330 So. 2d882, 885 (Miss. 1976) (quoting Blackbourn v. Tucker, 17 So. 737, 739 [1895]).

CHAPTER 9: A CRUEL AND INTOLERABLE BURDEN

Constance Curry's book *Silver Rights: The Story of the Carter Family's Brave Decision to Send Their Children to an All-White School and Claim Their Civil Rights* (Chapel Hill, NC: Algonquin Books of Chapel Hill, 1996) introduced me to the story of the Carter family's courage and bravery and informed this chapter. Jennifer Welch's stage adaptation of Curry's book, *Mrs. Carter and the Sunflower Seven*, brought this story alive to me in ways I never expected when I first read *Silver Rights* in 1996.

1. Federal Writers' Project of the Works Progress Association, *Mississippi: The WPA Guide to the Magnolia State* (New York: Viking Press, 1938), 408.

2. John Dollard, *Caste and Class in a Southern Town*, 2nd ed. (New York: Harper & Brothers, 1949), 62.

3. Hortense Powdermaker, *After Freedom: A Cultural Study in the Deep South* (1939; New York: Russell & Russell, 1968), 80.

4. William R. Ferris and John Dollard, "John Dollard: Caste and Class Revisited," *Southern Cultures* 10, no. 2 (2004): 7–18.

5. Keisha N. Blain, "They Called Her 'Black Jet,'" *The Atlantic*, April 28, 2022.

CHAPTER 10: "JUSTICE IS A BLIND GODDESS"

An essential piece of background for this chapter was "Instant Schools: The Frenzied Formation and Early Days of the Mississippi Private School Association," a 2020 doctoral dissertation by E. Gray Flora at the University of Mississippi. This dissertation, along with the documents and documentation Flora found in documents and interviews, was key to my understanding of how the segregation academy system in the Mississippi Delta came to be. Flora's work provides a clear understanding of how political and social clout was used to help create segregated private schools instantly during a pivotal moment in Southern educational history.

1. Hortense Powdermaker, *After Freedom: A Cultural Study in the Deep South* (1939; New York: Russell & Russell, 1968), 371.

2. National Center for Education Statistics, *School Composition and the Black–White Achievement Gap*, 2015, https://nces.ed.gov/nationsreportcard/subject/studies/pdf/school_composition_and_the_bw_achievement_gap_2015.pdf

3. Howell Raines, *My Soul Is Rested: Movement Days in the Deep South Remembered* (New York: Putnam, 1977), 301.

4. Lily Altavena, Rose Velazquez, and Natalie Griffin, "School Takeovers Leave Parents Without a Voice in Education," *Voting Wars* (News21 investigation), August 20, 2016, https://votingwars.news21.com/school-takeovers-leave-parents-without-a-voice-in-education/.

5. Ellen Ann Fentress, "Are You a Seg Academy Alum, Too? Let's Talk," *Bitter Southerner*, https://bittersoutherner.com/from-the-southern-perspective/are-you-a-seg-academy-alum-lets-talk.

6. James Baldwin, "Letter from a Region in My Mind," *New Yorker*, November 9, 1962.

7. Quoted in Kate Royals, "Bills to Expand School Choice Pending as Parents Rally at Capitol," *Mississippi Today*, January 23, 2018, https://mississippitoday.org/2018/01/23/bills-to-expand-public-to-private-school-options-pend-as-students-parents-rally-at-capitol/.

8. "Bowie—Freedom Schools, 1964, Jan. 14–Dec. 2," Harry J. Bowie Papers, 1964–1967, Archives Main Stacks, Mss. 31, Box 1, Folder 4, Freedom Summer Digital Collection, Wisconsin Historical Society, https://content.wisconsinhistory.org/digital/collection/p15932coll2/id/3794.

9. William Sturkey, "'I Want to Become a Part of History': Freedom Summer, Freedom Schools, and the Freedom News," *Journal of African American History* 95, nos. 3–4 (2010): 348–68.

CHAPTER 11: THE WRONG SIDE OF THAT FENCE

1. Alan Lomax, *The Land Where the Blues Began* (New York: The New Press, 2002).

2. Alysia Santo and Joseph Neff, "Mississippi Prisons: No One's Safe, Not Even the Guards," The Marshall Project, February 20, 2020, https://www.themarshall project.org/2020/02/20/mississippi-prisons-no-one-s-safe-not-even-the-guards.

3. Kathryn J. Edin, H. Luke Shaefer, and Timothy J. Nelson, *The Injustice of Place: Uncovering the Legacy of Poverty in America*, 2022, Poverty Solutions at the University of Michigan and Princeton University, https://poverty.umich.edu /research-funding-opportunities/data-tools/understanding-communities-of -deep-disadvantage.

4. John Dollard, *Caste and Class in a Southern Town*, 2nd ed. (New York: Harper & Brothers, 1949), 284.

5. Angela Y. Davis, *Are Prisons Obsolete?* (New York: Seven Stories Press, 2003).

6. Prison Policy Initiative, "Mississippi Profile," https://www.prisonpolicy.org /profiles/MS.html, accessed March 4, 2025.

7. Ellen B. Meacham, "Education Reform Act of 1982," *Mississippi Encyclopedia*, Center for the Study of Southern Culture, originally published July 11, 2017, last updated April 14, 2018, https://mississippiencyclopedia.org/entries/education -reform-act-of-1982/.

8. Jerry Mitchell, "Conditions at Mississippi's Most Notorious Prison Violate the Constitution, DOJ Says," ProPublica, April 21, 2022, https://www.propublica .org/article/conditions-at-mississippis-most-notorious-prison-violate-the -constitution-doj-says.

CHAPTER 12: YOUR BLUES AIN'T LIKE MINE

An essential resource for anyone seeking to understand the impact of blues tourism is B. Brian Foster's *I Don't Like the Blues: Race, Place, and the Backbeat of Black Life* (Chapel Hill: University of North Carolina Press, 2020). Foster's observations and analysis were essential to understanding the way the blues does and does not resonate with many Black Clarksdale residents.

1. Margery Kerstine, *Merchants on Issaquena: Avenue of the Blues in Mississippi* (Clarksdale, MS: Kerstine's Enterprises, 2020).

2. Charles Peabody, "Notes on Negro Music," *Journal of American Folklore* 16, no. 2 (1903): 148.

3. Albert Murray, "The Storyteller as Blues Singer," in *Albert Murray: Collected Essays and Memoirs* (New York: Library of America, 2016), 698.

4. Quoted in William R. Ferris, *Blues from the Delta* (New York: Da Capo Press, 1984), 42.

5. David W. Johnson, "'Fixin' to Die Blues': The Last Months of Bukka White with an Afterword from B. B. King on Bukka White's Legacy," *Southern Cultures* 16, no. 3 (Fall 2010): 15–34, available at link.gale.com/apps/doc/A237941083/AONE?u=oregon_oweb&sid=googleScholar&xid=f342fae1.

6. Johnson, "'Fixin' to Die Blues.'"

7. Albert Murray, *Stomping the Blues* (New York: Vintage Books, 1982).

CHAPTER 13: CASINO LIGHTS

In thinking about the social impact of casino gambling on Tunica, Mississippi, Tracy L. Farrigan's dissertation, "The Tunica Miracle, Sin and Savior in America's Ethiopia: A Poverty and Social Impact Analysis of Casino Gaming in Tunica, Mississippi" (Penn State University, 2005), helped clarify what I saw on Tunica's landscape as well as the history of the land itself. Farrigan believes, as I do, that despite the success of the casino industry in Tunica County, where much has changed, much has tragically remained the same for the majority of the poor in this region. *Resorting to Casinos: The Mississippi Gambling Industry* (Jackson: University Press of Mississippi, 2006), edited by Denise von Herrmann, also served as background reading for this chapter.

1. David L. Cohn, *God Shakes Creation* (New York: Harper & Brothers, 1935).

2. Federal Writers' Project of the Works Progress Association, *Mississippi: The WPA Guide to the Magnolia State* (New York: Viking Press, 1938), 264–65.

3. *Clarion-Ledger*, July 21, 1985.

4. Kiese Laymon, *Heavy: An American Memoir* (New York: Scribner, 2018), 233.

5. Chico Harlan, "An Opportunity Gamed Away," *Washington Post*, July 11, 2015, https://www.washingtonpost.com/sf/business/2015/07/11/an-opportunity-gamed-away/.

6. Associated Press, "Closed Casino Hotels in Mississippi Could House Unaccompanied Migrant Children," May 23, 2024, https://apnews.com/article/tunica-harrahs-casino-mississippi-immigrant-migrant-children-9167517ca54554cedo1954cc3536cafb.

7. Audie Blevins and Katherine Jensen, "Gambling as a Community Development Quick Fix," *Annals of the American Academy of Political and Social Science* 556, no. 1 (1998): 109–23.

8. Stephanie N. Mehta, "Legalized Gambling Lifts a Depressed Town," CNN Money, March 15, 2007, http://money.cnn.com/magazines/fortune/fortune_archive/2007/03/19/8402375/index2.htm.

9. Violet Jira, "Tunica School District Returns to Local Control Monday, After Nearly a Decade," *Mississippi Today*, June 27, 2024, https://mississippitoday.org/2024/06/27/tunica-school-district-returns-to-local-control-monday-after-nearly-a-decade/.

CHAPTER 15: A VEILED MIRROR

1. Duncan Cooper, "LaToya Ruby Frazier: How to Make Your Photos Matter," *Fader*, April 28, 2015, https://www.thefader.com/2015/04/28/latoya-ruby-frazier -interview-how-to-make-your-photos-matter.

2. James C. Cobb, *The Most Southern Place on Earth: The Mississippi Delta and the Roots of Regional Identity* (1992; New York: Oxford University Press, 1994), 333.

3. Justin Randolph, "The Making of Appalachian Mississippi," *Southern Cultures* 26, no. 4 (2020): 90–109.

4. David Kohn, "The 300-Million-Gallon Warning: Are the Nation's Abandoned Coal-Slurry Ponds Environmental Disasters Waiting to Happen?" *Mother Jones*, March/April 2002.

5. Harry M. Caudill, *Night Comes to the Cumberlands: A Biography of a Depressed Area* (Boston: Little, Brown, 1963).

INDEX